Praise for Pat Alacqua and OBSTACLES TO OPPORTUNITY

"With over thirty years in the C-suite of iconic sports and entertainment organizations, I've faced countless challenges and change agents. Pat Alacqua and his Entrepreneur to Enterprise Program are among the best at facilitating meaningful change. We met when I was CEO of the National Basketball Association's (NBA's) Atlanta Hawks. We quickly became friends and later collaborated on innovative projects... Pat is unmatched in startup operations—from conception and planning to anticipating every detail through implementation. I highly recommend him across all business types and industries."

—DR. BERNIE MULLIN, Founder and Chair of The Aspire Group; formerly CEO of the Atlanta Hawks (NBA), Atlanta Thrashers (NHL), Philips Arena; and formerly Chief Marketing Officer of the NBA

"Pat can dig into the weeds and really think through process and operational efficiency and is a master at that, but he doesn't lose sight of the strategy. When you have somebody smart and they're on your side and willing to be honest with you, and they have a lot of integrity, you just... can't go wrong."

—JANE GENTRY, CEO Adviser and Business Strategist

"The way that Pat approached challenges or the 'problems' in my business was with a sense of creativity that excited me. It brought the fun back into the process and as a result, I was able to show up better as a leader. I was more energized because I knew every single action that I took was moving me toward my goal. And I'm forever grateful to him for that... there is no better thought partner to have than Pat."

—DEZ THORNTON, Communications Consultant, Speech Coach, and Speech Writer

"Pat's attention to detail, his thoughtful questions, and his focus on tackling the issue at hand allow me to clarify and focus on exactly what I need to be successful. Each time I approach a hurdle or problem, knowing I have a plan in place and the guidance to execute it, increases my confidence in taking action."

—ANDREA GALLO, Risk Management C-Level Executive

Obstacles to Opportunity

OBSTACLES
TO
OPPORTUNITY

Transforming Business Challenges into Triumphs

Stories and Strategies From Leaders Who've Mastered It

PAT ALACQUA

Obstacles to Opportunity:
Transforming Business Challenges into Triumphs
Stories and Strategies From Leaders Who've Mastered It

Copyright © 2025 Entrepreneur To Enterprise

Printed in the United States of America

Obstacles to Opportunity
Pat Alacqua

Paperback ISBN: 978-1-960299-64-2
Hardcover ISBN: 978-1-960299-65-9

TABLE OF CONTENTS

Foreword by C.J. Stewart.. 1

Introduction.. 5

Section 1. Leadership Journey Overview 7

Chapter 1
My Leadership Journey... 9

Chapter 2
Entrepreneur to Enterprise Pathway.. 20

Chapter 3
The 3Cs Process to Faster Results Overview 23

Chapter 4
The 3Cs Success Path 26

Chapter 5
Components of the Leadership Experience 30

Chapter 6
Leadership Hurdles and How to Jump Over Them................................ 39

Section 2. From Challenges to Triumph: Real-Life Leadership Stories 47

Section Introduction 49

PART 1: Simplicity Is Key 51

The challenges that arise when growing a business can appear overwhelming. By simplifying the approach, breaking things down piece by piece, and staying true to their values, these leaders mastered the art of problem-solving with clarity, focus, and determination.

Chapter 7
Play-By-Play Communication Strategies with Legendary Sportscaster, Bob Rathbun 53

Chapter 8
Harnessing Mental Might with Mental Performance Consultant, Danny Ourian....... 58

Chapter 9

Batting Against Barriers with Baseball Visionary, C.J. Stewart................................66

Chapter 10

Tackling Teamwork with Fitness Innovator, John Busing.......................................73

Chapter 11

Lead Simply, Lead Strong..80

PART 2: Time to Take Action 83

Once a challenge has presented itself it's often easy to get stuck in the goal of overcoming it and not the steps required to do so. These leaders discovered that simply taking action took them from facing a hurdle to leaping over it.

Chapter 12

Turning Passion into Action with Real Estate Guru, Alester Spears...................85

Chapter 13

Action-Oriented Leadership with Healthcare Tech CEO, John Marron............94

Chapter 14

Turning Plans into Progress with Trade Show Pro, Tom Iacovone.....................99

Chapter 15

Empowering Success in Sports Brand Building With 'The Professor,' Dr. Bernie Mullin 106

Chapter 16

Balancing Empathy and Action with Executive Sales Strategist, Trey Hinson...............114

Chapter 17

Turning Decisions into Momentum 123

PART 3: Zoom Out to Zoom In 127

Through each growth phase of business, it's important to keep the big picture in mind. Challenges, however, often require a much more micro focus. The following leaders recognized that by first looking at the greater problem and then breaking things down into smaller, achievable milestones they could develop solutions that were both impactful and sustainable.

Chapter 18

Crafting Success One Stitch at a Time with Master Haberdasher, José Perez................129

Chapter 19

Putting Words into Action with Messaging Mastermind, Dez Thornton...................136

Chapter 20

Navigating New Frontiers with Operations Pioneer, Cara Roach 144

Chapter 21
Pushing Limits and Finding Balance with Resilient Leader, Mitch Ried *151*

Chapter 22
Captaining a Collaborative Crew with Global Business Leader, Jeff Hannah *159*

Chapter 23
Leading Through Adversity with Strategic Sports Executive, Brendan Donohue *167*

Chapter 24
Scaling New Heights with Staffing Expert, Leigh Ann Alacqua *176*

Chapter 25
Turning Challenges into Triumphs with Military Leader and Author, Deji Ayoade ... *184*

Chapter 26
Widen Your Lens, Sharpen Your Focus *196*

PART 4: Plans, Perspective, and People 199

It's important to remember that the fundamentals of business are often what helps propel you through challenges. Developing effective strategies, gaining a clear perspective on your goals, and relying on the team of people around you are imperative in moving through the inevitable growth roadblocks.

Chapter 27
Acting on Strategy with Leadership Expert & CEO Adviser, Jane Gentry *201*

Chapter 28
Building a Strategic Playbook with Sports Innovator, Lou DePaoli *210*

Chapter 29
Work-Life Harmony with Psychologist, Advocate, and Podcaster, Dr. Stephanie J. Wong *216*

Chapter 30
Resilience Through Uncertainty *223*

Section 3. Becoming Your Own Leader: The Ultimate Challenge Story 227

Section Introduction 229

Chapter 31
Leadership Persona Pathway *231*

Chapter 32
Building Your Leadership Muscles *240*

Section 4. Key Insight Takeaways 249

Chapter 33
Amplifying Your Performance...*251*

Chapter 34
Essential Insights for Sustained Growth *259*

Chapter 35
The Journey to Enduring Success—How I Can Help *263*

Acknowledgments 266

About the Author 268

Foreword

I needed to find the exit.

In the early days of founding our youth sports development organization, L.E.A.D. Center For Youth, I attended a high-profile networking event hosted by the Atlanta Sports Council (ASC). As I stood against the wall watching some of the biggest players in Atlanta's sports community milling around the room, I started to question why I was there. I didn't know anybody, and nobody knew me. Even though I had created somewhat of a name for myself as a professional hitting instructor with my Diamond Directors platform, this was an entirely different scene. Besides, if the momentum I had generated thrust me into the forefront of L.E.A.D., my wife, Kelli, was the brains of the operation.

We both decided that the ASC event would be the first step in fostering the kind of relationships we needed to build L.E.A.D. At its core, the vision of L.E.A.D. was to develop an engine that could help empower a generation of at-risk Black youth. The complete blueprint for this strategy, which involved helping these young people lead and transform the city of Atlanta through baseball and tennis, was still tucked somewhere in the recesses of my mind.

After retreating to the restroom to systematically roll through the excuses over and over again in my mind of why I shouldn't be there, why I should leave, and what possessed me to show up in the first place, I made a beeline for the exit. About halfway to the door, someone called out my name. Bill McClellan, the then director of finance for The Home Depot, approached me like we were old friends. In the course of our conversation, in which I was sure I completely whiffed on explaining the context of what we were trying to do with L.E.A.D., Bill saw something in me that I didn't see in myself.

From my perspective, I was completely unprepared and woefully insecure about what role L.E.A.D. could play in Atlanta's underserved communities. At that moment, I felt like I lacked the mental framework and confidence needed to articulate our vision and how it could help transform a segment of the community that needed transformation. From Bill's perspective, he saw a conviction in me that had potential.

The meeting, which inspired a long-lasting friendship and mentorship, led to one of the most consequential introductions of my career. At the time, Pat Alacqua was running the Suwanee Sports Academy in Suwanee, Georgia. After acquiring it and becoming managing partner and CEO, Pat was instrumental in turning the academy and its programs into one of the foremost player development facilities in the country, primarily focusing on an athlete's mental, physical, and emotional growth on and off the court.

Pat's mentorship proved instrumental. He challenged me to think more deeply and systematically, moving from a transactional mindset—where interactions were simply exchanges—to one that focused on transformation. He helped me identify my strengths and gain confidence in my ideas, pushing me to engage in continual self-reflection. Over time, I learned to operate at a ten, reaching new levels of awareness and strategic thinking. The journey, I would later discover, was not just about improving my thinking skills; it was about shaping a holistic approach that would define how I would mentor others. It instilled a balance of mental, emotional, and strategic strength. This strategic thinking evolution from insecurity to confidence not only made me more of a capable leader but also a mentor who was uniquely equipped to guide others through their transformations. The process grounded my approach in my own journey of growth and resilience.

Our paths crossed at a time when I was looking for answers—a roadmap to help me understand how to lead, how to build, and how to create something meaningful. The key to the uniqueness and power of Pat's mentorship is that he not only helped me find answers but how to ask the right questions. He did not come to me with a set of instructions; he came with a mirror. What I would see in that mirror changed everything for me.

Where I was once unsure and unchallenged in my direction, Pat helped pull the universe together for me. Before my conversations with him, L.E.A.D., while having some legs, needed a more concise direction. With every step I took, I was haunted by questions that lingered in the background. Was I leading well? Was I creating the impact I wanted? I knew the mechanics of my job, sure, but I did not know how to think, how to be decisive without doubt, and, above all, how to create the future I envisioned. From our first conversation, that all changed.

I remember one of our earlier conversations where Pat told me that transforming a business begins with transforming yourself. At the time, I didn't fully understand what that meant. But I was about to. With Pat, transformation was not a buzzword, but a process—one where you must dig deep and uproot what does not serve the purpose. I came to him with questions about business strategies and left with questions about my values, my vision, and my role in the world. More than a coach, he was a catalyst for change.

The foundation of this change—in the standard and commitment that Pat places on his teachings—is his 3Cs process: CLARIFY, CHART, and COALIGN. Each step became a mirror that reflected back the parts of myself I had not examined closely enough. The first C—CLARIFY—was deceptively simple. Pat asked me to define, in clear and precise terms, what I wanted to achieve with my work. Not just surface-level ambitions, but the core: Why I was doing this, who it would serve, and what I believed about the work I was doing. I remember sitting down with a blank sheet of paper, trying to distill the goals I'd held for years into a sentence that spoke to my purpose.

With each step, Pat asked me hard questions—ones that would often stop me in my tracks. He was not content with superficial answers. He probed, challenged, and encouraged me to dig deeper, past the easy explanations and into the heart of what mattered. "If it doesn't move your heart, it won't move your head," he said. That struck me because it was a call to reconnect with the reason I started my journey in the first place. It was about building something that didn't just make sense financially but made a difference in the world.

True leadership is not about quick wins or surface-level gains; it's about conviction. And conviction, Pat instilled in me, is not an abstract feeling, but a commitment that you make to yourself and to those you lead. I quickly learned to connect with that conviction, to find a deeper purpose in my actions, and to transform that purpose into tangible results.

As we moved through the CHART phase, Pat guided me to take that conviction and give it form. He helped me to map out what success looks like—not in broad strokes, but with a clear, actionable roadmap. In this phase, I learned that clarity isn't just about seeing the destination, it's about understanding the steps it takes to get there. He helped me identify my strengths and weaknesses, not to label them as good or bad, but to use them as markers along the journey.

His approach to charting was practical but deeply philosophical. It was about understanding that every step in the journey is connected and that even the challenges serve a purpose. He encouraged me to embrace setbacks as opportunities and to see obstacles not as barriers but as stepping stones. Under his guidance, I came to understand that the path to success isn't a straight line, but a series of choices—each shaped by clarity and conviction.

One of the most transformative parts of this phase was the way Pat helped me redefine my relationship with failure. Failure, Pat believes, is not something to fear or avoid, but is a teacher. Failure is a guide that can help refine your vision. "Every failure is a chance to realign with your purpose," he often said. The lesson was powerful. In time, it helped me move past the fear of making mistakes and embrace the growth that came from them.

The final C—COALIGN—was where everything came together. Pat believed that true success is never achieved alone. It is about building a community, a network of people who share your vision and are willing to walk the path with you. Here, he taught me the importance of aligning with others, of building relationships that were grounded in shared values and mutual respect.

The coalign process helped me see the power of collaboration, not as a means to an end, but as a source of strength and resilience. He encouraged me to seek out partners who would challenge me, who would push me to be better, to think bigger, and to act with integrity. I learned that leadership isn't about going it alone; it's about creating a space where others can thrive alongside you.

My journey with Pat was not just about business. It was about personal transformation, about becoming the kind of leader who doesn't just build a successful organization but creates a lasting impact. Pat taught me that the true measure of success is not found in profits or accolades—it is found in the lives you touch, the change you inspire, and the legacy you leave behind.

For anyone reading this book, you are not just getting a guide to business success—you are getting a blueprint for transformation. Let me be clear here: Pat's process is not easy. It is a journey that will ask you to look inward, confront your own doubts and limitations, and build something meaningful from that place of vulnerability.

If you are ready to take that journey, this book will be your guide. Pat's wisdom, his insight, and his unwavering commitment to personal and professional growth have changed my life, and I believe they have the power to change yours as well.

In a time when people want and need to change the world, those transformations are not about changing what you do, but about changing who you are.

Corteney "C.J." Stewart

Co-founder/Chief Visionary Officer, L.E.A.D. Center For Youth
Co-owner, Diamond Directors Player Development

Introduction

"Success is not final, failure is not fatal: It is the courage to continue that counts."
—WINSTON CHURCHILL

Purpose of this Book and Who Should Read It

Challenges in business are inevitable whether you're just starting out or in the throes of growing a successful company.

This book is for business leaders seeking insights to overcome challenges and accelerate career and business growth—from aspiring leaders to seasoned executives. The strategies and real-life stories shared here offer tools to take a structured approach toward business success.

Whether you're leading a startup, an established company, or heading a department, you'll gain actionable insights and inspiration to overcome obstacles and achieve your goals.

Structure of this Book

The chapters share stories of leaders and provide actionable steps and best practices to apply in your business journey. Each chapter gives you the tools and insights to overcome challenges faster.

Section 1. The Leadership Journey

This section covers my journey and key foundational concepts I believe can help you along your career and company-building path, including the Entrepreneur to Enterprise Pathway, the 3Cs Process to Faster Results, and the importance of gaining access to leaders who share their leadership stories, with the goal of helping you overcome your own big challenges.

Section 2. From Challenges to Triumph—Real-Life Leadership Stories

This section presents inspiring stories from leaders who have overcome significant challenges. Each of the four parts within this section focuses on different aspects of tackling business hurdles, from simplifying the approach and taking decisive action to maintaining a big-picture perspective and leveraging fundamental business strategies.

Section 3. Becoming Your Own Leader: The Ultimate Challenge Story

This section encourages you to reflect on your own leadership journey and offers guidance on building your leadership muscles, navigating your pathway, and evolving as a leader. You'll document your biggest challenges, explore the Leadership Persona Pathway and how you can move forward faster, and engage in practical exercises to apply the 3Cs method for faster results.

Section 4. Insight Takeaways

Unlock the secrets to sustained growth in this final section, where the fusion of collaboration and facilitation takes center stage. Discover the compelling reasons why mastering facilitation accelerates results and how this skill can transform your performance. Prepare to delve into powerful insights that will not only enhance your personal growth but also elevate your company's success to new heights. Embrace these essential strategies and set the stage for enduring achievement.

The Difference Maker

This book stands apart with my disciplined frameworks and a results-driven approach. It provides practical strategies from real-world experience that you can implement immediately.

I invite you to embark on this journey with me. We will explore how to better tackle challenges along your career path and in your business, learn to get out in front of them, and collaborate on how to reach your desired outcomes. My goal is to energize and guide you as you tackle challenges throughout the book.

Up Next

In "My Leadership Journey," I share the key moments, challenges, and successes that shaped my path from small-town entrepreneur to guiding business leaders through their toughest challenges. This next chapter offers a deep dive into the experiences that influenced my leadership approach and the lessons that will set the stage for the practical strategies and insights ahead.

►SECTION 1◄

Leadership Journey Overview

**PAT
ALACQUA**
BUSINESS GROWTH
STRATEGIST

Chapter 1

My Leadership Journey

Ideas without the disciplined thinking needed to implement them
put you on the road to nowhere.

As an entrepreneur, business growth strategist, and operating executive, I have a passion for business building and helping other leaders reduce their learning curve during their journey of growth. From the first steps to full scale, I focus on ways in which entrepreneurs, emerging leaders, and seasoned executives can elevate their businesses by giving them the tools to conquer the inevitable challenges that arise along the way.

My approach is designed to connect with leaders at every stage of their career and business-building journey because the core challenges of leadership and growth go beyond titles and industries. Whether you're establishing a new business, scaling an existing one, or navigating complex transitions, the insights and strategies in this book are crafted to support your journey.

My own challenge story began in a small town in South Jersey, just outside of Philadelphia, Pennsylvania where I grew up as an only child to two wonderful parents. We sometimes struggled with very little money, but I had a good childhood because my parents ensured I had everything I needed. I always wanted to have my own business and couldn't wait to start my journey out of high school. Little did I know that my desire to be an entrepreneur would lead me to discover a real passion for using my own *been there, done that* experience to help others build their businesses.

As far back as I can remember, I've always been a person obsessed with forward progress. After building Nth Degree, my company in the tradeshow and events industry, and experiencing the sacrifices and hard-won lessons that come with growing and eventually selling a business, I finally reached a point where I could look in my rearview mirror and reflect. One of the things that I often ponder is: What does it really take to build a sustainable organization?

You see, I got most of my business lessons from the school of hard knocks. I learned things the hard way—through long nights, major setbacks, and high-stakes decisions. One of the many things I appreciate about business is that it's the great equalizer. No matter one's path or pedigree, all leaders face the same challenges. Over the years, I've sat and listened to leaders tell stories of how they earned their business battle scars, and their stresses and successes always reminded me of my own journey.

Although I had to blaze my own trail, upon reflection, I realized that my road would have been a lot rougher if mentors, peers, and others who walked the same path had not shared their best practices and secrets to success. That was the turning point for me—recognizing and fully appreciating the proverbial hand-up from those leaders who had been where I was trying to go. Gradually, my deep sense of gratitude for their wise counsel turned into a yearning to pay it forward. This desire to help others avoid the pitfalls I had encountered grew stronger with each phase of my career, fueling my ultimate purpose as a mentor and guide.

I got my feet wet with my first entrepreneurial endeavor when I started a small residential concrete business with my cousin Frank. It was a crash course in learning fast as we took on small jobs like installing driveways, sidewalks, and patios for homeowners. It was also my first experience gaining insights and tips from someone who had already been where I wanted to go on my own business-building journey, helping reduce my learning curve for the challenges I faced in that business, and for years to come. That someone was my uncle. He was an accomplished professional with years of experience and knowledge in the type of concrete work we did for our customers. We didn't know what we didn't know, but he helped us learn to anticipate so that we were ready to handle any type of project we took on.

This experience planted the first seed of my belief in mentorship, a role that would become one of the most fulfilling aspects of my career. Realizing how much faster I could grow with the guidance of someone more experienced, I began developing my appreciation for those who helped me along the way.

As time went on, I felt a growing responsibility to pay it forward—to become the kind of mentor I had been fortunate to have at different points on my journey. Over time, this desire evolved into one of the most fulfilling aspects of my career: helping other leaders navigate their own journeys by sharing the insights and lessons I had gained.

Reflecting on this time, I see that the lessons went far beyond just how to complete a project. It was about understanding discipline—knowing that success often lies in preparing thoroughly for the unknown. That value of discipline has been a cornerstone throughout my journey.

Early on, I learned that building a foundation of self-discipline sets you up for growth, regardless of the business's size or scope. A clear, disciplined approach to each project ensures that you're prepared for unexpected challenges and can adapt when needed.

This early lesson in discipline became a guiding principle that would shape my approach in every business endeavor that followed, from building Nth Degree to my later turnaround work with Suwanee Sports Academy to my other ventures as well as all my activities while working with and coaching other leaders.

My second business was a trade show and events company I co-founded just a few weeks past my twenty-fourth birthday. My two partners and I named the company Installation and Dismantle, and often referred to as I&D Inc., which we later changed to I&D Group. Years later, we ultimately repositioned the company to what it is today: Nth Degree. We built a global event marketing and management company to help customers create and execute successful trade shows and event programs worldwide.

During our tenure as owner-operators we created a national and internationally recognized brand, implemented operational and financial processes and policies to manage through growth transitions, repositioned the business, successfully implemented a leadership succession plan, and capitalized on the value we built by selling the business. Nth Degree remains a leader in its sector today. It was a true journey of learning and success for me.

Throughout my venture of business-building with Nth Degree, there were many unexpected challenges that I never imagined at the onset. I would not have overcome these challenges without the insights of people who had been where I needed to go and were willing to share the things they learned on their own journey.

Sensing a theme? There is tremendous power in the stories of others. History may repeat itself, but you don't have to repeat the mistakes of others when insider stories are readily available. I could write another book focused only on those challenges I faced and the knowledge, experience, insights, tips, and proven problem-solving approaches that I learned from others who faced similar challenges to experience the success we had.

The following are just some of the solutions and successes we had. I share these so you can imagine, and relate to, the challenges we faced and overcame while building Nth Degree.

Customer-Centric Approaches: We created new service approaches in the tradeshow industry to meet changing customer needs, pioneering customer service and business-building processes that industry-wide organizations emulated.

Resource Development: We developed resources, systems, and financial policies with the controls to transition a single service offering to a multi-divisional business operating in a decentralized organization worldwide.

Sales Process Innovation: We pioneered sales processes and organizations when sales organizations didn't exist in the industry for our services.

Technology Utilization: We utilized technology and built management systems to operate the business of the business, including the show floor labor management system, an industry first.

HR Organization: We created an HR organization to manage more than 350 full-time and part-time staff and thousands of employees working on projects worldwide.

Company Rebranding: We recreated the company into a global events marketing firm, including changing its name to Nth Degree, as our initial offering matured and new competition entered the marketplace.

Strategic Relationships: We implemented processes to formulate collaborative strategic relationships worldwide, ensuring accountable service to customers exhibiting abroad.

Legal Navigation: We navigated antitrust legal strategies, paving the way for precedent-setting broader customer choice of providers in the industry.

Union Labor Relations: We led and collaborated with other service companies to manage union labor relations and contract negotiations, steering industry-wide changes to create more effective working conditions and enabling tradeshow exhibitors to receive higher service levels throughout the United States.

Exit Strategy: We implemented our successful exit strategy by selling the company to a private equity group.

Another highlight of my Nth Degree journey was when my partners and I were elected to the Exhibitor Appointed Contractors Association Hall of Fame in 2006 in recognition of contributions and innovations developed as an industry-leading provider of services. This honor was a recognition of all the great people who worked with us and played a part in the success of Nth Degree.

Many of those people are still having a real impact on the tradeshow and event industry today. They've taken key leadership roles in companies in the industry, and many have founded and operated their own businesses, where they are successfully navigating their own business-building journeys. In a full circle moment, all of them leveraged the experience and knowledge gained from their time working with us.

Growing Nth Degree, as with all my business-building experience over the years, was both satisfying and, at times, painfully frustrating. I learned by stumbling through firsthand what it took to start a business, navigate multiple growth phases (including national and international expansion), and then reposition and pivot for a changing marketplace. I had many experiences I wouldn't trade for anything throughout my learning journey. I proudly exited the trade show and events business after passing it into the competent hands of a great leadership team.

Looking back on these successes, I recognize that they were possible only by embracing resilience—the value of adapting to each challenge, no matter how daunting, and staying committed to the goal. Resilience is critical in scaling a business. Staying committed during tough transitions—whether it's growth, rebranding, or succession planning—will help you stay focused on the larger vision, even when facing unexpected hurdles.

This resilience was tested even further after selling my interests in Nth Degree as I continued my journey when, together with a group of investors, I bought a Sports Academy in Suwanee, Georgia. Suwanee Sports Academy was a classic turnaround situation, hemorrhaging cash without a plan in place to stop it. We faced the pressing reality of turning around a business under intense financial pressure. Each step required persistence and a willingness to adapt to new challenges in a different industry, which reinforced resilience as an essential part of my approach to business growth.

We created a player development company focused on athletes' mental, physical, and emotional growth to enhance performance on and off the court, from beginner stages to the pro level, and provide the best path to higher achievement.

After acquiring the business, we developed and implemented a turnaround plan. We successfully applied a new business model that established sustainable profitability, ultimately creating a nationally recognized brand in the youth sports space and within college and professional basketball. We crafted and executed a leadership succession plan, exiting the business through a sale to one of the leaders we had primed.

This journey not only leveraged what I had learned throughout my previous business-building opportunities but also introduced me to new people with new approaches to overcoming challenges. Leaders, inside and outside the company, who were willing to share the lessons they had learned which then helped me move forward faster as I tackled my own challenges.

Working in the youth sports industry revealed to me just how universal many business challenges are, regardless of the field. The need for disciplined strategy, effective resource management, and resilient leadership is a constant across industries. This realization broadened my understanding of how my experiences could serve leaders in a wide range of sectors.

I was fortunate to yet again have a great team that helped us have a real impact not only on our community but also on other leaders throughout the youth sports landscape who learned from what we were accomplishing so they could leverage our solutions for their own success.

These are just a few of the challenges and solutions we navigated as we moved through our success path for Suwanee Sports Academy:

Creation of Offerings: Developed and perfected programming content and launched a suite of offerings in multiple sports so customers could choose what they needed when considering a player development program.

Unlike our work at Nth Degree, where we focused on pioneering approaches within an established industry, Suwanee required a complete reimagining of how to reach and engage a youth-oriented audience. This strategic pivot meant building an entirely new brand identity and positioning it to stand out in the youth sports landscape.

Branding Strategy: Created a corporate identity package and a branding and marketing communications strategy to build high-impact local, regional, and national recognition.

Sales Processes: Developed sales processes and systems to sell all offerings including high-end recurring revenue programming. This model received national recognition for basketball player development.

Resource Access: Creatively provided access to resources not typically available and affordable to small companies. These resources included a focus on creating a marketing infrastructure to communicate the business's unique offerings effectively.

With a smaller-scale organization than Nth Degree, we had to creatively stretch limited resources, accessing tools that could support a leaner model without sacrificing quality.

Technology Utilization: Employed technology infrastructure and applications to help improve and manage the business of the business while differentiating Suwanee Sports Academy in the marketplace.

Staffing Model Development: Effectively transitioned to a variable staffing model that provided Suwanee Sports Academy with greater financial flexibility.

Management Systems: Created planning and management systems to manage staffing and customer growth, including non-financial and financial processes such as budget and cash flow management.

Leadership Development: Primed managers from within the sports academy, helping the academy transition from an entrepreneurial company to a successful professionally managed enterprise. This enabled us to develop and implement a succession plan leading to realizing the asset value we created through the sale of the business.

This experience broadened my understanding of different industries and reinforced my belief that leaders across sectors face universal challenges. When moving into a new industry, remember that while the products or services may change, core business principles—like strategic resource allocation and brand positioning—remain the same. Cross-industry challenges often require the same disciplined thinking.

It was in this phase that my mission to help others became even more profound, and I began helping leaders in other industries navigate their business growth journeys. I encountered leaders navigating similar hurdles, and I had the privilege of sharing lessons learned from my journey.

After selling my interests in the Suwanee Sports Academy, I continued my business-building journey on new paths as well as by helping entrepreneurs and company leaders successfully navigate their transitions through different stages of the Entrepreneur to Enterprise journey.

I'll never forget a particular mentoring moment that confirmed I was in alignment with my passion and purpose. I was guiding a CEO through the difficult transition from the entrepreneurial startup phase to a professionally managed enterprise—the most stubborn growth phase that every entrepreneur worth their salt must conquer. Seeing the emotional lows she experienced; I shared my own experiences. When I saw a glimmer of light in her eyes as I planted a seed of hope, I felt a sense of fulfillment unlike any other. I knew then that my purpose was evolving into a legacy of empowering others to succeed.

Mentoring has become an essential part of my journey—a way to extend my impact beyond what I could accomplish alone. Through each leader I help, my legacy grows, grounded in the knowledge that the skills and insights I pass on will continue to shape businesses and lives long after my direct work is done.

As I reflect on my overall professional journey to date, I have an immense desire to share the names and stories of every person who contributed to my success in paving a fulfilling career. Unfortunately, the limitations of space within this book just won't allow it. So right now I simply want to emphasize that *none of us can do it alone.*

It's both rewarding and humbling to know that my experiences resonate with others and improve their odds of success. Not only that... I'm continuing to learn and grow as a leader. The transition from being a major player to a coach and mentor did not come without some apprehension because I'm an operator at heart. I often asked myself if I could handle being disconnected from the hands-on, day-to-day work that gave me so much satisfaction.

However, over time, I've learned that my perspective, combined with a collaborative approach of asking the right questions rather than always having the answers, while leveraging my own experiences as a business operator, has had an enormous impact on the leaders I mentor.

In these moments, I see how integrity comes to the forefront. It's about staying true to my word and honoring the commitments I've made to those I mentor, creating trust that fuels their growth. Integrity isn't just important in mentoring—it was a guiding principle in every business relationship I built. Whether negotiating contracts, leading teams, or working with partners, I found that integrity anchored trust and set the standard for lasting success.

A simple way I learned to define integrity is this: doing what we say we will do when we say we will do it. And if something prevents that, we manage expectations by resetting them for what others can expect. In all these moments, staying true to my word and honoring commitments has created a foundation of trust that fuels growth, for those I mentor and those I work with alike.

We can all be much more successful in overcoming significant challenges by accessing those who have been where we are going and are willing to share what they have found to be valuable solutions. I could not have been as successful in the roles I've played without this willingness by others to share personal insights, tips, and proven approaches with me.

You might say this is my *why* for writing this book. You see, a question I get all the time from entrepreneurs, CEOs, operating executives, and decision-makers at all levels is "Why do you do what you do?" A key driver for me is that I learned business building through trial and error during various growth transitions that proved satisfying, yet frustrating. I found that this frustration doesn't always come from failure but often from the inevitable growing pains that accompany success.

It truly energizes me when I can have an impact. People describe me as a problem solver and, more importantly, a problem identifier, with a keen sense for uncovering and solving issues before most even know the problem is on the road ahead. To this day, my trial-and-error experience has led me to create a sequenced approach for tackling any big business challenge and creating the fastest path to a solution, from concept to strategy through implementation to results. I'm energized by the impact that this approach can have, and I'm passionate about helping others anticipate and overcome roadblocks on their journey.

Today, my focus is on helping others create something they can take pride in. Something that transforms their lives and careers. That's bigger than any business I could have ever built on my own. That's legacy! There's a strong sense of fulfillment in watching others grow, knowing I've played a part in helping them achieve their own vision. Seeing their successes unfold is a reminder that legacy isn't just what we accomplish ourselves, but the impact we leave in the lives we touch. For me, that's the ultimate reward.

Throughout this book, I will share more of what I have learned during my career as well as the stories of other successful leaders from all stages of their careers. I'll introduce you to many admirable leaders who shared their stories so you can learn from their challenges and what solutions and processes they discovered that worked best as they moved their careers and companies forward. Such a generous gift of knowledge and experience has allowed me to succeed on my own journey and I know it will do the same for you.

A quick closing story for you. A CEO once recommended me to another CEO who needed some interim help. I told him the role had to be fun if I was to consider it. He told me there were so many challenges that he couldn't say anything would be fun about the role. There were just so many problems to work out.

My reply? "Sounds fun!" I think he thought I was crazy. Let me tell you, that's how I'm wired. Fun to me is gaining clarity for a challenge, figuring out the best path to desired outcomes, and getting everyone aligned to ensure successful implementation. Maybe I am a little crazy. But this energizes me. And I would like nothing more than to help you get on your fastest path to reaching your desired outcomes.

If you are reading this book to explore how you can better tackle challenges in your job and company, you are in the right place. You could be embarking on entrepreneurship, leading a team, or running a successful company; regardless of your leadership level, challenges require the same kind of disciplined thinking and focused approach.

- **You may be unsure** about the best approach to overcoming these challenges, and seek actionable guidance, impactful ideas, and tried-and-true tips.
- **You may need to discover** what you don't know and uncover the questions that need answering.
- **You may want to** involve your team for input, buy-in, and alignment but don't quite know how to do that smoothly and successfully.
- **You don't** want to go through your own trial and error experience; instead, you would like to learn a proven method for tackling challenges and mastering the leadership pathway.

Throughout this book, you'll learn actionable steps, discover inspirational insights, and gain powerful directives to implement in your own business-building journey. If you are responsible for taking on significant challenges for your company in any capacity, the advice and guidance in the following chapters will prove invaluable to your success.

My wish is for you to find success in tackling business challenges and to feel empowered, knowledgeable, and excited while doing so. The road to success can be challenging enough without having to face the challenges alone, especially when there is an approach that can guide leaders like you through them with ease. I aim to give you access to the stories of successful people sharing their insights, tips, and lessons learned from tackling their significant challenges. I want to help you find the *right* solutions to move your career and company forward and upward... faster.

Up Next

Explore the **Entrepreneur to Enterprise Pathway**, a roadmap for growing your business from inception to a thriving enterprise. In the upcoming chapters, we'll dive into the pathway's critical phases, the 3Cs Process to Faster Results, and leadership stories that offer insights for overcoming your biggest challenges. Get ready for actionable strategies to navigate your business journey with confidence.

Chapter 2

Entrepreneur to Enterprise Pathway

Every challenge conquered and problem solved becomes
a stepping stone to a stronger, more resilient enterprise.

Every business embarks on a transformative journey through five distinct growth phases—from an idea to an entrepreneurial venture, to a startup operation, to a proven business, and ultimately to maturing into a sustainable and successful enterprise. This progression is what I term the "Entrepreneur to Enterprise Pathway," a crucial framework for any business leader—whether an aspiring entrepreneur, an emerging leader, or a seasoned executive.

Navigating the Growth Phases

The journey along the pathway is marked by a series of interconnected challenges that are critical to both personal career development and company success. Overcoming these challenges requires a collaborative approach—deemed the most efficient path from ideation to outcome. This involves:

- **Asking the Right Questions:** To understand the core of each challenge.
- **Clarifying Challenges and Outcomes:** To ensure everyone's efforts are aligned.
- **Developing a Customized Plan:** To foster a learning environment conducive to growth.

Such collaboration not only helps bridge knowledge gaps but also empowers you, the leader, with the necessary insights to effectively address any significant challenges that arise.

Primary Challenges Along the Pathway

As you progress along the Entrepreneur to Enterprise Pathway, you will encounter five primary challenges. These are common across all businesses and are pivotal in transitioning from one phase to the next:

1. **Recognizing Customer Needs**
   - Develop solutions that are adaptive to changing needs.
   - Understand that initial success will bring about further challenges as needs evolve.
2. **Managing Resource Stretch**
   - When daily operations intensify, and resources seem stretched, it's crucial to bolster operational support and management systems to maintain short-term and long-term profitability.
3. **Instituting Professional Management**
   - The transition from an informal startup atmosphere to a structured, disciplined organization is necessary as the company expands and complexities increase.
4. **Adapting Organizational Culture**
   - As the company grows, the original culture may shift. Leadership must be proactive in managing these changes to maintain alignment with the company's goals and values.
5. **Anticipating Future Challenges**
   - Stay ahead of problems before they fully emerge. Understanding and anticipating these challenges is key to smooth transitions to further stages of growth.

Utilizing the Framework

Each company's journey along the Entrepreneur to Enterprise Pathway will vary, but these five challenges provide a robust framework for anticipating and tackling obstacles. Your ability to link recurring problems or opportunities to these challenges will enhance your strategic approach, making your pathway through each phase more navigable.

As you reflect on your current position within these phases, consider which challenges are most pertinent to your situation. How will you address them? Engage with this pathway actively and use it as a guide to steer your business toward sustained success.

Up Next

Discover the 3Cs Process to Faster Results, a streamlined method for tackling business challenges. In this chapter, you'll learn the 3Cs—Clarify, Chart, and Coalign—to identify problems, define outcomes, align your team, and take action. Get ready to master the balance of decision-making, ask focused questions, and close knowledge gaps to accelerate your success.

Chapter 3

The 3Cs Process to Faster Results Overview

In the midst of chaos, clarity is the first step toward
decisive action and impactful outcomes.

In business, addressing challenges efficiently and effectively is crucial, but pinpointing these issues and making aligned decisions for prompt action can be difficult. This necessitates a streamlined method that focuses on extracting only the essential information, clarifying your challenge, defining desired outcomes, aligning your team, and determining the sequential steps to success.

I experienced a need for this in my own business-building journey, and it led me to create my 3Cs Process to Faster Results. The 3Cs provide a powerful framework for business leaders to tackle challenges that emerge during business growth. It's a systematic approach, designed to equip leaders like you with the right decision-making skills for impactful actions, thereby setting you on the fastest and most effective path to business-building success.

The 3Cs are:
- **CLARIFY Your Challenge:** Identify your problem or opportunity precisely, allowing you to prioritize effectively among all competing priorities for focused attention and resources.
- **CHART Your Course:** Outline your destination, identify potential roadblocks, and establish non-negotiables for your journey.
- **COALIGN Your Team:** Ensure that decision-makers and key influencers are in sync with the planned course of action.

I have also sharpened my skills in three essential ingredients to get the most out of my 3Cs process, and I want to emphasize them for you.

The Three Essential Ingredients Are....

1. **Balancing Science and Art.** We often spend so much time focused on the science, which means the way something worked for someone else or in another situation, that we tend to ignore needed adjustments for implementing it in our current situation.

   It's important to always consider the art to make the necessary adjustments. If you only focus on how something worked in other situations, you ignore the clues to making the right adjustments to meet your current requirements.

2. **Ask Laser-Focused Questions.** The question is often more important than the answer. We are encouraged in our jobs to have the right answers when needed. The puzzling thing is that we must get good at knowing what we don't know when it comes to tackling challenges and then asking the right questions.

   Asking laser-focused questions extracts the relevant information in today's world of information overload. The right questions create the fastest path to desired outcomes when addressing problems or seizing an opportunity.

3. **Close Knowledge Gaps.** Engaging your team and key influencers in the discovery and learning process ensures that everyone gains the essential context and understanding needed to effectively address and bridge knowledge gaps. This approach is crucial for fostering successful collaboration and implementation.

Gaining proper alignment comes from productive collaboration, which only happens through dialogue and feedback. Then, someone can take action, with everyone rowing in the same direction.

I leverage my 3Cs process and three essential skill ingredients to create the fastest path to results for any significant challenge.

You see, I've built my own businesses and helped others grow theirs, and it was often a struggle to evaluate one challenge from the next, especially among all the competing priorities that can arise at any point. This often led to lost opportunities, disappointing outcomes, and regrets. Through trial and error, I discovered how to synthesize and organize only what is important and then created a process that can be replicated by any leader or manager.

Think of it like a whittler. Someone who cuts, trims, or shapes a piece of wood by carving off the bits that are not needed, leaving only a carving that resembles what they envisioned before starting. My 3Cs process whittles away all the noise of today's information overload. It simplifies and reduces the overwhelming parts, saving time, money, and resources on the way to thoughtful, efficient, and effective decisions when addressing a problem or opportunity.

Let's now talk about what the 3Cs *aren't*. I've often found that talking about what something is *not* can be just as important as what it *is*, and I reveal this to entrepreneurs and business leaders when helping them take on a challenge. So, I'll address the perception versus the reality.

People are quick to perceive my 3Cs to be a long-term strategic planning process. It is not. The reality is it's a disciplined thinking process for taking action *now*. Intended as a customizable tool for disciplined planning and action, the 3Cs process should be used for where you and your business are today, not three to five years from now. It is a systematic step-by-step approach for decision-makers and stakeholders to facilitate strategy development and gain alignment, giving your team the direction needed to complete an implementation plan more efficiently, more cost-effectively, and *faster*.

At its core, this is a comprehensive and strategic think-and-act method designed to help businesses CLARIFY big challenges, CHART a path, and COALIGN collaborators for successful implementation.

There's so much to teach about my 3Cs process and how it can help you overcome your biggest challenges. In fact, look out for a comprehensive guide on it in the future. For now, dive deep into the *what* and the *how to* with my online course. Learn more at PatAlacqua.com.

Up Next

Embark on the 3Cs Success Path, applying the 3Cs framework in five essential steps to tackle any business challenge. This chapter guides you from overwhelmed to impactful outcomes, ensuring team alignment and a clear path forward. Discover practical steps and real-life examples to transform challenges into achievements, driving your business forward efficiently.

Chapter 4

The 3Cs Success Path

Success is a journey that requires clarity, a well-charted course, and a united team.
Only then can you transform challenges into achievements.

THE 3Cs SUCCESS PATH

START	CLARIFY	CHART	COALIGN	RESULTS
①	②	③	④	⑤
Feeling overwhelmed & unsure about tackling the challenge	Decide whether to tackle the challenge	Choose & develop the 'how to' path to achieve result	Involve others for feedback & alignment	Feeling energized by realizing results, FAST.
	Determine what can be gained or lost	Identify desired outcome(s) & obstacles	Share charted course & adjust as needed	
	Consider competing priorities	Document what must & cannot happen	Transfer to key team to finalize planning details prior to implementation	
		Consider required resources		

Let's walk you through the 3Cs Success Path for tackling a challenge. Your challenge might be a problem you need to address or an opportunity you want to reach for. The 3Cs process has been designed to help you reach your desired outcomes for any challenge.

There are a total of five steps on your success path to tackling any challenge. You will use the 3Cs process to navigate this path.

Getting started with Step One is where most people feel overwhelmed and unsure about tackling their big challenges when considering all the competing priorities they are facing at any given point in time.

Sometimes you don't know where to start and don't have the confidence to implement successfully. If you have a solid approach to tackling your challenge, you can more easily stay focused on what you know and trust that your approach and process will fill in the gaps for what you don't when moving forward.

Let's fast-forward to what you should be feeling when realizing the results of your success path. After navigating these five steps, you should feel energized by the impact of leveraging the fastest path to your desired outcomes.

Now let's address the steps in between.

Step Two is where you **CLARIFY your challenge**, whether it be an opportunity or a recurring problem. This stage is when you're busy with all your responsibilities but need to make an intentional decision on whether to tackle a big challenge. It is about getting clear on your problem or opportunity and what you can specifically gain or lose because of this challenge. You are also considering the overwhelm of any competing priorities for you and your business and you'll need to determine whether this is the right time to tackle this challenge.

Everything is built on this base. The clearer you are here, the more effective everything else becomes.

Step Three is where you **CHART your course**. As you continue your big challenge journey, this step is when you already know the scope of what you gain by tackling the challenge or, equally important, what you can lose if you choose not to act.

At this point, you're now ready to confidently take the path that will get you the results you seek. You will identify the desired outcomes for taking on this challenge and the obstacles that stand in the way of success. You'll document what must happen and what cannot happen along the journey, and consider the resources required for success. Clearly **CHARTING your course** will provide great context as you involve your team and other key stakeholders for their input and alignment.

Step Four is all about how to **COALIGN your team**. At this point, you are ready to involve your team and key stakeholders for their feedback and alignment on how you have initially charted the course. You will share your desired outcomes and non-negotiables for the path you take for how to get there, discuss required resources for your problem or opportunity, and adjust as you consider the feedback you receive.

You can then turn things over to your project manager and key team members for the final planning details, including team role definitions, action items, timelines, accountabilities, specific budget dollars, and tracking progress and results while adjusting where needed.

This will substantially improve your chances for successful implementation and reduce delays. Everyone is now rowing in the same direction from the start, saving time and money, and mitigating the risk of implementation.

Step Four is the bridge to getting started implementing. You are now ready to make things happen by transforming all the ideas into reality. Many companies fail when it comes time for the implementation stage. Ideas are often the easy part. Making them happen ultimately demonstrates real success. It's time to get clear on your project implementation plan and then execute that plan.

Once you have successfully used this process and have made it a part of your disciplined thinking and planning process, you truly have a sustainable foundation for moving your business forward fast.

A quick story I want to share with you. One I tell often to emphasize a key point in tackling challenges. Years ago, I was given advice by the president of Porsche, here in the United States.

This is what he drew out for me.

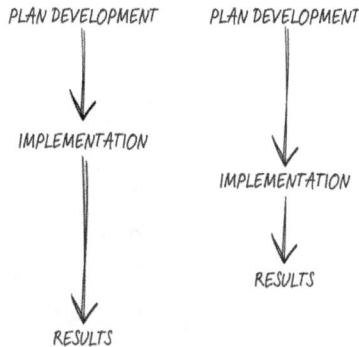

PLAN DEVELOPMENT   PLAN DEVELOPMENT

↓   ↓

IMPLEMENTATION

↓   IMPLEMENTATION

↓

RESULTS

↓

RESULTS

He then asked me, "In any situation, what would be your preference if you were getting started leading an initiative, which path would you want to take?"

I said, "Of course, I would want the path where I got the benefit of the results faster."

His response was, "I agree. But why is it that everyone would answer just as you and I have, but then put themselves on the other path? Why? Because they spend so little time mapping out their path to the destination they want to reach that they stay stuck in the implementation stage and never get there."

Even though the core point of the story is so simple and somewhat obvious, it still resonates with me today. It is for this reason that my 3Cs process for choosing the fastest path to desired outcomes when tackling a big challenge is so impactful when applied in a disciplined manner over and over. This is when business building truly moves your company from an entrepreneurial one-to-one that is a blend of entrepreneurism and disciplined management. This blended balance is key to any sustainable business transforming from the beginning stages to becoming a sustainable enterprise.

Once again, you can get all the details about my 3Cs process and how to implement it on your own by visiting www.PatAlacqua.com.

Up Next

Explore **Components of the Leadership Experience**, where you'll uncover the key challenges leaders face. This chapter covers the shift from *doer* to *leader*, the power of collaboration, problem avoidance, and breaking through plateaus. Get ready for insights and practical advice to confidently navigate your leadership journey and drive both personal and organizational growth.

Chapter 5

Components of the Leadership Experience

Great leaders are forged in adversity,
transforming obstacles into stepping stones and setbacks into triumphs.

Let's jump into the components of a leader's journey to success. These are four general challenges all leaders face at one time or another throughout their careers.

1. Transforming from Doer to Leader: Mastering The Mental Game
2. The Power of Collaboration
3. Problem Avoidance
4. Breaking Through Plateaus

Think about how each of these might apply to your own business journey and the ways in which you have, or could, navigate your path around these challenges.

Let's get started with the first one.

1. From Doer to Leader: Mastering the Mental Game of Leadership

Have you ever been puzzled over why some individuals falter when they transition into leadership roles despite their earlier successes? Moving from a doer to a leadership position can be overwhelming for many entrepreneurs and business leaders. Although management systems that focus on the business from a broader perspective are widely discussed, the requisite psychological adaptations are often underestimated.

Let's get into the three crucial mental challenges individuals encounter when stepping into managerial and leadership roles:

- Impact on how we feel about ourselves
- Modulating the need for authority
- Managing the urge for approval

By comprehending and tackling these hurdles, prospective leaders can smooth their pathway to leadership. The term doer describes someone primarily engaged in hands-on task completion and is responsible for specific outputs. Such individuals are typically highly proficient in their roles, finding personal gratification in their direct achievements.

Conversely, leaders undertake managerial or leadership duties within an organization. Their role centers on orchestrating teamwork, mentoring, setting strategic visions, decision-making, and realizing shared objectives. Leaders adopt an overarching view, prioritizing the collective over individual achievements.

The evolution from doer to leader signifies a fundamental shift in mindset and responsibilities, transitioning from immediate task execution to a broader, more influential role. While the role of a doer provides personal satisfaction, evolving into a leader demands the development of new competencies and addressing psychological barriers related to team management, task delegation, and complex decision-making.

Now, let's focus on the three mental challenges crucial for those advancing into leadership or for existing leaders aiming for greater fulfillment in their roles.

First, let's discuss the **impact on how we feel about ourselves**. The change from an active role player or doer to a leader can alter self-perception. The direct link between effort and result weakens, which might reduce feelings of self-worth.

Take Sarah, a skilled project manager who advanced into a leadership position but encountered self-doubt, affecting her confidence and decision-making. She can overcome this by engaging in self-reflection and recognizing her past achievements. Receiving feedback from peers and mentors can also provide a balanced view of her skills while adopting a growth mindset and practicing self-affirmations can help restore her self-esteem.

Next, we address **modulating the need for control**. Traditionally, doers maintain complete oversight and perform tasks autonomously. However, leadership necessitates entrusting others with responsibilities.

Consider Mark, an experienced entrepreneur who initially sought to control all aspects of his venture. This control impeded team collaboration and creativity. By practicing delegation and fostering trust, Mark can alleviate these concerns. Defining clear roles allows team members to assume responsibility, easing the transition from micromanagement to a more collaborative environment.

Finally, **managing the urge for approval**. The desire for approval from others can compromise a leader's ability to make firm decisions or tackle performance issues.

Jessica, for example, who became a team leader, found her need for approval conflicted with her managerial duties. Cultivating an environment of open dialogue and mutual respect can help leaders like Jessica maintain a balance between being personable and exerting necessary authority.

In conclusion, transitioning from a doer to an effective manager and leader involves more than mastering operational systems. It's about mental transformation. Embracing these challenges can enable leaders to confidently assume their new roles, blending control with empowerment and team success. Leadership is an ongoing journey of personal and professional growth, where nurturing both can have a profound impact on teams and entire organizations.

Let's now dive into the next key component for making the transition to an effective leader.

2. Unleashing the Power of Collaboration: A 6-Step Proven Template for Success

Unleashing the power of collaborating with others can propel us toward our desired outcomes so much faster and smarter when taking on business challenges. In a world that thrives on interconnectedness, collaboration has become so important to our success when taking on business challenges. By working together, we can accomplish far more than what we could achieve alone.

Collaboration is not just a buzzword; it's a mindset that cultivates synergy and unlocks real potential. Embracing collaboration can move your career and company forward... faster.

There are five reasons why collaboration is so important to success in today's world of business challenges that we can expect on the road ahead.

1. **Collective Wisdom:** Collaboration allows us to tap into the collective wisdom of a group. We can uncover innovative solutions and overcome big challenges so much more effectively.
2. **Greater Creativity:** Collaboration acts as a stimulant for creativity. When people from different backgrounds come together, unique perspectives blend, sparking new ideas and approaches.
3. **Amplify Problem Solving:** Exchanging feedback, and leveraging

each other's strengths, give us an approach to address problems from various angles to find the best solutions.

4. **Faster Learning:** Working alongside talented individuals allows us to continue our own learning journey and acquire new skills. We can all benefit by leveraging the strengths of others.

5. **Relationship Building:** Collaborating with like-minded individuals, helps us build meaningful relationships.

Making collaboration a fundamental part of our approach to tackling business challenges helps us all move our careers and companies forward.... faster.

I'm often asked to help leaders explore their collaboration potential with others. I use my 6-Step Collaboration Template to explore synergies to see if there is potential to leverage those synergies for their mutual benefit.

Let's walk you through the template, but first, I want to emphasize one thing with you: *balancing the science and the art of any proven solution.* You see, we all hear about solutions, tools, or models that have worked for others, and then wonder if they will work for us.

It could be a...

- Diet to improve health or manage weight...
- Workout to build strength...
- Template that allows you to just fill in the blanks to close sales faster...
- Checklist for what to do to increase margins...
- The list goes on and on....

What's often misunderstood is that anything that has worked for another situation will typically work for you, but only once it's customized and adapted to your situation. The best solutions are ones that are proven. You don't want to recreate the wheel, but you need to consider how to personalize any successful approach to fit your situation.

A quote from Thomas Edison really drives this point home. He once said...

"I regard it as a criminal waste of time to go through the slow and painful ordeal of ascertaining things for oneself, if these same things have already been ascertained and made available by others."

That's what I mean by the science. And when a method is adapted to work for an individual, that's what I call the art.

So, what I want you to remember as I share my template for exploring the real collaboration potential with anyone is that this template has proven to work over and over for me, but I typically adjust it to fit each situation when I explore collaboration opportunities with others. Be sure to think about how you can adjust it for your situation. You will also note that I have integrated my 3Cs process into my collaboration process.

You will be able to use my 6-Step Collaboration Template as your roadmap every time you explore collaboration with others to reach desired outcomes. All that being said, let me walk you through each step now.

Step One: Desired Outcome/s for Collaboration. This is where each potential collaborator identifies what they want to get from the collaboration.

Step Two: Obstacles or Roadblocks in the Way. Be sure to have each person think about what they anticipate getting in the way of reaching desired outcomes.

Step Three: Non-Negotiables. Have each person consider their own views on what must happen and what cannot happen when any implementation roadmap for reaching outcomes is ultimately completed.

Step Four: Potential Synergies. This is where each potential collaborator considers how they can add value to the other collaborators as well as how each of the others can add value for them.

Step Five: Final Preparation for Decisions. Once each person has clarified and documented their own thinking for Steps One through Four, then have everyone review all the feedback documented by each person. It is here that everyone then adds or adjusts whatever resonates with them during this review.

Step Six. Collaborators Meet—Align and Prioritize. At this point, you're ready to update the planning document and distribute it so everyone can come to a final planning session with the same context needed to meet and make decisions together on the synergies that have the highest probability of success to reach desired outcomes for all collaborators.

When Step Six is completed, the most efficient and highest-impact next steps can be determined and scheduled for action.

The real value of any framework or template lies in how well it helps synthesize and organize the actionable knowledge gained through the thinking and dialogue that takes place. So, when working through this 6-Step Collaboration Template, be sure to document your thoughts before moving to any next step. This gives you a way to take everyone's thinking and make it more tangible for discussion and alignment. You'll increase the probability of a successful implementation process, so everyone realizes the value provided by all collaborators.

I hope you get value from my 6-Step Collaboration Template. Use it to build your mindset and actions for cultivating synergy and unlocking real potential for tackling business challenges through collaboration. Embracing collaboration will move your career and company forward... faster.

Let's now move on to the third key component of the leadership experience.

3. From Reactive to Proactive: Mastering the Art of Problem Avoidance

Life presents us with numerous challenges and obstacles that demand our attention. Often, we find ourselves trapped in an endless cycle of problem-solving, tirelessly fixing things in an attempt to restore normalcy. But what if there's a better approach? What if we break free from this cycle and find a path to lasting success?

Let's discuss the art of problem avoidance.

When I refer to problem avoidance, I mean the proactive identification and sidestepping of potential issues before they arise. I am not suggesting in any way that you ignore problems. In fact, by addressing issues proactively, you can often avoid bigger headaches down the road.

Problem avoidance is a highly effective approach that empowers us to allocate more time and resources to seize opportunities that propel us forward. Instead of constantly putting out fires and dealing with problems as they emerge, we become architects of our own success, building a solid foundation that resists setbacks.

Problem avoidance involves proactive thinking, risk assessment, and preemptive measures to mitigate potential roadblocks. It allows us to create the freedom and confidence needed to capitalize on opportunities others might overlook until they become so disruptive that they have a more significantly negative impact than necessary.

Let's consider an example to understand the effectiveness of problem avoidance better.

Imagine you're planning a project that involves multiple stakeholders.

Traditional problem-solving would include addressing issues arising during the project's execution. However, by adopting a problem-avoidance mindset, you would assess and anticipate potential challenges before they become critical.

Through proactive measures like risk assessment, collaboration with stakeholders, and continuous improvement of processes, you identify the possibility of communication breakdowns due to conflicting objectives.

Recognizing this potential problem, you take steps to foster open communication, establish clear goals, and develop contingency plans. As a result, you avoid the issue altogether, ensuring smooth collaboration, timely delivery, and overall project success.

In contrast, if you had relied solely on problem-solving, you would have had to spend significant time and resources resolving the communication breakdowns and dealing with their consequences.

This example highlights how problem avoidance can lead to more effective outcomes by preventing issues from materializing in the first place. By proactively addressing potential problems, we save time and resources and create an environment conducive to innovation, collaboration, and growth.

Now, let's dive into four strategies that can help shift our mindset from reactive problem-solving to proactive problem-avoidance:

1. **Assess and Anticipate:** Take the time to evaluate potential risks and challenges in advance, allowing you to develop preventive measures.
2. **Learn From Past Experiences:** Analyze Previous Problems And Identify Recurring Patterns To Avoid Similar Pitfalls In The Future.
3. **Foster a Culture of Collaboration:** Encourage open communication and teamwork, as diverse perspectives can uncover potential issues before they become critical.
4. **Invest in Continuous Improvement:** Regularly review and update processes, systems, and policies to stay ahead of emerging challenges.

Remember, problem avoidance is a journey. By embracing these strategies, we unlock a future of opportunities where success becomes the norm, and we face the unpredictable confidently.

Through problem avoidance, we foster an environment that cultivates innovation, collaboration, and growth. Teams that prioritize problem avoidance become more productive, and experience reduced stress levels, leading to higher job satisfaction and overall well-being.

The choice is yours. Will you be a problem solver trapped in a perpetual cycle, or will you be a problem avoider, unlocking the doors to a world of endless possibilities? It's time to step forward, embrace problem avoidance, and pave the way for a brighter future. Together, let's make it happen.

Last, but not least, the fourth component of your leadership experience journey.

4. Breaking Through Plateaus: Propelling Your Career and Company Forward

Did you ever think that staying ahead of the curve in the fast-paced business world can sometimes feel like running on a treadmill? No matter how fast you go, the scenery remains the same. As ambitious leaders, we constantly seek new avenues, hoping that our next step might be the one that propels us forward.

I remember a time in my own journey when, despite my best efforts and long hours, the growth graph seemed to flatten out. It's that sinking feeling, leaving you wondering if this is as good as it gets. In today's world of competing priorities and constant overwhelm, a question that frequently lingers in the back of our minds is...

How do we stay ahead of the curve?

The big obstacle we often stumble upon is feeling stuck. Despite pouring our hearts and soul into our endeavors, it sometimes feels like hitting a brick wall. We find ourselves up against limited opportunities, fierce competition, and saturated markets. Standing out feels almost impossible. When faced with this common challenge, many resort to conventional strategies like refining existing skills or expanding their network. While these strategies aren't wrong (and can even offer some relief) they sometimes fall short of sparking the significant growth we seek. As comforting as they are, these traditional pathways might not always address the core issues holding us back.

There's a world out there brimming with innovation, adaptability, and emerging trends. Relying solely on what we know can make us miss out on the magic of what we don't. To truly propel forward, a fresh perspective is vital. We need to think differently, to see our challenges not as immovable obstacles but as puzzles waiting to be solved. This shift involves taking a moment to reflect, understanding where we feel trapped, and then seeking out new avenues of growth.

Growth Mindset: One mindset that's been a game changer for me is the growth mindset—a belief that every challenge is a learning opportunity. It's about realizing that our most significant growth often happens just outside our comfort zones.

Innovation: Another crucial element is innovation. The world around us is evolving at a breakneck speed. Keeping pace means we should be open to new ideas and technologies and actively seek them out, challenge industry conventions, and foster a culture where creativity thrives.

Partnerships/Collaboration: Building strategic partnerships has also been an invaluable asset on my journey. Collaborating with those who offer fresh perspectives and expertise can be a beacon of mutual growth.

Remember the early days of our careers, filled with ambition and excitement? It's time to reignite that passion. And for those emerging leaders, it's time to ignite it for the first time. By embracing a growth mindset, leaning into innovation, forging strong partnerships, and staying agile, we can break free from being stuck and truly soar. Countless individuals and businesses have done just that. From disruptive startups to industry giants, their stories inspire and remind us of the endless possibilities that lie ahead.

The path to true success is paved with challenges, introspection, and adaptability. We can unlock our boundless potential with the right mindset, tools, and insights from those who have been where we are going.

Up Next

Explore **Leadership Hurdles and How to Jump Over Them**, where you'll learn to turn obstacles into opportunities. This chapter offers practical tools to handle internal team issues and external changes, helping you emerge stronger. Discover how to make tough decisions, maintain team harmony, and stay true to your values while avoiding burnout. Get ready to lead with conviction and adapt to any challenge.

Chapter 6

Leadership Hurdles and How to Jump Over Them

Leadership is about turning obstacles into opportunities.
Embrace challenges, adapt swiftly, and lead with conviction.

Leadership comes with its bumps in the road. Both internal team issues and external changes can make the journey bumpy. This chapter will provide you with tools and strategies to start navigating these hurdles and emerge stronger.

Major Hurdles in Leadership

Rolling with the Punches

Change is constant. New technologies, market fluctuations, and global events can disrupt your plans. Leaders must stay adaptable. The ability to roll with the punches ensures you're prepared for unexpected shifts.

Strategies to Adapt

- Establish a routine to monitor changes (e.g., monthly check-ins). This will keep you informed and ready to pivot when necessary.
- Implement incremental steps rather than drastic shifts to manage change. Small steps prevent overwhelming your team and maintain steady progress.
- Develop a flexible framework that allows for rapid prototyping and testing of new ideas. This iterative approach helps you quickly adapt to changes and implement effective solutions.

Tough Calls on the Fly

Decision-making under pressure is a crucial skill. Sometimes, leaders must make significant decisions with limited information. The ability to make tough calls on the fly ensures you can act swiftly and confidently in critical moments.

Decision-Making Frameworks
- Develop a Quick Decision Kit to identify critical tools like core values, KPIs, risk assessment charts, and decision-making models.
- Create a checklist of essential information for decisions.
- List trusted advisers for quick input.
- Develop templates for everyday decisions, such as pros and cons lists or decision trees.
- Forge pre-determined protocols for emergency scenarios to guide decision-making.

Make Decisions with Conviction

Acting decisively fosters trust and stability within the team. Stick to your core values and principles. Confidence reassures your team and maintains momentum.

Incorporate scenario planning into your decision-making process. You can make more informed and confident decisions under pressure by anticipating and preparing for various outcomes.

Keeping the Peace and Talking It Out

Teams, like families, can experience conflicts and misunderstandings. Managing these dynamics maintains harmony and productivity. Addressing conflicts early and cultivating open communication prevents issues from escalating.

Conflict Resolution and Communication Strategies
- Create an environment where issues are addressed early.
- Hold regular check-ins or team meetings to voice concerns. This encourages transparency and prevents conflicts from festering.
- Implement an open-door policy for team members to approach leaders with concerns.

Foster a Culture of Open Dialogue
- Encourage team members to express their thoughts through regular meetings or feedback tools. This not only fosters open dialogue but also strengthens the bond between you and your team.
- Give the speaker full attention, acknowledge their points, and respond

thoughtfully.
- Train team members to give and receive constructive feedback, focusing on specific behaviors and outcomes.

Creating a 'No Surprises' Environment
- Regularly discuss challenges and progress to prevent surprises. Transparency builds trust and keeps everyone aligned.
- Implement conflict resolution training programs for your team. Help them build the skills to handle disagreements professionally and constructively, reducing the likelihood of conflicts escalating.

Staying True to Your Roots

As companies grow, maintaining core values can be challenging but essential. Consistently anchoring meetings with the company's mission keeps the team aligned and motivated.

Methods to Maintain Core Values
- Celebrate achievements that align with core values.
- Integrate core values into your performance review process. Evaluate and reward employees based on how well they embody the company's values daily.

Not Burning Out

Balancing work and life is vital for sustained energy and focus. Prioritizing self-care ensures leaders can perform at their best and set a positive example for their teams.

Self-Care Practices
- Schedule regular breaks and reflection periods to recharge and prevent burnout.
- Develop a wellness program for your team. Offer resources such as fitness memberships, mental health support, and workshops on stress management to promote overall well-being.

Toolkit for Overcoming Hurdles
Make A Game Plan—Planning Techniques

Create a detailed roadmap with clear objectives and steps. A well-defined plan provides direction and clarity. Revisit and tweak your strategies. Regularly update your plan to reflect changes. This ensures your strategy remains relevant and practical. Use data analytics to inform your planning process. By leveraging data insights, you can make more accurate predictions and adjustments to your strategy.

Learn from the Pros

Seek advice from experienced leaders. Mentorship offers valuable insights and shortcuts to success.

Networking Tips
- Join industry groups and attend events to expand your knowledge and open opportunities for collaboration.
- Leverage online platforms for mentorship opportunities.
- Establish a mentorship program within your organization. Encourage senior leaders to mentor junior employees, fostering knowledge transfer and leadership development.

Never Stop Learning

Dedicate time each week for learning new skills. Continuous learning keeps you ahead and enhances your capabilities.

Recommended Resources
- Online courses: Flexible and accessible, allowing you to learn independently.
- Industry publications: Staying updated with the latest developments helps you remain competitive.
- Create a learning culture within your team: Encourage knowledge sharing through regular lunch-and-learn sessions, internal workshops, and collaborative projects.

Earning the Gold Stars
Build Trust and Credibility

Demonstrate your ability to navigate challenges and earn your team's trust. Find a way to share success stories.

- Highlight achievements to build morale and camaraderie. Celebrating

success reinforces positive behaviors and motivates the team.
- Develop a recognition program that allows peers to acknowledge each other's contributions. Peer recognition can boost morale and foster a supportive team environment.

Stretching Your Comfort Zone

Embrace new challenges to expand your capabilities. Facing difficult situations promotes growth.

Personal Anecdotes
- Share your experiences of stepping out of your comfort zone. Personal stories encourage others to take similar steps.
- Set stretch goals for your team. These ambitious targets push individuals beyond their comfort zones and drive innovation and growth.

Big Wins Ahead

Recognize and celebrate both small and large achievements to boost morale.

Setting Ambitious Goals
- Encourage your team to aim high and strive for excellence.
- Use milestone celebrations as opportunities for team building. Plan events or activities that celebrate success and strengthen team cohesion and collaboration.

Here's the thing. Those hurdles you're jumping over? They're stepping stones to becoming the kind of leader who doesn't just survive but thrives. It's about using those tools, soaking up wisdom from those already there, and treating each challenge as an opportunity to grow.

Embrace the bumps in the road as your launch pad to something greater. Keep pushing forward, keep growing, and you'll find that the bumps you once saw as obstacles will become the milestones you look back on with pride. Kudos to the challenges that shape us, the tools that guide us, and the victories that define us!

As we've explored, leadership is shaped by our ability to confront challenges, stay adaptable, and cultivate the skills to drive both personal and organizational growth. Now, it's time to widen our lens and learn from a diverse group of leaders who have overcome their own significant hurdles.

The stories that follow will provide you with a unique perspective into how business challenges have been met with innovative strategies, collaboration, and relentless focus. These leaders' journeys will light your path, turning their hard-earned triumphs into inspiration and actionable insights for your own growth.

Up Next

Dive into our **Challenge Stories**, where leaders share their toughest challenges, key lessons, and successes. As you read, reflect on your own business journey and how these insights can impact your career.

BONUS RESOURCES

Visit our Resource Center today to
access resources that will help you
overcome challenges and grow faster.

Create your free account at
PatAlacqua.com/bonus-resources
and unlock these valuable insights now!

PAT
ALACQUA
BUSINESS GROWTH
STRATEGIST

SECTION 2

From Challenges to Triumph:
Real-Life Leadership Stories

PAT
ALACQUA
BUSINESS GROWTH
STRATEGIST

Introduction

*"The stories of those who've overcome great challenges light our path,
turning their triumphs into inspiration and their wisdom into our guide."*

Learning from others' challenges has been invaluable in my career, and I am passionate about sharing the trials, errors, and solutions that have helped successful leaders reach where many aspire to be.

Shared wisdom provides a bridge over our challenges, offering tools to navigate our path with clarity and confidence.

The Good Stuff from Leadership Stories

1. **A Guide to Success:** Leaders' stories act as routes on a map, showing us how to win and avoid their mistakes. They also remind us we're not alone in our struggles.
2. **New Perspectives:** Leaders' stories spark fresh ideas and help us avoid their mistakes.
3. **We're Not Alone:** It feels good to hear that other people have had their struggles. It's a reminder that we're all in this together.
4. **Keep Getting Better:** These stories show us that being a leader means constantly learning and getting better at what we do.
5. **It's Okay to Be Real:** The best stories show leaders being honest about when things get tough. It tells us that it's okay to be ourselves and that this honesty can help build a place where everyone trusts each other more.
6. **Success is More Than Just Winning:** Success isn't just about money or fame. It's also about overcoming doubts, working well with others, and sticking to what's right, even when it's hard.
7. **All the Wisdom:** Every story adds more to the big pile of know-how we can all use. It's like a shared secret recipe for being a great

leader.

8. **Mixing Ideas Up:** When leaders look at what people in totally different jobs are doing, they can bring some of that magic back to their work.

9. **History Has Clues for Us:** Looking back at what leaders did before us can teach us a lot and help us figure out where we want to go next.

In the following chapters you'll have access to:

- A backstage pass to the firsthand knowledge and experiences of fellow business leaders, from the challenges they faced to how they overcame them.
- Anecdotal stories, ideas, tips, and best practice tools you can use to get faster results when tackling your own challenges.
- The uniquely valuable perspectives of experts who've not only learned how to reach success but know the importance of sharing their journeys with others.

My vision for this book, and particularly these stories, is to forge a collaborative route to success powered by the insights of those who've navigated the business landscape's challenges and opportunities.

Through real-life challenge stories, I aim to spotlight the decision-making process and problem-solving acumen of astute business minds. Powerful narratives are more than guidance; they're the compass for entrepreneurs and executives, guiding them toward informed and effective action.

While reading through these stories continue to keep in mind your own experience facing—and working through—challenges and consider how some of these tips could apply to your business. In a later section, you'll have the opportunity to take a deeper dive into ways you can look at your own challenge story and begin to implement equally helpful strategies.

Let's get started!

PART 1: SIMPLICITY IS KEY

The challenges that arise when growing a business can appear overwhelming. By simplifying the approach, breaking things down piece by piece, and staying true to their values, these leaders mastered the art of problem-solving with clarity, focus, and determination.

Chapter 7

Play-By-Play Communication Strategies with Legendary Sportscaster, Bob Rathbun

Effective communication is about listening deeply, understanding fully, and responding thoughtfully to build meaningful connections and achieve lasting success.

Bob Rathbun is the longest-tenured TV play-by-play announcer in the NBA's Atlanta Hawks history. He has received numerous awards, including the Cynopsis Sports Media honor and thirteen Southeast Regional Emmy Awards. An eight-time National Sportscasters and Sportswriters Association (NSSA) Sportscaster of the Year, he also received the Positivity in Broadcasting Award from Positive Athlete Georgia in 2017.

Bob's basketball work has included calling games for TNT, NBA TV, CBS, ABC, and ESPN. He has anchored The Basketball Tournament for ESPN and hosts *A Trophy Life*, the podcast of the Naismith Awards. He sits on the national Naismith Awards Board of Directors and Board of Selectors.

Since 1988, Rathbun has called games for the Atlantic Coast Conference (ACC) and (Southeastern Conference) SEC. He also voiced the Women's National Basketball Association's (WNBA's) Atlanta Dream for ten seasons. His baseball resumé includes Fox Sports South's voice of the Atlanta Braves, radio for the Detroit Tigers, and TV for the Baltimore Orioles.

Bob's accolades include Sportscaster of the Year honors in Virginia and Georgia, a Distinguished Service Award from the ACC, and a Distinguished Alumni Award from Catawba College. He is a member of multiple Sports Halls of Fame.

Throughout his decades-long career in sports broadcasting Bob has learned valuable lessons on the significance of improving our interactions in both personal and professional settings. His approach to enriching these interactions is rooted in thoughtful communication, a deep commitment to personal engagement, and an understanding of the potential long-term professional impact our words and actions can have. Moreover, Bob highlights the indispensable role of research in both understanding the past and preparing for future challenges.

Let's dive into Bob's story, where he brings a unique perspective on communication, resilience, and leadership, and artfully illustrates how the forging of stronger, more meaningful connections can have a direct impact on success.

What do you do to improve the quality of your interactions?

To improve the quality of interactions, it is crucial to manage the influx of information that comes at lightning speed in today's world. Once you hit send on a message, whether it is a tweet, a post, or an email, you cannot take it back. Impulsive actions driven by emotions can lead to trouble and harm relationships. Therefore, it's essential to think before communicating online and limit time spent on social media to focus on more productive activities.

Another way to enhance interactions is through research. While online research is valuable, the most insightful discoveries often come from talking to people directly. Engaging in one-on-one conversations with players, coaches, colleagues, or employees can uncover a treasure trove of information and personal stories.

By showing genuine interest and actively listening, you can build rapport and trust, leading to better communication and collaboration.

In business settings, taking the time to get to know team members, bosses, and colleagues on a personal level can strengthen relationships and foster open communication. Asking questions, listening attentively, and cultivating real in-person connections are essential for effective interactions and building a positive work environment.

Therefore, it is essential to limit reliance on technology and prioritize face-to-face interactions to improve the quality of communication and relationships.

Can you share your approach to discovering and qualifying opportunities for yourself?

I've always relished the chance to share insights during my public speaking engagements, especially when they intersect with my experiences in sports. Many of my audiences are sports fans, drawn to hear stories from the world of athletics. But the parallels between sports and business are striking. While the settings differ, the lessons of leadership, teamwork, and striving for success resonate across both arenas.

At the Atlanta Hawks, the pursuit of victory is a daily focus. Whether it is players honing their skills, coaches refining their strategies, or staff members working collaboratively, everyone is driven by the goal of winning. This mindset permeates our organization and informs our actions each day.

Translating this sports mindset to the boardroom is invaluable. Effective leaders inspire their teams to be fully engaged and committed to the company's mission. Just as athletes strive to excel on the field, employees should be motivated to contribute their best efforts to achieve organizational goals.

I embrace opportunities to discuss these principles because they are universally applicable. Sports serve as a rich source of examples and lessons that can be readily applied to various business scenarios. It is both enjoyable and rewarding to explore these connections and inspire others to adopt a winning mindset in their professional endeavors.

In today's information age, how important is research to getting the results you want?

Research is paramount to achieving the results you want. Whether it's in broadcasting NBA games or leading a business, immersing yourself in information is akin to drinking from a fire hose. The key is learning to distill that information down to what's truly meaningful. When preparing for a game, I have a checklist of about twenty-five things I go through, focusing on what I need to know rather than reading every word of everything.

For those starting out, curiosity about the *why* is essential. Understanding the history of your field is crucial for broadcasters and leaders alike. Sports, for example, didn't begin with ESPN; knowing the history of the game adds depth to your understanding. Similarly, in business, knowing about a leader's background, experiences, and mentors provides valuable insight into their decision-making and leadership style.

When researching, dive into the past to better understand the present and anticipate the future. Ask questions about upbringing, family, education, and career trajectory. Understanding the journey of individuals allows you to relate to them better and predict their actions.

As a leader, taking advantage of these opportunities to learn about your team members creates stronger connections and more effective leadership. Thus, embracing research and learning from the past is essential for success in today's information age.

What tips can you offer entrepreneurs and emerging leaders for creating and sustaining a lifelong learning journey?

I believe it starts with a commitment to personal growth, a lesson I learned during my undergraduate years at Catawba College in North Carolina. At nineteen, I transferred from UNC Charlotte to Catawba and dove into full-time work at a radio station. There, Dr. Carl Hall, head of the speech department and my mentor, guided me on a journey of self-improvement. He emphasized the importance of continuous learning, particularly in broadcasting.

Dr. Hall and I worked tirelessly on refining my voice, stage presence, and performance in the studio and during play-by-plays. Through independent studies, I would record games, review them with Dr. Hall, receive feedback, and then implement improvements in subsequent broadcasts. This iterative process laid the foundation for my lifelong commitment to learning and growth.

As a leader, effective communication is paramount. One must first acknowledge and take ownership of their role as a communicator before guiding others. Utilizing modern tools like cameras and microphones, individuals can record and review their presentations instantaneously. This self-awareness allows for reflection on one's delivery, message clarity, and overall effectiveness.

By mastering the art of communication, you can convey your message with greater impact and influence. These lessons are invaluable for anyone seeking to enhance their speaking skills and leadership abilities.

Talk about the things people can do to become better communicators.

Two things come to mind. The first is quality in-person communication. When you are representing yourself, it is crucial that you register and receive feedback from your audience, whether you're in a boardroom with five people or you're speaking to a group of 500 or even 5,000.

It does not matter if you are an articulate speaker, and you practiced and you know your material or not. Your focus should not just be on giving the speech or transferring the information; you want to be able to read your audience as to how that information is being received.

You do not want heads down checking their messages; you want them to be engaged with you. And I think there are some techniques you can implement to hold their attention, things like walking around, getting out from behind the podium, engaging with your audience. But most importantly, you want to make sure that you're seeing in your audience that they are receiving what you're saying.

The second is asking for feedback and listening to it. That's why I'm such a big fan of recording presentations, so you can go back and watch them and see for yourself. Did I do the job that I thought I did in trying to impart this information to my audience?

So, when the questions come, make sure that you are a good listener and truly hear and understand their questions, concerns, opinions, and points that they want to make because you've triggered something in them that wants to further the conversation. And these are the moments where oftentimes I will learn something that I did not consider before.

So the art of giving a good presentation lies also in being a good listener. Even if you are in a small conference room or at a round table, the lessons I think are the same. You want to get their feedback first through their body language and then later, when you ask for and listen to what your audience has to say.

Bob's insights from the realm of sports broadcasting and leadership remind us that whether on the court or in the boardroom, success stems from continuous learning and adaptability. Let's carry forward these lessons, striving to improve not only our communication skills but also our ability to connect and lead effectively in all areas of life.

Up Next

Meet Danny Ourian, assistant director of Applied Sport and Performance Psychology at Dominican University and founder of Hoops Minded. In this chapter, explore how Danny's approach blends psychology with athletic training to boost mental performance. Learn his insights on overcoming frustration, effective collaboration, and lifelong learning, and discover how mental training can drive peak performance and personal fulfillment, both on and off the court.

Chapter 8

Harnessing Mental Might with Mental Performance Consultant, Danny Ourian

The mind is the most powerful muscle. By training it as rigorously as the body, we unlock the true potential for peak performance and personal fulfillment.

Danny Ourian is an eminent figure in the world of sports psychology. Embarking on a journey from the basketball court to the academic arena, Ourian has honed his skills not only as a coach but also as a mentor and educator, influencing countless individuals with his dedication to mental fitness and well-being. His innovative approach to mental performance coaching has redefined traditional training methods, proving the transformative power of mental training and its essential role in achieving sustained high performance and personal fulfillment.

Let's explore how Danny has integrated rigorous psychological principles with athletic training, providing athletes and professionals alike with the tools to excel both in sports and in life.

The stories shared on Danny Ourian's Hoops Minded website offer glimpses into his multifaceted persona. But the stories only scratch the surface of who he truly is and why his work resonates with so many. Beyond the title of basketball coach, Danny embodies a unique blend of mentor, teacher, coach developer, and certified mental performance consultant, who just happens to hold an MA in sports psychology.

What sets Ourian apart is his unwavering commitment to detail, coupled with an infectious positivity and a fearless approach to pushing his players and clients beyond their comfort zones. Throughout his career, he has traversed the globe, coaching basketball in diverse settings, from serving as a program director for PeacePlayers International in the Middle East to co-founding Global Game

Changers, a company focused on sports development solutions worldwide.

Today, he serves as the assistant director of Applied Sport and Performance Psychology at Dominican University of California, leveraging his expertise to empower athletes and professionals alike.

Danny Ourian's journey to becoming a leader in mental skills training began during his master's studies at John F. Kennedy University. His research on emotional regulation among high school basketball coaches laid the groundwork for a groundbreaking curriculum titled, "Hoops Minded." This innovative approach combines on-court skills development with tailored mental coaching, addressing the unique needs of each individual athlete.

Central to Danny's philosophy is the recognition of the parallels between athletics and business. He understands that both arenas require individuals to navigate pressure, set goals, and manage performance. While the public scrutiny may differ, the psychological demands remain consistent. Ourian emphasizes the importance of mindfulness and living in the present moment, urging his students to focus on the task at hand while drawing lessons from past experiences.

For Danny Ourian, preparation is paramount. He advocates for a proactive approach to managing thoughts and emotions, recognizing that both positive and negative thoughts are natural components of any endeavor. By cultivating mindfulness and acknowledging emotions, individuals can regain control and channel their focus toward achieving their goals.

Danny's approach to mental skills training transcends the boundaries of athletics, offering valuable insights applicable to all aspects of life. Through his holistic methodology, he empowers individuals to harness their full potential, both on and off the court. As he continues to explore the intersections between sports psychology and professional development, Danny Ourian remains dedicated to guiding others toward peak performance and personal fulfillment.

What typically frustrates you when taking on a challenge and how do you go about finding a remedy?

I've found that most frustration in new challenges stems from some lack of understanding of the task or its details somewhere along the line. If everything was understood, there would be no frustration, but that isn't always clear. I sometimes forget to look inward carefully at the details of what is being asked of me to truly get to the heart of the ask and to check for understanding.

In order to work through this frustration, I'll often start by simply learning about the task, the project, or the challenge. I'll read it, review it, and comb for details. Then, if there is time and space to do so, I'll sit with it. I will take a passive approach, whereby I don't immediately try to tackle it.

I'll leave it for a day and then come back to it the following day with fresh eyes. Behind the scenes, our minds are developing an understanding of what is needed and where the gaps are. Then, if I find I continue to lack understanding at some point in the challenge, I'll seek out consultation or support from trusted colleagues. Typically, in working with others, I've been able to remedy that frustration and approach the challenge collaboratively.

What have you found to be both an efficient and effective approach for your collaboration?

I find that an efficient and effective approach to collaboration starts with a clear understanding of the problem at hand. I believe in priming my colleagues or business partners beforehand, ensuring we're aligned on what needs to be discussed to address the root issue efficiently.

Listening plays a crucial role in my collaboration strategy. I actively seek out the guidance of others, valuing their expertise and insights. I make it a point to ask follow-up questions to gain a deeper understanding and insights into their perspectives.

Moreover, I don't limit myself to just one perspective. I leverage a diverse range of professionals with varied backgrounds, drawing from my coaching network, basketball experience, and academic connections. This diversity of opinion has been instrumental in helping me navigate challenges effectively and will continue to be a valuable resource moving forward.

In essence, embracing diverse perspectives is key to successful collaboration. By leveraging a range of viewpoints, we can approach challenges with greater creativity, innovation, and effectiveness.

When seeking consultation or support on tackling a business challenge, what have you found to be the most efficient and effective approach?

Clarity is paramount. It is essential to have a clear understanding of the problem you are aiming to address. I always ensure to prime my colleagues beforehand, outlining what specific aspects we will be discussing to make the most of our time.

Listening is another crucial aspect of my approach. I value the input and expertise of others, so I actively listen to their perspectives and insights. I make it a point to ask follow-up questions whenever I encounter something I don't fully grasp or would like further clarification on.

I also believe in diversifying the pool of individuals I seek advice from. Drawing from a variety of backgrounds and experiences enriches the discussion and provides a broader range of perspectives. Whether it is tapping into my coaching network, leveraging my basketball background, or engaging with academic peers, diversity of opinion has proven to be instrumental in approaching challenges from multiple angles.

Embracing a diversity of opinions ensures you will get a well-rounded understanding of the issue at hand, enabling you to develop more comprehensive and effective solutions.

What are the best ways to free yourself from the silo you work from and seek collaboration?

First, I prioritize reaching out to others, regardless of whether they are directly involved in my project or not. By seeking their perspectives and understanding their work, I gain valuable insights that can inform my own approach. This cross-pollination of ideas often leads to innovative solutions and fresh perspectives.

Second, I recognize the importance of physical movement and sunlight, especially when working remotely. Taking short breaks for a brisk walk outdoors not only rejuvenates me but also stimulates creativity and problem-solving. I have noticed that even during these breaks, my mind continues to subconsciously process tasks, leading to new insights and solutions.

Creating opportunities to work in different environments, such as coffee shops or coworking spaces, also can enhance collaboration. Being around other people, even if we are not directly interacting, can create a conducive atmosphere for brainstorming and idea generation.

In the end, my go-to strategy is leveraging my trusted network of colleagues and mentors. I regularly engage with this group, bouncing ideas off them and seeking their advice on various challenges. This informal board of directors, as some might call it, provides invaluable support and perspective, helping me navigate complex problems more effectively.

How do you draw a sense of connection from the people you work with?

Fundamentally, we are designed to connect and socialize. In today's fast-paced work environment filled with meetings, emails, and deadlines, it is easy to fall into the trap of treating interactions as transactions—focused solely on extracting what we need and moving on. It is easy to get caught in that trap.

But true connections go beyond mere efficiency. They involve genuinely caring about others and actively listening when they speak. Instead of diving straight into business agendas, taking the time to inquire about someone's well-being, their family, or what they have been up to can make a significant difference.

When we ask, "How are you?" are we truly prepared to listen and empathize with their response, especially if it is more nuanced than a simple, "I'm fine"? In a world where business can sometimes feel cold and impersonal, infusing our interactions with warmth and genuine concern for one another can make the work we do more meaningful.

In our work environment, we make it a point to ask each other how we are doing and genuinely mean it. We listen attentively, reflect on each other's feelings, and summarize what's being shared. These counseling skills, inherent to sports psychology and mental performance, are invaluable in fostering authentic connections.

What is your strategy for turning a struggle with a task into a more effective experience?

Navigating the challenges of balancing tasks and responsibilities can be daunting, especially when time feels limited. For me, efficiency and effectiveness are paramount in maximizing productivity within the constraints of a busy schedule filled with work and family obligations.

One strategy I find particularly effective is time blocking. I designate specific periods for focused work and intentionally schedule these on my calendar. During these blocks, I make a conscious effort to minimize distractions, such as avoiding checking emails, which can often derail deeper work. By closing my email browser and committing to single-tasking on the project at hand, I can maintain concentration and productivity.

I also rely on to-do lists to prioritize tasks for each day. I jot down my key priorities and organize them based on their importance, allowing me to tackle them systematically throughout the day. Regularly revisiting and updating this list keeps me on track and ensures that I address critical tasks in a timely manner.

What are the challenges you sometimes face when a challenge stands in your way? What is the process that gets you through the situation?

Drawing from principles of sports psychology, particularly mindfulness, acceptance, and commitment, the first step for me is to conduct a thorough assessment. This involves getting to know the individual, asking key questions, and gathering insights from relevant parties such as parents or coaches. Through interviews, observations, and questionnaires, I aim to gain a comprehensive understanding of their challenges and goals.

Once we have identified the specific goals, we focus on setting achievable objectives within a defined timeframe, typically spanning over several sessions. We prioritize two to three mental goals and break them down into actionable process goals. These steps are crucial for guiding the individual toward tangible progress in areas like confidence or motivation.

The core of my methodology revolves around mindfulness, acceptance, and commitment. While mindfulness helps individuals cultivate awareness and presence, acceptance is often a challenging concept, especially for athletes accustomed to a never-accept-defeat mindset. I emphasize accepting the present circumstances and approaching challenges with skillful strategies rather than brute force.

Finally, commitment is where the real work begins. We dive into identifying core values and translating them into actionable behaviors. By aligning actions with values and committing to consistent practice, individuals can cultivate integrity and live a more authentic life.

One of the primary challenges in this process is getting athletes to recognize the importance of mental skills training and committing to the necessary work. Similar to physical training, mental training requires dedication and persistence. By advocating for a systematic approach to mental performance, we aim to normalize and integrate mental training into athletes' routines, ensuring they are equipped to perform at their best when it matters most.

What are some of the challenges you face in getting people aligned with your approach?

Sometimes there are challenges resulting from misconceptions or resistance to new concepts. The framework of mindfulness, acceptance, and commitment is rooted in sports psychology but may be unfamiliar or unconventional to some individuals, especially those accustomed to more traditional training methods.

One hurdle is helping athletes understand the importance of mental skills training and integrating it into their overall regimen. This can be challenging, particularly for athletes who prioritize physical conditioning over mental preparation or who are skeptical about the effectiveness of psychological techniques.

Another obstacle is overcoming the ingrained mindset prevalent in sports culture, which often emphasizes toughness, resilience, and pushing through obstacles without acknowledging vulnerability or the need for acceptance.

Convincing athletes to embrace the idea of acceptance—to acknowledge challenges and work with them rather than against them—can be a significant challenge.

Committing to the process of mental skills training requires dedication and consistency, similar to physical training. Some individuals may struggle with maintaining focus or motivation, especially when faced with setbacks or competing priorities.

To address these challenges, I emphasize the practical benefits of mental skills training and provide tangible examples of how it can enhance athletic performance. I also strive to build rapport and trust with athletes, demonstrating empathy and understanding while guiding them through the process. I also work to create a supportive environment where athletes feel comfortable exploring new techniques and strategies without judgment.

Overall, the goal is to shift perceptions and attitudes toward mental skills training, promoting its acceptance and integration as a fundamental aspect of athletic development and performance optimization. Through education, guidance, and ongoing support, I aim to empower athletes to unlock their full potential both on and off the field.

Talk about the mental elements business professionals have in common with athletes. What high-performance tips can you offer on the similarities?

In both sports and business, high performance requires effective management of pressure and preparation for crucial moments. As professionals, we can learn valuable lessons from athletes in optimizing our mental game.

One key strategy is mindfulness, which helps maintain focus and intentionality amid pressure. Additionally, adopting a pre-performance routine, like the PREP acronym, can enhance readiness and performance.

PREP stands for:

- **P**ick a Quality – Set an intention or goal for your performance, triggering the desired behaviors.
- **R**elease Distractions – Identify and let go of external stressors or concerns to stay present.
- **E**nergy Management – Gauge your energy level and adjust it accordingly to match the demands of the situation.
- **P**review Situations – Visualize yourself in the upcoming scenario, engaging all senses and adopting a first-person perspective.

By integrating these high-performance tips into our professional lives, we can better manage pressure, enhance focus, and elevate our performance to achieve our goals.

Talk a little about why mindfulness can help performance.

Mindfulness is a centuries-old concept that has gained popularity today. While it appears more as a buzzword, its essence remains powerful and timeless. At its core, mindfulness involves cultivating a non-judgmental awareness of one's inner and outer experiences, fostering a deep presence in the present moment.

Being mindful means being attuned to both internal and external phenomena without attachment or judgment. It is about being fully engaged in the here and now, rather than dwelling on the past or worrying about the future. This heightened state of awareness can significantly impact performance, whether in sports or business settings, by enabling individuals to operate at their best.

Formal mindfulness practice involves setting aside dedicated time for meditation or reflection. Taking just ten minutes a day to sit quietly and focus on the present moment can yield profound benefits. There are various resources available, including apps and guided meditation recordings, to support this practice.

Informal mindfulness practice can be seamlessly integrated into daily life. Whether stuck in traffic or waiting in line, these everyday moments serve as opportunities to tune into our thoughts, emotions, and bodily sensations. By observing these experiences without judgment, we cultivate a greater sense of presence and resilience in navigating life's challenges.

Danny Ourian's journey from a basketball coach to a prominent figure in mental performance consulting illustrates his dedication to fostering growth and resilience, not just in athletes but in individuals across various disciplines.

Up Next

Join us in exploring the journey of C.J. Stewart, former pro baseball player and founder of Diamond Directors and the L.E.A.D. Center For Youth. See how C.J. uses his passion for baseball to empower at-risk youth, turning the sport into a tool for social change and personal development. Discover how sports can drive lasting impact on individuals and communities, and learn from his experiences overcoming challenges to build a powerful platform for youth empowerment and community engagement.

Chapter 9

Batting Against Barriers with
Baseball Visionary, C.J. Stewart

True impact is achieved by leveraging our passions to uplift others, transforming challenges into opportunities, and empowering communities to rise together.

CJ Stewart is a figure whose life and work transcend the boundaries of sports to address deeper societal issues. As a former professional baseball player and a dedicated mentor, Stewart has leveraged his experience in sports to empower young individuals, particularly African American youth, using baseball as a tool for social change and providing pathways for underprivileged youth to transform their lives. His efforts focus on not only enhancing their athletic abilities but also on building their leadership skills, academic performance, and civic engagement.

CJ Stewart's innovative approaches to mentorship and community engagement illustrate the powerful impact sports can have in fostering resilience, discipline, and success beyond the field.

It has always been about the challenge. For as long as C.J. can remember, he has been challenged to rise above the odds, the barriers, the doubters, whatever or whoever got in his way. As a kid, Stewart grew up in one of Atlanta's most dangerous apartment complexes, Hollywood Brooks, located on Hollywood Road in Atlanta's Bankhead Highway area.

He used baseball to overcome the challenges (and statistics) and eventually went from John A. White Park all the way to Wrigley Field after the Chicago Cubs drafted him. His stint, for all the reasons a young man who admittedly lacked discipline could imagine, abruptly ended.

But his story didn't. Living a life framed by the phrase, "Where you start doesn't determine where you finish," Stewart used baseball again to rise up. Creating the organization, Diamond Directors, the former professional baseball player started helping others find the discipline and drive that he lacked. What Stewart saw were too many Black teenagers drawn into this depressing cycle of crime and poverty. Baseball, he knew, could help re-direct and incentivize them.

The road to becoming a known compassionate, engaged member of his community was paved with all the challenges he expected, and more. But with the help of a handful of mentors and community support, he pushed on. He created a process-focused methodology designed to improve baseball performance by identifying and improving specific areas in the development process—AT-BATS, a proven, trademarked, comprehensive system of professional training and development.

His legacy as one of the top baseball development professionals in the country is paved with success stories, including a list of the game's top amateur, collegiate, and professional players. Jason Heyward (Los Angeles Dodgers); Dexter Fowler (Chicago Cubs, World Series Champion); Andrew Jones (former Atlanta Brave); Pete Alonso (NY Mets); Kyle Lewis (Seattle Mariners); Andrew McCutchen (Pittsburgh Pirates); and the list goes on.

But that wasn't enough. Along with his wife, Kelli, he founded the L.E.A.D. (Launch, Expose, Advise, Direct) Center For Youth. The nonprofit organization's mission is to empower an at-risk generation to become ambassadors and leaders to transform their city. Of young men who complete L.E.A.D.'s ambassador program, 100 percent have graduated from high school, 93 percent have enrolled in college, 90 percent have received college scholarship opportunities, and 14 percent have entered the military or workforce.

Along the way, C.J. continues to build relationships with local community leagues and with the top-shelf travel baseball programs, which draw the elite young talent. This is the foundation he works from, which is knowing the entirety of the baseball landscape in one of the most fertile areas of the game in the United States.

To make it all work, Breaking Barriers Atlanta (BBATL) is the fundraising mechanism, the process for sustaining L.E.A.D. Center For Youth. BBATL leverages the relationships Stewart has built in the ecosystem of baseball in the Atlanta metro area and then builds even more relationships. BBATL gives corporate sponsors a platform to connect their brand to active involvement in L.E.A.D. civic programming, which will help at-risk kids bust down barriers.

The programming for BBATL includes using trained teenage Black coaches to teach the game and its fundamentals to the children of predominantly White stakeholders, or the children of corporate partners. The aim is to not only teach the game but to expose these more affluent children to what Black kids deal with on a daily basis, which CJ Stewart calls the "curveballs of crime, poverty, and racism."

"This is life-saving work," Stewart says. "Too many of our young men are being raised in homes and schools where they make their own standards, and they're not held accountable for anything. We spend so much time chasing test scores that we neglect to set a foundation of core values and standards that lead to greater accountability and, ultimately, greater success. L.E.A.D. gives our young men an opportunity to walk in my shoes and go much farther than I did."

Is there anything you wish was faster and easier as you went through your process to create L.E.A.D.?

I wish everything could start out simplistic, but it inevitably becomes complex before it simplifies and becomes actionable. During the initial stages of creating L.E.A.D., I had to break down my ideas into manageable steps, which required a lot of detailed thinking.

While this process felt challenging, it helped me internalize and communicate my vision more effectively. Despite the complexity, I'm grateful for the experience because it allowed me to articulate my vision with conviction, even if others didn't fully understand it at first.

As we progressed through the process and involved more people, I found that the initial complexity paid off. By thoroughly thinking through the challenges upfront, we reached a point where our goals became simpler and more actionable. This clarity made it easier to bring others along and delegate tasks effectively.

While I'm known for my emotional approach as a visionary, I've earned the respect of my team by demonstrating that I've put in the time to make our objectives clear and achievable. This balance between emotion and intellect has been crucial in leading the team toward our goals.

Talk about the 3Cs process you employed for tackling your challenges.

When I think about confidence, it's not just about believing in something; it's about having a track record of success. That's why when I used the 3Cs process—Clarify, Chart, and Coalign—I approached it with confidence. For me, having a structured sequence is essential. It's not just a cliché; it's a fundamental truth that meaningful endeavors require a clear process.

The confidence in this process comes from knowing that we're going to clarify why we need what we need, identify the key stakeholders, chart out a path, and finally, coalign our efforts. However, coaligning can be particularly challenging because it involves ensuring that everyone involved is on the same page.

To illustrate, I'm not a skilled cook, and what scares me most about cooking is not having a recipe. I need precise instructions—measurements, oven temperatures—because I rely on following directions. Similarly, in business and tackling challenges, having a clear process is like having a recipe. It provides the necessary steps to turn a vision into reality.

Reflecting on my journey, both personally and professionally, I've realized that having a roadmap is crucial for success. It sets a clear starting point and outlines the steps needed to reach our destination.

With the 3Cs process, I approach challenges with confidence, knowing that we have a well-sequenced plan to guide us toward our goals.

What would have happened if you didn't get started following the 3Cs approach?

If we hadn't followed the 3Cs approach, it would have been like navigating without a map. We would have relied on luck and hope, which are not reliable strategies, especially when it comes to raising funds for a nonprofit. It would have led to frustration, especially in terms of recruiting and retaining board members who understand and support our mission.

In a city like Atlanta, where sports play a significant role, corporations are keen on associating their brands with sports teams. However, one of the critical issues is the recruitment, promotion, and retention of Black men in these corporations.

Articulating our mission effectively is crucial to gaining buy-in from both board members and corporations. Through the 3Cs process, I was able to communicate our vision with conviction, knowing that it resonated intellectually and emotionally with our stakeholders.

By following this process, we were able to socialize our ideas among our board and staff effectively. I made it clear that if anyone didn"t agree with our approach, we needed to find something better. This conviction, backed by a well-structured process, enabled us to gain the necessary support. Without it, we would have been in survival mode, which is not conducive to effectively serving the needs of Black boys from low-income households.

Is there anything you wish was faster and easier as you go through a business process?

I wish everything started out simple, but it often gets complex before it becomes actionable. Breaking down ideas into steps helps internalize them, avoiding reliance on memory. While some may prefer to tackle challenges as they arise, I, as a visionary, anticipate future obstacles to address them proactively.

This detailed thinking, while challenging, enhances my ability to communicate with conviction, even if others don't fully grasp my vision immediately.

Despite the initial complexity, I appreciate the learning experience. As we progress and involve more people, the process becomes simpler. Starting with complexity pays off by making subsequent stages easier. When tasks reach a simple stage, I am fully committed to moving forward without complicating matters further.

In involving others, I recognize the need to balance intellect and emotion. While I bring emotion as a chief visionary officer, I also demonstrate the effort invested in simplifying the process.

By anticipating needs and aligning tasks with individuals' strengths, I ensure they feel empowered and capable. This journey from complexity to simplicity is integral to effective collaboration and achieving our goals.

Talk about some of the struggles you had when pulling together the BBATL program. When did you decide you needed help?

The struggles were real and significant. As L.E.A.D.'s chief visionary officer, I recognized that fun without funding was impossible. With year-round programming and hundreds of boys to serve, the challenge of securing necessary funds through grants and foundations kept me up at night. In Atlanta, despite the city's wealth, there's also significant need, adding to the complexity.

The key struggle revolved around leveraging our program participants as assets to raise funds. This dilemma consumed our time as we sought solutions internally. However, we soon realized the futility of this approach. We had to make a choice: either waste time and risk losing money by trying to solve the problem ourselves or seek help from proven experts who could provide structure and clarity to our ideas.

When I reached out for help in building the structure for BBATL, despite the hard work involved in refining my thinking, I started to sleep better. Being able to find somebody to help me talk through everything allowed us to acknowledge the complexity of our situation while simplifying our approach. While the process was challenging, it was ultimately fruitful.

My wife Kelli, who serves as our executive director, and I, both African American nonprofit leaders, understood the broader context. Black-led nonprofits face significant funding challenges in America, a systemic issue that won't change overnight.

What was standing in the way of turning your vision for BBATL into a reality?

Primarily the challenge of effectively communicating my ideas. As a visionary, I tend to struggle with articulating my thoughts clearly, which makes it difficult to build consensus and move forward. Through a collaborative thought process, I was able to express my ideas while having someone who could capture, simplify, and sequence them effectively, keeping the conversation flowing.

This collaboration allowed me to identify what was truly important and what needed to be prioritized. I could then go back to my team. I was no longer stuck. The vision for BBATL has been packaged in a way that allows for immediate action and fundraising efforts, satisfying our executive director's objectives.

Simultaneously, there are ample growth opportunities envisioned for the next decade, which keeps me engaged and motivated. The challenge has shifted from communicating the vision to planning for what comes next, a welcome shift from feeling stuck in the initial stages of ideation and communication.

Describe where you are now as opposed to where you were?

As of 2024, our organization, now seventeen years old, has evolved into a major league organization and has developed a robust fundraising platform that resonates with Fortune 100 companies. This platform allows us to showcase how they can invest in their future employees by supporting our programs. It's no longer just about charity; these companies see an opportunity to make a tangible impact by contributing to the development of 250 Black boys from Atlanta's inner city.

Our year-round programming focuses on equipping these boys with the social and emotional skills they need to thrive, ultimately shaping them into what we call "major league citizens"—individuals who are gainfully employed and productive members of society. With our refined approach and fundraising platform, we now approach companies with a sponsorship mindset rather than merely seeking charitable donations. This shift has elevated our organization to a new level of impact and sustainability.

———————————

C.J. Stewart's ongoing mission to break down barriers of inequality and create opportunities for youth in his community illustrates a remarkable journey from a professional sports career to impactful community activism. His work continues to inspire and challenge us to consider how sports can serve as a powerful tool for community development and social justice, making a lasting difference in the lives of many.

Up Next

Join us as we explore the journey of John Busing, former National Football League (NFL) player and founder of MOVE+breathe. Learn how John transitioned from professional football to leading in fitness and sports performance training. Discover his experiences overcoming challenges, promoting holistic health, and building a community-driven platform focused on personal growth, discipline, and wellness. See how his passion for helping others live healthier lives has fueled his success and inspired those around him.

Chapter 10

Tackling Teamwork with Fitness Innovator, John Busing

True strength lies in the harmony of mind and body. Embracing both unlocks our full potential to overcome challenges and achieve excellence.

John Busing's inspiring professional evolution spans from the football field to the forefront of fitness and sports performance training.

John's transition from athlete to entrepreneur reflects a deep commitment to fostering holistic health and athletic excellence, and his story highlights a profound understanding of the challenges and triumphs of adapting to life beyond professional sports. Using the discipline and teamwork ingrained in him through his football career to inspire others, Busing has not only carved a niche in the fitness industry but has also established a community-focused platform that emphasizes personal growth, discipline, and wellness strategies focused on the body and mind.

In 2006, everything changed for John Busing. After working his whole life toward his dream, the dream came true. Signed as an undrafted free agent out of Miami (Ohio) University in 2006 by the Cincinnati Bengals, the 6-foot-2-inch, 218-pounder had arrived in the NFL. He spent the first three seasons of his NFL career with the Bengals, posting twenty-five tackles in twenty-seven games, nineteen of which as a core member of the special team's unit.

Eventually signing as a free agent with the Houston Texans, where he logged a career-high in tackles—thirty-two—and his first interception, John ended up finishing his career with the New York Giants.

Adjusting to life off the field, John worked as a sports performance trainer spending the next ten-plus years helping provide elite athletic training to a wide range of athletes in the northern suburbs of Atlanta.

And then came MOVE+breathe, which he started with his wife and business partner, Lauren. Meeting while collaborating together in their work with athletes, the Busings created a brand dedicated to combining her expertise in yoga, breath work, and rolling methods, with his forte in improving athletic performance.

Today, the duo continues to bring the best of all worlds to its passionate consumer base, building a brand that complements and intersects its grace and grit.

What typically frustrates you when taking on a challenge and how do you go about finding a remedy?

I think if you asked me that at different points in my career, I would probably say different things. I think a problem that's probably frustrated and plagued me for longer than I would like to admit is just a little bit of indecisiveness, being in that middle area where, in the face of a challenge, I'm trying to make a decision but can't, and that indecision is what holds me back, what keeps me stuck. And, in fact, I often think I would be better off making the wrong decision, that at least that would push me in a direction where then I could make a correction, learn from it and move on from there.

I believe that's one thing that is a universal issue—overanalyzing the situation to the point where no real action can be taken. I think as humans we are indecisive because while we are comfortable with what we know, we don't know what we don't know, and that part scares and paralyzes us. You may have an intuition or a gut in the beginning, but then you start to question yourself like, "Well, you know, I've never done this before, am I sure that's the right decision, but are we sure that's the way we want things to move or the direction that we want things to go in?"

In business, people often try to make the perfect decision when really all that needs to be happening is just a decision, period. You can then move forward, and if you need to make an adjustment in the future you make that adjustment from that point and continue on.

This is something that I personally work on and, while it frustrates me, I am grateful to know what the solution is. Instead of staying stuck, I have to figure out why I'm having the issue, how to get past it, and then take the action needed to do so. I tell people this all the time, you've got to get a little bit uncomfortable in order to grow, right?

Like you have the information at hand, you are trying to make the best decision that you can and if it does not work out, okay, it's not the end of the world, we're going to make an adjustment. We are smart enough. We've got the right tools; we have the right people on the team to help us figure things out from that point. Focusing on this angle of tackling challenges will help to make facing them a whole lot easier from the start.

Just to give you a little anecdotal perspective, I often watch the interviews after games, when they stick a microphone in front of somebody and I hear them say "OK, why did this happen?" or "Why did you lose?" "What are you going to change for next week?"

So many of the answers come back to, "Well, you know what? We've got to get back to practice, to our process, to the way we prepare." In so many words they are saying what I've said here: We have to trust that. Trusting in the process, and knowing that you have a strong foundation to build from, that is the key.

What typically keeps you stuck? How do you get past these sticking points?

In my experience, indecisiveness often has been a major obstacle. Overanalyzing situations and striving for the perfect decision can lead to getting stuck in the middle without taking any action. But I have come to realize that making any decision, even if it's not perfect, is often better than remaining stagnant. Taking action allows for learning from mistakes and making adjustments along the way.

Uncertainty plays a significant role in causing indecision. It's natural to question ourselves when faced with new or unfamiliar situations. However, I've learned that growth often requires stepping out of our comfort zones and embracing discomfort. Trusting in our abilities and past experiences can help alleviate the fear of making the wrong decision.

Drawing parallels to sports, I find that trusting in the process is key. Just like in athletics, where immediate answers may not always be available after a loss, having faith in the preparation and approach is essential. While the outcome may not always be favorable, trusting in the process allows for adjustments and improvements over time.

So, while indecision can be challenging, trusting in the process and being willing to learn from mistakes helps in overcoming sticking points and moving forward toward achieving goals.

What do you wish was easier tackling challenges and why do you find it hard?

I think communication can be difficult and get in the way of you succeeding faster and more seamlessly when challenges arise. This is one of the things I have personally had the opportunity to reflect on.

When I started out building a previous business my partner at the time and I had very similar interests and philosophies on where we were going with the company. It is one of the reasons we created a partnership to begin with but over time some of our business goals began to change. My partner was becoming more interested in another segment of the industry, whereas I was staying true to what we had started the business for and why we had started it. His new focus was taking away from our original goals.

That was probably the first indication that we may not be in alignment perfectly like we were before. Sensing that was one thing, but my lack of communication on it really caused issues down the line. I came from a sports mentality in thinking the one thing I can always control is how hard I work, that I may not be able to control what the opponent does or what the coach's decision is going to be but I can determine the amount and quality of the work I'm going to put in.

So my mindset was, "Okay, I'll do more work, work harder, longer hours, and that will fix the issue" instead of going in there and communicating, saying to my partner, "Hey listen, you know, we've got this thing going on and my plate's already really full. Like, what can you do to help out in this situation?"

Because this is a partnership. Not bringing up those issues when they were happening, not addressing them head-on, and having those tough conversations early on ended up leading to bigger problems down the line. We ended up ending the partnership. I think that would have happened no matter what. But could we have saved ourselves eighteen months of painful back and forth? Most likely.

So I think if communication comes easier then the problems you face can be handled honestly and quickly, leading you to the end result you are seeking in a much faster way.

What do you wish would occur faster in business?

There is a general formula you can follow: identifying the decision, gathering relevant information, identifying solutions, weighing the evidence, and then making a choice among those. That's the basic framework you can use to tackle any challenge, opportunity, or problem.

You want to try and take something that's maybe seemingly complex and make it a little bit simpler. Get to the root of the issue of what you're trying to figure out or accomplish. This can be done in your head—on a more gut or instinctual level. You should be very analytical.

I like to look at both. I'm more analytical, as I mentioned before, so I try to quantify things. I also want to know what my gut is saying in those situations. I think having the numbers gives me confidence to back my decisions that I feel initially.

As a business leader, there are lots of challenges you must consider, lots of different scenarios. You are thinking about the bottom line. The impact on your customers. The impact on your employees. You're thinking about the impact on you as a business owner.

When facing challenges, you have to take everyone and everything into account. It comes down to trying to please everybody, at least for me, in those situations. You're trying to make everything work for the business and your clients—both at the same time—and not necessarily driving the best results.

What was the toughest obstacle you faced when tackling a big challenge in your career? How did you overcome it?

The toughest obstacle was the challenges that come with a partnership, particularly how the business should look. In the beginning, an old business partner who I talked about earlier, and I shared the same vision, but over time that changed, as well as how we viewed the division of responsibilities and how things should operate.

Ultimately, the partnership dissolved. At the end of the day, while that was the best thing to do, it could have been a lot easier. It could have been done sooner. The whole experience caused me to probably spend at least twelve months going through this process—time that held me back from moving forward. One of the hardest things to do was tell my business partner that things were not working out—that it was time to split up. You want to let the other person know that in the long run, this is the best option.

At that time, we were looking to start some new things, so the whole thing was a big risk on both of our parts. There is a bit of a safety net when you have a partner, at least in some situations. Ultimately, it ended up being for the best, but at the time, it was a really challenging and stressful situation.

For me, the process of making those challenging decisions meant going back to what my core values are. When we started the business, we had a clear direction of who we were, where we were heading, and what we were trying to accomplish. As time goes by, you can lose track of those things. It was a tough lesson to learn, but it was a lesson learned, and over time I eventually went back and reviewed what went wrong. It became a great opportunity to get better, to clearly define the division of responsibilities and expectations, as well as improve my communication skills.

By going back and revisiting them, you are making sure you are still honoring those principles. That has worked for me and our business. Staying true to who we are, making sure we are not trying to do something else or not trying to be something we are not. That has given us the best results.

What's the core message you would offer other leaders and decision-makers before they tackle their next big challenge?

There is a general formula you can follow: identifying the decision, gathering relevant information, identifying solutions, weighing the evidence, and then making a choice among those. That's the basic framework you can use to tackle any challenge, opportunity, or problem.

You want to try and take something that's maybe seemingly complex and make it a little bit simpler. Get to the root of the issue of what you're trying to figure out or accomplish. This can be done in your head—on a more gut or instinctual level. You should be very analytical.

I like to take a look at both. I'm more analytical, as I mentioned before, so I try to quantify things. I also want to know what my gut is saying in those situations. I think having the numbers gives me the confidence to back my decisions that I feel initially.

What advice can you offer for people working together? Where does that balance of ideas come from?

When working together, it is important to appreciate each other's differences and strengths. Partnerships thrive when there is a balance of ideas stemming from diverse perspectives and approaches. Recognizing that different styles can be complementary is key.

Effective communication is paramount. Establish clear processes for communication, including regular check-ins and open dialogue. Commit to addressing issues promptly and transparently.

Ensure alignment not only in business goals but also in how the partnership operates. Discuss and agree upon decision-making frameworks, roles, and responsibilities.

Find ways to leverage each partner's strengths. Embrace the dynamic of one partner being more outgoing and idea-focused, while the other is more strategic and organized.

Regularly evaluate and adjust the partnership. Reflect on what is working and what isn't, and be willing to make necessary changes to keep the partnership healthy and aligned.

Remember that it is not just about business planning but also partnership planning. Neglecting communication and alignment issues can lead to conflicts down the line.

Learn from past experiences, both successful and unsuccessful. Use these lessons to refine how you approach communication and partnership dynamics in the future.

Why is having a passion for what you do so important?

Having a passion is crucial for several reasons. First, it brings fulfillment and joy to your work, making it something you genuinely love to do each day. For my wife and me, our business is not just a job, but a lifestyle centered around our passion for helping others live healthier and happier lives.

When you are passionate about your work, it becomes more than just a means of making a living—it becomes a mission to make a positive impact on others. At our business, MOVE+breathe, our goal is to create a community where people can improve their quality of life through yoga and strength training.

Passion also drives innovation and creativity. When you're truly passionate about what you do, you're more likely to think outside the box, experiment with new ideas, and find unique solutions to challenges.

Moreover, passion is infectious. By pursuing your passions wholeheartedly, you inspire others to do the same. Building a vibrant community of like-minded individuals who share our passion has been one of the most rewarding aspects of our journey.

Ultimately, having a passion for what you do fuels your commitment, resilience, and perseverance. It keeps you motivated during tough times and empowers you to overcome obstacles on the path to success.

So, whether it is through our business or any other endeavor, embracing your passions can lead to a more fulfilling and impactful life.

John Busing's journey illustrates the seamless connection between achieving peak athletic performance and cultivating a balanced, healthy lifestyle. His story is not just about transition but also about transformation, demonstrating how one can leverage personal strengths and passions to craft a fulfilling and impactful second career.

Chapter 11

Lead Simply, Lead Strong

"Simplicity is the ultimate sophistication."

—LEONARDO DA VINCI

In this chapter, we focus on the power of simplicity in leadership. By simplifying your approach, you can drive greater clarity, effectiveness, and impact. The leader stories you have just read in Part One navigated complex challenges by simplifying their communication, decision-making, and focus. Now, it's your turn to apply these lessons in your own leadership journey.

Key Takeaways

1. **Simplify Communication.** Effective leaders simplify their messaging, cutting out unnecessary details to ensure their teams are aligned on core objectives. Clear, direct communication reduces confusion and improves team performance.

2. **Clarify Mental Focus.** Mental clarity is crucial for resilience. Leaders who simplify their mental approach and eliminate distractions are better able to concentrate on key priorities and navigate challenges more confidently.

3. **Set Boundaries for Sustainable Growth.** Setting clear boundaries is essential to prevent burnout and sustain long-term growth. Leaders who protect their time and energy by simplifying their focus can more effectively pursue their strategic goals.

4. **Adaptability Through Simplification.** Simplifying your approach makes it easier to adapt in fast-changing environments.

By focusing on what truly matters, you can pivot quickly and take decisive action during times of transition.

Leadership in Practice

- **For Emerging Leaders:** Identify one area in your leadership where you can simplify—whether it's communication, task delegation, or decision-making. Take immediate action to reduce complexity.
- **For Seasoned Leaders:** Review your processes and identify where complexity has crept in. Simplify these areas to create more effective outcomes.

Simplicity in leadership is not a one-time action but a continuous practice. By regularly simplifying your approach and eliminating unnecessary complexity, you'll build a foundation for long-term success. The leaders in this part of the book embraced simplicity to sharpen their focus and maximize their impact. Now it's your turn—simplify your leadership to make space for what truly matters.

Up Next

Uncover more success stories from leaders who embraced action as the solution to overcoming challenges. Starting with Alester Spears, real estate consultant, and healthcare technology thought leader, we'll see how he navigated dual careers with resilience and grace. Learn from his journey through career shifts, balancing family, and finding fulfillment in both fields. His insights on mentorship, self-awareness, and staying true to one's passions will offer valuable lessons for your own path forward.

PART 2:
TIME TO TAKE ACTION

Once a challenge has presented itself it's often easy to get stuck in the goal of overcoming it and not the steps required to do so. These leaders discovered that simply taking action took them from facing a hurdle to leaping over it.

Chapter 12

Turning Passion into Action with Real Estate Guru, Alester Spears

True success is about staying true to your passions and values while navigating life's challenges with resilience and grace.

Through a robust blend of discipline, commitment, and entrepreneurial spirit, Alester Spears navigated the complexities of a dual career in healthcare technology and real estate with a grace and resilience inspired by his upbringing. Starting off on a conventional corporate path, his career took a significant turn when he recognized the potential within himself to forge his own path, much like the consultants he encountered. Alester demonstrates that it is possible to balance high professional aspirations with deep personal responsibilities, debunking the myth that one necessarily precludes the other.

If Alester could turn back the clock, he'd change the course he took a bit differently. Growing up watching his father, Major General Stanhope Spears, make waves in both corporate and political realms, Alester initially followed a conventional corporate trajectory.

But there are differences, especially the stark contrast between the corporate landscape of the '90s and his father's era. Loyalty seemed scarce at the C-level. Instead, the environment was replaced by a relentless pursuit of profit and growth. The old-fashioned way of doing business was replaced by email and cell phones, intensifying the pressure to be constantly available, irrespective of the time or day.

It wasn't until nearly two decades later that Spears experienced an epiphany familiar to many aspiring entrepreneurs. The reins, he discovered, were in his hands. The turning point came when Alester witnessed his healthcare IT company engage an external consultant who knew little about the industry or the company's specifics. Seeing the consultant's lucrative contract, Spears saw his path. Choosing to prioritize self-service over corporate allegiance, Spears leveraged his decade-long experience in healthcare IT to transition into a consultancy role, specializing in healthcare.

Yet, his heart yearned for a career in real estate, where he could harness the interpersonal skills inherited from his extroverted parents. He was fifty-three when he embarked on another career reboot. Around the same time, Alister's life would take another unpredictable twist with his father's Alzheimer's diagnosis, followed by his mother's health decline exacerbated by the pandemic. Balancing his real estate aspirations with caregiving responsibilities, Spears felt no regrets or hesitations, devoting himself wholeheartedly to his mother's care.

His new journey offered many invaluable insights, including debunking the notion that family commitments must be sacrificed for career pursuits. Part of the insights he drew from came from his parents, including his father's groundbreaking work as the adjutant general of South Carolina, a job he took at fifty-eight, and his mother's successful beauty shop, a career she revived after raising a family.

From Stan and Dorothy, Alester realized that entrepreneurship is more than a profession; it's a mindset. "Don't allow yourself to be pigeonholed. This is your life; steer it according to your terms."

In essence, his journey underscores the transformative power of self-awareness, resilience, and familial influence in navigating career transitions and embracing entrepreneurial pursuits. Through his experiences, he learned that the pursuit of passion need not be at odds with familial responsibilities, but rather, can harmoniously coexist, enriching both personal and professional domains.

What advice can you offer people about turning what's important to them—what they enjoy—into a career path?

This realization didn't come to me until years later. They say the hobbies you enjoyed as a child—those that kept you entertained at ten, eleven, or twelve years old—are where your passions lie. I distinctly remember as a kid, I loved exploring the houses being built in my neighborhood. It was a brand-new area, and seeing those houses in different stages of construction fascinated me. Sometimes my family joined me, as we were naturally curious about what was happening in the neighborhood.

Looking back, I realize a passion was born from those experiences. I didn't realize it then, but when I was seeking a career, I understood that what you did in your free time as a child can guide your career choices as an adult.

So, I would encourage people to do some self-analysis, some self-awareness. Reflect on what brought you joy as a kid in your spare time. From there, consider how you can turn that into a career because passion drives excellence.

Think about how you can leverage your skills to align with that passion and become the best version of yourself. For example, my childhood interest in exploring homes and neighborhoods aligns well with my career in real estate today.

What tips can you share for discovering the right mentor?

Business mentors have greatly influenced my life across various career stages. Initially, upon securing my first job out of college, I recognized the significance of relationships in advancing my career trajectory. As I progressed through different roles and companies, I made it a priority to observe and connect with individuals in positions higher than mine. Identifying those whom I admired and shared common interests with was key, as it made building relationships more enjoyable and fruitful.

Leveraging these connections, I sought advice, expanded my network by meeting their contacts and reciprocated by offering assistance whenever possible. Exceptional mentors not only provide guidance but also open doors to new opportunities. They may extend invitations to join them in their career advancements, recognizing your value and the strength of your relationship.

I particularly admire self-made individuals who have risen from humble beginnings to achieve remarkable success. Their perseverance, ambition, and hard work serve as inspirational examples of what can be accomplished through determination and dedication. Conversely, individuals whose success seems to have been effortlessly bestowed upon them may lack the depth of experience and resilience earned through overcoming challenges.

In addition to professional guidance, my parents have been influential mentors, imparting valuable lessons not only in business but also in personal development and the pursuit of one's aspirations. Their example underscores the importance of embodying the qualities and values one aspires to uphold in life and career.

How were you able to identify your own strengths before moving your career forward?

Both of my parents were very social, relationship-building individuals. They both approached it differently. As a child, I benefited greatly from their teachings in strong social skills—how to meet people, be inclusive in conversations, and ensure nobody felt left out in a group. I further developed these skills in college and beyond.

It became evident to me that my natural inclination leaned toward the sales side of business. Making friends came easily to me, and I was inherently an extrovert and social being. Thus, I recognized that relationship-building and social skills would be my strengths moving forward.

When I entered corporate America, I realized that working for a corporation is largely a social game. While performance matters, so does being a team player, collaborating with other departments, and providing constructive solutions rather than just pointing out problems. Leveraging my social skills and knack for building relationships greatly assisted me in my corporate career.

Now, in my real estate endeavors, these skills remain invaluable. Real estate is inherently a social career. It requires meeting people, understanding their wants and needs, and ensuring they feel included in the process, whether it's finding a permanent residence or a vacation home. My love for the outdoors and working with people in homes aligns perfectly with my skill set in relationship-building and social skills. Overall, these abilities have continued to serve me well throughout my career transitions.

What tips can you offer for people who find it hard to take action?

When it comes to taking action, fear often plays a significant role. Many people hesitate to act due to fear of making the wrong choice or facing criticism from others. This fear can be paralyzing, preventing individuals from pursuing their goals and aspirations.

In my own experiences, instances where I failed to take action were typically driven by fear. Whether it was financial concerns or worries about societal expectations, fear held me back from living authentically and making decisions aligned with my true self. But I've come to realize that overcoming fear is essential for making the best choices for oneself.

It is important to acknowledge that mistakes are inevitable, and they can serve as valuable learning opportunities. Some of the most significant lessons and personal growth have stemmed from making errors and learning from them. Instead of dwelling on past missteps, it's crucial to embrace them as part of the journey toward success.

Rather than allowing fear to dictate our actions, I encourage people to do their due diligence and make informed decisions. This entails conducting thorough research, seeking advice when necessary, and trusting in one's abilities to navigate challenges. If a mistake is made along the way, it's essential to view it as a steppingstone rather than a setback.

Talk about the importance of doing what you say you will do.

The importance of following through on commitments cannot be overstated. When individuals make promises or commitments, others rely on those assurances to plan and make decisions. Failure to fulfill these commitments not only leads to disappointment but also undermines trust and credibility.

In the corporate world, I've encountered situations where promises were made to address various challenges, only for those promises to go unfulfilled. This lack of follow-through not only created frustration but also hindered progress and achievement of goals. It's essential for individuals and teams to deliver on their commitments to maintain credibility and uphold their integrity.

Personally, I strive to adhere to this principle in both my professional and personal life. I prioritize honesty and transparency, avoiding overpromising and under-delivering. Whether in sales roles, managerial positions, or as a business owner, I understand the impact of my words on others' expectations and outcomes.

By consistently following through on commitments, I uphold my integrity and build trust with those around me. This trust forms the foundation of effective collaboration and relationships, enabling me to achieve success in my endeavors. Honoring commitments allows me to maintain peace of mind and rest easy knowing that I've upheld my word and acted with integrity.

What is your best advice for people thinking about switching careers?

Switching careers can be a significant and rewarding decision, but it requires careful planning and strategic communication. First and foremost, it is essential to be proactive in communicating your career transition. Utilize social media platforms like LinkedIn and Facebook to update your profiles and share your new career direction with your connections. This helps ensure that people perceive you accurately and understand your current focus.

Take advantage of networking opportunities to inform colleagues, acquaintances, and friends about your career switch. Whether you're attending industry events, social gatherings, or simply running into people in various settings, use these interactions as opportunities to share your new career path and express your willingness to assist them in any way you can.

Remember that transitioning careers is a process, and it may take time for others to fully recognize and acknowledge your new professional identity. Be patient and persistent in reinforcing your new career narrative and continue to actively engage with your network to establish yourself in your chosen field.

Ultimately, embracing your career change with confidence and enthusiasm will inspire others to support and engage with you in your new venture. By effectively communicating your transition and demonstrating your commitment to your new path, you'll pave the way for success in your new career endeavor.

Why is it important to strike the right balance between caring what people think of you and being your own person?

Finding a balance is crucial for personal growth and fulfillment. Growing up in a culture where there is an emphasis on minding one's own business, I was conditioned to be overly concerned about others' perceptions. This mindset initially affected my confidence, especially in my corporate career, where I felt the need to constantly measure up to others' expectations.

The fear of rejection, particularly in sales situations, often led to self-doubt and hesitation. I found myself overanalyzing every interaction, worried about saying the right thing or appearing a certain way. This mindset, while stemming from a desire to please others, ultimately became a hindrance, causing me to stumble and feel trapped by my own insecurities.

But with age and exposure to different cultures and environments, I began to realize the futility of worrying excessively about others' opinions. I came to understand that everyone is preoccupied with their own lives and concerns, and most people aren't overly concerned with what others think of them. This realization allowed me to shed the burden of seeking validation from others and focus on being true to myself.

I learned to prioritize authenticity and integrity in my interactions, both personally and professionally. Instead of fixating on others' perceptions, I shifted my focus to building genuine connections and adding value to every interaction. This shift in mindset liberated me from the shackles of self-doubt and allowed me to embrace my individuality confidently.

Now, I approach each day with the mindset of doing my best and staying true to my values. I've learned to let go of unnecessary worries and trust in my abilities to navigate life's challenges. By prioritizing authenticity and self-assurance, I've found greater peace of mind and fulfillment in both my personal and professional endeavors.

What are the keys to successfully project managing any kind of initiative?

It begins with meticulous planning. Throughout my career, whether in healthcare consulting or real estate, I've adhered to this fundamental principle. When presented with a problem or challenge, I meticulously analyze available solutions and formulate a comprehensive plan to address it. This plan serves as the blueprint for my approach, guiding every step of the process.

Effective communication is another vital aspect of project management. Utilizing a customer relationship management system ensures that I maintain organized and efficient communication with clients and stakeholders. Whether through email, phone calls, or other channels, tracking interactions enables me to stay informed and responsive to their needs. This approach was integral to my consulting business, where proactive outreach and engagement were essential for acquiring and retaining clients.

Also, creating a detailed business plan is crucial for both professional and personal endeavors. At the beginning of each year, I craft a comprehensive plan outlining my goals, strategies, and tactics. This plan serves as a roadmap for achieving success, providing clarity and direction in pursuit of my objectives. Just as I did in healthcare consulting, I approach my real estate business with a systematic playbook, tailored to meet the specific needs and objectives of each client.

Consistency and adaptability are also key principles in project management. By following standardized processes and refining them based on feedback and outcomes, I ensure a disciplined and effective approach. However, I also remain flexible, ready to adjust strategies and tactics as circumstances evolve. This balanced approach allows me to navigate challenges and capitalize on opportunities effectively.

How do you find the right balance between going with your gut and relying on instinct?

In business, my approach typically involves gut instinct. I reflect on what I believe could be the solution based on past experiences and knowledge. This initial instinct serves as a starting point, providing me with a broad perspective on the situation.

However, relying solely on intuition is not enough. It is essential to back up these instincts with thorough research to ensure the proposed solution is viable. Research plays a crucial role in validating and refining initial gut reactions. I examine what others have done in similar situations, analyze past experiences, and explore strategies implemented by other companies. This comprehensive approach helps in crafting a well-informed solution.

While gut instincts provide a valuable foundation, they must be supplemented by objective analysis. Tools like SWOT analysis—assessing strengths, weaknesses, opportunities, and threats—can aid in this process. By evaluating the proposed solution from multiple angles, I ensure alignment with both my initial instincts and the realities of the situation.

Flexibility is key throughout this process. If new facts or insights emerge during research, I remain open to adjusting my approach accordingly. Adapting to new information is essential for making informed decisions and achieving optimal outcomes. In the dynamic landscape of business, change is constant, and embracing it is vital for success.

What can be done to ensure there is always a win-win when dealing with others?

In any business dealings or personal relationships, it is crucial to strive for a win-win outcome. One-sided victories often lead to negative repercussions. Ensuring mutual benefit fosters sustainable and positive relationships. Trusting your instincts can guide you in assessing whether a deal benefits all parties involved. Sometimes, it's even possible to achieve a win-win-win scenario, benefiting multiple stakeholders.

Fair treatment and equitable outcomes are paramount. Negotiations require a spirit of compromise, where both parties give and take. Ultimately, everyone should feel satisfied with the arrangement. It is essential to consider each party's needs and priorities to create a mutually beneficial outcome. If one party feels shortchanged, it undermines the win-win dynamic.

Surveying the situation, understanding the stakes, and prioritizing fairness are key. Whether forging new relationships or negotiating deals, ensuring everyone's interests are met is fundamental. It is not about exploiting others for personal gain but rather fostering collaborative and mutually beneficial arrangements. When all parties walk away feeling positive about the outcome, it is a true win-win.

What does the phrase, "paddle your own canoe" mean to you? Why is that important?

The phrase, "paddle your own canoe," embodies the idea of taking responsibility for your own journey and destiny. We are each the captains of our own ships, navigating the waters of existence toward our desired destinations. While we may receive support and assistance from others along the way—whether it be family, friends, or mentors—it is ultimately up to us to steer our course.

Building a network of trusted individuals is essential, as they can provide guidance, encouragement, and assistance when needed. However, it is important to maintain awareness that not everyone may have our best interests at heart, and discernment is crucial in choosing whom to rely on. Trust is earned over time, and it is essential to surround ourselves with individuals who genuinely support our goals and aspirations.

At the end of the day, the responsibility for our actions and decisions lies solely with us. We cannot blame others for the outcomes of our choices. Therefore, it is imperative to approach life with thoughtful consideration and deliberate planning. By doing so, we can ensure that we are actively shaping our own destinies and living authentically.

Life is precious and fleeting, and we only have one opportunity to make the most of it. Embracing the concept of "paddling our own canoe" reminds us to seize control of our lives, pursue our dreams with determination, and take ownership of our futures. When we reach the end of our journey, we want to look back with pride, knowing that we navigated life's waters with purpose and autonomy.

Alester Spears's story is a powerful reminder of the enduring impact of familial influence and the profound personal fulfillment that comes from pursuing a career that resonates deeply with one's personal values and interests.

Up Next

Explore the remarkable journey of John Marron, a healthcare IT visionary and CEO/COO with a history of driving success. In this chapter, learn how John's leadership style—focused on inspiring rather than intimidating—has reshaped organizations, creating a culture of accountability and empowerment. His experiences navigating obstacles and delivering results offer valuable lessons in building a dynamic and agile business environment.

Chapter 13

Action-Oriented Leadership with Healthcare Tech CEO, John Marron

Leadership is about inspiring action, creating accountability, and ensuring clear communication. When these align, they form a powerful engine for transformation and success.

The dynamic and impactful career of John Marron, a seasoned leader in the healthcare IT sector exemplifies an inspiring path and a leadership style that is both transformative and results-oriented.

Rooted in a preference for inspiration over intimidation, John's business philosophy was profoundly influenced by the failures he faced early in his career. These experiences instilled a belief in the power of positive reinforcement, the importance of building a culture where team members feel safe to take risks and innovate, and the ability to turn challenging situations into opportunities for growth, improvement, and transformation.

John Marron grew up in a business era where bosses led by intimidation. So, when he took a stop at a small midwestern firm, he was surprised to learn that inspiration, not intimidation, could work. Gateway EDI was a revenue cycle management firm for the healthcare industry—the kind of company where leadership said it was okay to fail from time to time.

Over the course of his career, with that edict squarely in his pocket, Marron's healthcare technology career leaned on a bias toward action. He is a builder, whether his responsibilities rest in an established leadership role or when he is on an interim executive assignment. As a healthcare technology leader, he applies his general management and CEO/COO leadership skills in turnaround and growth situations for companies seeking to tap into his business-building experience.

His track record of success comes from providing operational strategic and technological leadership in different types of challenging environments. The tenets for his success can be found in his six-point building blueprint, which includes accountability, empowerment, communication, collaboration, transparency, and urgency.

The people under him, or beside him, crave their repurposing. And while he doesn't demand they post his six-point plan in their cubes as a manifesto, he admits to enjoying seeing the tenets taped next to their computers as a guide. "I come with leadership and themes that I communicate, and people want that, and they want to participate in it."

What typically frustrates you when taking on a challenge and how do you go about finding a remedy?

Let's assume by challenge we are talking about a crisis or a problem to be solved. That said, my frustrations come from indecisive behavior, lack of a plan, and a failure to execute.

People often are overwhelmed by problems or challenges, which means they either shut down and take no action or do the opposite—for example, jump right in and flail about with no clear plan. That creates an inability to execute. My action steps are to take leadership, ensure calm, create an accountable plan with benchmarks, communicate the plan, and measure/status.

What do you want more of and/or less of in business?

The key is to have less bureaucracy and more action. You must have a bias to action and execution. This is what makes a difference and ensures things get done. Micromanaging, which is a smaller form of bureaucracy, and interference will slow down execution and reduce even the best plans to rubble.

This leads to a need to form smaller and more accountable teams, and fewer meetings, especially group meetings. Too often project managers will schedule weekly updates with ten-plus people that serve no purpose other than checking a box.

It is really important for businesses to have that bias-to-action mindset—to look for the solution to the problem. A bias to action with accountability and results ensures something gets done and on time.

I was brought up in a business, a large insurance company, that was a bit of a bureaucratic empire. The processes to get things done were too long and there were too many people involved. Even the small- to medium-sized companies I worked with showed similar traits.

Too many people involved have no real value. You need action steps. When I talk about bureaucracy and having less of it, I want less people attending and being involved in the project. I want fewer pages in the document. There is no need to make it look thicker. Action steps are what drive results and get us to where we are trying to get to. This is especially important for smaller companies.

The best tip I can give is don't favor activity, favor action and execution. Getting away from activity will move you toward action and results every time.

What do you wish was easier when tackling challenges and why do you find it so hard?

The biggest hindrance to problem-solving is often communication, and understanding, of all of the stakeholders in a business. Communication lays the groundwork for appropriate resources, funding, and action from management, partners, and colleagues. All must understand the challenge in the same way, to ensure the right focus is applied.

Too often the senior team ignores the message, perhaps not properly delivered, and is late in approving resources, both human and financial. Similarly, if your partner or client is not equally invested, their response and action can hinder the ability to overcome the challenge.

What do you wish would occur faster in business?

I remember sitting in the CEO chair and expecting my board to make decisions, as opposed to expecting them to assist me by removing the obstacles to make the decisions. I like to see the decision-making process happen faster. Give me the information I need to take the next step.

To do that, you need to break the information down into pieces that are relevant to you. So, while I don't need you to make a decision, I need you to help me. I needed one of those board members to speak to the customer. You have to understand communicating with your stakeholders. What are you trying to get from them?

It's about action and involvement. You need to eliminate the need to form large teams, overanalyze the problem, and meet on it often. Smaller, agile teams, clear leadership, and an executable plan will drive results.

Too often fear paralyzes and we lose empowerment and therefore no owner, and no one in charge. So we form groups, misery loves company, and meet often and talk about it. This way everyone owns it, and when everyone owns it—no one does. Meetings with notes give a false pretense of action and teams create a false sense of ownership.

If you are going to take a problem to your CFO, bring him a financial problem. Don't bring him a technology problem. Too often, when you're communicating, you try to communicate everything. Break it down into small pieces, and understand your peers, your board, or your senior executives' capabilities and their strengths. Use their strengths and don't try to make everything so grandiose— here's everything and I need all the answers. Execution suffers and time is wasted for everyone.

What was the toughest obstacle you faced when tackling a big challenge in your career? How did you overcome it?

Lack of understanding from needed stakeholders and therefore a failure to attack the problem, accept the risks, and execute a manageable plan. Often, the solution to critical problems will require some decision and action from those above you, whether that be a manager, C-suite executive, or even a board. Sometimes their involvement becomes necessary, but a lack of understanding of the nature of the problem creates either no decision or the incorrect one.

The way to avoid this is constant and clear communication, over-communicating actually, to ensure the stakeholders needed are involved and up to speed on the problem and its nuances. This will require short, but efficient updates and Q&A, but should not be confused with creating a committee or other bureaucratic vehicle, but rather used as a checkpoint to ensure everyone is on board.

A lot of time, we think communication means leaders communicating down into the organization are important. Many believe that really makes a difference. But when I talk about communicating, I mean to all your stakeholders.

So, you have to look at it as two important communication components. One is with your customers and making sure they understand what's important in the communication cycle. The second, and most important, is communicating. When you talk about talking with all your stakeholders, it is everyone from the CEO, the CFO, and the board. I've been fortunate enough to be CEO of companies and then it's the board. I've been GM and COO and then it might be the CEO or the CFO as you communicate up.

You must have the buy-in of the senior executives for funding and resources. If they don't understand all the aspects of what you are trying to do, that's where the struggles come into play.

When we talk about communication, we are not talking old school. For example, "Did you see that email I sent?" Talk early and often. It's building that story and making sure they truly understand what you need. Communication with your customers is one thing, but communicating with the stockholders is very different and important.

———————

John Marron's story is a compelling narrative of a leader who not only challenges the status quo but also actively reshapes it to foster a more dynamic, responsive, and effective business environment. His leadership philosophy serves as a guide for current and aspiring leaders in any industry, emphasizing that real progress is achieved through action, accountability, and clear communication.

Up Next

We turn to Tom Iacovone, a former championship coach turned leader in the exhibit and trade show industry. His journey highlights grit, discipline, and the drive to overcome obstacles in implementation. Iacovone's leadership and commitment to seeing initiatives through offer valuable lessons in solving complex challenges and achieving success.

Chapter 14

Turning Plans into Progress with Trade Show Pro, Tom Iacovone

True leadership shines in identifying problems and relentlessly pursuing solutions.
Success is defined by the grit and discipline to carry plans across the finish line.

Let's turn our attention to Tom Iacovone, a distinguished figure in the field of exhibit and trade show management, whose career is punctuated by his pragmatic approach to solving complex challenges. Tom's journey underscores a core professional truth: the path from identifying problems to implementing solutions is fraught with obstacles, yet it is where true leadership shines.

By applying the same principles of hard work, drive, and tenacity he exhibited on the sidelines as a championship-winning high school football coach, Tom seamlessly transitioned from high school teacher and coach to the private sector. He began his new journey working for an Atlanta-based tradeshow and event management company.

After a few years of learning this new industry, Tom moved back to his East Coast roots to work with an exhibit builder in New Castle, Delaware. In just a few short years, Tom and a partner acquired the company and renamed it Avalon Exhibits.

After years of success as owner and operator of Avalon, in 2007 he merged his firm with Art Guild, a full-service provider of face-to-face marketing and educational programs, which was founded 100 years ago. The company creates and manages trade shows and event programs across the country. Tom is the VP with responsibilities in leadership, internal culture management, revenue growth, operational efficiencies, and customer satisfaction.

Throughout his career, Tom Iacovone has consistently emphasized the importance of moving beyond the identification of problems to actively fostering robust implementation strategies. He argues that the real challenge in any organization is not just in crafting a vision or setting goals, but in the grittier work of carrying plans across the finish line.

Tom's leadership philosophy is characterized by a bias toward action, an insistence on accountability, and a commitment to clear, communicative leadership.

What typically frustrates you when taking on a challenge and how do you go about finding a remedy?

One of the most frustrating is encountering obstacles during the implementation phase. It is a common pattern not just within our company, but across many organizations. While identifying problems and brainstorming solutions often come relatively easily, the real challenge lies in executing those solutions effectively. Implementation is where many companies hit a roadblock, and the process can become bogged down, hindering progress.

The implementation phase is critical, yet it also is where many initiatives falter. It is easy to get caught up in the planning and ideation stages, but when it comes to putting plans into action, complications often arise. There is a structured process for implementation, but navigating it smoothly is easier said than done. Challenges can emerge, such as competing priorities, resource constraints, and unexpected obstacles, which can derail progress.

One of the biggest frustrations is the speed at which the world moves. Amid the hustle and bustle of daily operations, it is all too easy for implementation efforts to take a back seat. Clients continue to demand attention, new problems arise, and the urgency of the present often overshadows the importance of addressing long-standing issues. Before you know it, months have passed, and the problem remains unresolved, gathering dust on the shelf.

To remedy this, it is crucial to maintain focus and momentum throughout the implementation process. This may involve assigning dedicated resources, establishing clear accountability, and regularly monitoring progress. Having someone to champion the initiative and keep it at the forefront of everyone's minds can help prevent it from falling by the wayside amid competing priorities.

Maintaining ongoing communication and tracking progress also can help ensure that initiatives stay on track and reach successful conclusions.

What do you want more of and/or less of in business?

I always want more clarity, and to be able to focus on identifying and prioritizing challenges. It is essential to avoid getting overwhelmed by trying to tackle every problem at once. Instead, breaking down challenges into smaller, manageable tasks allows for more effective problem-solving.

Prioritizing these tasks is key to ensuring that efforts are directed toward the most critical issues and avoiding a sense of being bogged down by competing priorities.

I also want less of a tendency to take on too much at once without considering the broader landscape of priorities. It is easy to get caught up in the excitement of starting new initiatives or addressing immediate concerns, but without careful consideration of how these efforts align with overarching goals and existing commitments, it can lead to overwhelm and inefficiency.

When faced with multiple challenges, it is important to assess each one within the context of the overall priority landscape. This involves making deliberate decisions about where to focus resources and attention, as well as recognizing what challenges may need to be deprioritized or deferred for later consideration.

By strategically choosing which challenges to tackle and approaching them in a systematic and focused manner, businesses can increase their chances of successful implementation and meaningful progress.

What do you wish was easier when tackling challenges and why do you find it so hard?

I wish implementation were easier. The biggest hurdle often lies in translating ideas and solutions into actionable steps. While identifying problems and brainstorming solutions may come relatively easily, executing those solutions can be challenging. The implementation process requires a structured approach, which can be difficult to establish and maintain.

One of the main reasons implementation is hard is because the pace of the world doesn't slow down. Time flies, and before you know it, months have passed without progress in addressing the identified challenges. Clients continue to demand attention, new problems arise, and it's tempting to prioritize immediate needs over long-term solutions.

It is crucial to remain vigilant and track progress to ensure that identified problems don't languish unresolved. Having someone dedicated to driving implementation and keeping the team focused can help overcome this challenge. Without consistent effort and attention to implementation, problems may persist and even worsen over time.

How do you make decisions on what issues you are going to emphasize?

What I do is list what I perceive as the problems and then bring in ten or twelve key stakeholders, not just high-level ones, but people at every level. We identify problems using a SWOT analysis, looking at strengths, weaknesses, opportunities, and threats. Then, we prioritize the problems.

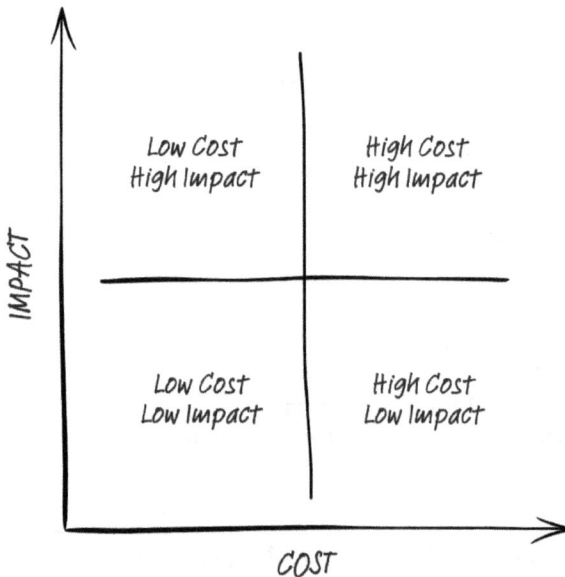

I have always found a great way to prioritize problems is to divide your problems into four quadrants: high impact and low cost, high impact and high cost, low impact and low cost, and low impact and high cost. The low-hanging fruit, which is easy to implement and has a high impact, is where you start. Then, you focus on the high impact but high cost quadrant, which can bring positive changes but requires significant investment.

We focus on those two quadrants because trying to solve every problem would be overwhelming. We pick out the high-impact problems and analyze where they fall in the quadrant. Then, we devise solutions.

What typically gets you stuck when taking on challenges?

Many companies, including ours, excel at identifying problems and brainstorming solutions. However, when it comes to putting those solutions into action, things often slow down or come to a halt. Implementation is where the process tends to bog down.

There is a structured process for implementation in every company, but it is not always easy to follow. Many companies and individuals struggle with executing solutions effectively. The fast-paced nature of the world exacerbates this challenge. Time flies, and before you know it, months have passed without progress in addressing the identified challenges.

It is easy to get sidetracked by the demands of the present, such as client orders and immediate problems, and postpone addressing longer-term issues. This tendency to prioritize the urgent over the important can lead to unresolved problems lingering on the shelf.

To overcome these challenges, it is crucial to stay focused and track progress diligently. Having someone dedicated to driving implementation and keeping the team on track can help ensure that identified problems are addressed effectively and in a timely manner.

What do you wish would occur faster in business?

I wish companies would realize that the key to getting things done faster is to have a plan and implement it correctly. You really must have a plan in which your goals and objectives are clearly defined. Make sure these goals and objectives are reasonable and attainable and set a corresponding agenda and timeline that is also reasonable and attainable.

More than anything, you have to go into the process with an open mind. You have to listen and do so effectively. The last thing you want to do is get so caught up in your own ego that you are not listening. You alone do not have all the answers.

Similarly, do not solicit advice from only like-minded individuals; ensure you are inviting a wide variety of thoughts and ideas into the mix so you expand the potential for real change, growth, and sustainable problem-solving.

You also have to make sure the team you pull together is well-prepared, and they work ahead of time on their thought processes. Follow up on every homework assignment you make. These things are all essential, and the sooner we recognize it, the sooner we can get to the end result we are all seeking.

I have been blessed with some very thoughtful and intelligent mentors over the years. One of the main axioms that stands out is "Failure to plan is planning to fail." More than anything, you have to have a plan. Success doesn't happen by accident; it takes effective and coordinated planning. It means you have to know where you are headed and how you are going to get there. To see that path and travel it, you need a plan.

Having a strategic plan should be a part of your core company values, which is a long-term vision. You need strategic imperatives to achieve the vision—identifying and solving problems are the easy part, but you need a plan to implement them. And that must be ingrained in your core values.

What was the toughest obstacle you faced when tackling a big challenge in your career? How did you overcome it?

One of the toughest was when we discovered we might not have all of the solutions. At one point, I sent out an agenda to about ten stakeholders within the company with all the problems I saw. I asked each of them to review these issues and then to add to the list as they saw fit. I wanted everyone to be prepared to discuss this in depth and in detail.

There were lots of issues that needed addressing, including reworking our foreman system. We had to look at reorganizing the entire structure. Adding to that was an aging workforce. That meant we would have to dig deeper with the union to find solutions. There were shipping, receiving, and warehousing issues and problems with purchasing. The entire system was in need of review and rework. We had a number of remote workers, so we needed to find a balance that didn't impact our performance and our ability to get things done.

To make things even more challenging, because of what was happening, our clients were waiting until the last minute to make decisions, which forced us to do the same. While we tried to rank these issues by importance, as you can imagine, the difference of opinion was rampant. Our stakeholders all had different priorities, and it became challenging to get people to be open-minded.

Opening your mind to change can be an obstacle. What we were facing was a high volume of jobs. Many were new builds. It was one of the busiest times in our company's long history, and we were not prepared. Among the specific challenges we faced was that, like most companies, we had a shortage of project managers. After nearly eighteen months of being relatively dormant because of COVID, the amount of work at one time put a tremendous amount of stress on the organization.

Our biggest issues to this day tend to be issues all companies face. We are very good at identifying problems, and we are equally good at offering solutions. Unfortunately, the challenges lie with implementation. When I sent out that agenda with all the problems as I saw them and asked everyone to review and add to the list, I was hoping we would be prepared to discuss them in depth and in detail. What happened was that every stakeholder had their own specific problem and priority.

We knew we had to identify and implement what needed to be done or the entire process would just turn into a wasted exercise. Identifying and solving problems should be easy, but where too many companies fail is in the implementation process. There are myriad reasons for that—company politics, costs do not justify end results—and there is just a failure to launch.

The solution should always be to identify the problems in quadrants: high priority/low cost, high priority/high cost, low priority/low cost, and low priority/ high cost. In essence, you grab the low-hanging fruit first and move systematically through the process.

Tom Iacovone illustrates the intricate dance between planning and execution within the business context. His strategies for overcoming implementation roadblocks and his advocacy for a focused, accountable approach provide valuable lessons for professionals across industries, emphasizing that true success is not just about identifying problems but effectively implementing solutions.

Up Next

Explore the journey of Dr. Bernie Mullin, founder of The Aspire Sport Marketing Group and former NBA executive. His leadership, rooted in empowerment and ethics, has transformed sports marketing. Learn key lessons on leadership, mentorship, and creating opportunities in the sports and entertainment industry.

Chapter 15

Empowering Success in Sports Brand Building With 'The Professor,' Dr. Bernie Mullin

Leadership is about providing opportunities and empowering others.
True success lies in the growth and success of those we mentor,
driven by ethics, integrity, and innovation.

Dr. Bernie Mullin, a.k.a. Dr. B, is a towering figure in the sports and entertainment industry whose career has been defined by a profound commitment to leadership, mentorship, and innovation. Mullin's journey through the complex terrain of sports management showcases a leader who deeply values the growth and development of his team and who has revolutionized the approach to sports marketing in a way that has significantly impacted the careers of countless professionals. His philosophy that "leadership is about providing opportunities" has enabled him to mentor a multitude of individuals, equipping them with the skills to excel in their careers.

The Professor

Driven by his strategically wired academic thinking and an artful business sense, there is a reason they call Bernie Mullin 'The Professor.' The nickname was solidified after he co-wrote the book, *Sport Marketing*, along with Dr. Bill Sutton and Dr. Steve Hardy. Considered the Bible for sports marketing, the best-selling book, now in its fourth edition and features a web study guide, continues to direct students to a better understanding of the theoretical backbone that is sports marketing.

That Mullin has spent the next forty-plus years systematically working with professional sports, collegiate athletics, and entertainment venue operations at the highest levels of the game employing those techniques is no accident. He continues to be a credit to his profession, proof of which can be found in his mentorship to a number of the industry's highest-profile leaders.

Over the years, specializing predominantly in startups and turnaround situations, Dr. B helped refocus, build, and drive proven-winning organizations on the field, court, and ice. By helping develop and lead a number of high-profile peak organizations, the lad from Liverpool set the bar as high as it can go. His work can be seen with the Pittsburgh Pirates, who hired him in 1986 as its SVP of business operations. His path included stints with the Colorado Rockies (SVP of business, 1991–1993); the Denver Grizzlies (president/general manager, 1993–1995); the University of Denver (vice chancellor of athletics, 1995–1999; the National Basketball Association (SVP of marketing and team business operations, 2000–2004); and the Atlanta Hawks, Atlanta Thrashers, and Philips Arena president/CEO, 2004–2008.

In 2016, he eventually founded the sports marketing firm, The Aspire Group, where he acted first as CEO, and later as chair. Aspire went on to become one of the leading outsourced revenue-generating firms globally in the space, generating more than $250 million in new and enhanced client revenues per year, and $1.5-plus billion in total revenues since its inception. Mullin's firm accomplished this while serving 300-plus global brands with 200 employees working in seven countries in seventeen different sports. The culmination of his efforts hit an apex when he sold The Aspire Group to a group that involved Playfly Sports, a leader in sports media, marketing, and technology.

Through Bernie Mullin's story, we learn that the essence of effective leadership lies in a commitment to ethical practices, the empowerment of others, and the relentless pursuit of innovation.

When the scores of people Bernie has mentored over the years thanked him for helping them succeed, his response was one you'd expect from a leader whose list of such individuals is quite long. "I reminded them that they were the ones who zigged and zagged through the doors that were opened."

Mullin believes that one of the most important tenets good leaders should have is their people. In the grand plan that leadership holds, the spoils of victory and success rest in the ones you surround yourself with. "It's more about them patting themselves on the back—all I did was provide the opportunity."

Ethics. Honesty. Integrity. More ethics. These are the characteristics Mullin says are what should drive the people who drive your business. Focus more on your people and you are focusing on the very ingredient that drives success. As simple as that tenet sounds, it is way more sophisticated in the scope of all the lifelines

Mullin has given to those he has worked with over the years.

What typically frustrates you when taking on a challenge? How do you go about finding a remedy?

When you are working with ownership groups involving all different kinds of backgrounds and personalities, one of the frustrating parts is when they won't let you do your job. You have to find ways to get things done.

When I left the University of Massachusetts in 1986 to go work for the Pittsburgh Pirates, they had fourteen owners. Of those, eleven were CEOs or chairs of some of the biggest corporations in Pittsburgh. They were huge companies—Westinghouse, Pittsburgh National Bank, PNC Bank, Mellon Bank, and Pittsburgh Paint and Glass, etc.—that were fantastic to work with. The other two investors were what you call self-made men.

At the time, the Pirates were drawing 7,000 fans a game. They were in last place, losing 100 games and $10 million a year. The turnaround job was a big undertaking. With all those voices in my ear, I eventually settled on three approaches:

1. Stop sailing in the wrong direction at a speed of going downhill rapidly.
2. The turnaround had to be in the right direction (you had to make them see those are two very different things).
3. You just have to start moving forward at pace, making decisions, and then seeing how the decisions play out.

It took five to six years, but we did it. In year three, the Pirates were winning divisions (at the time, the National League East). The turnaround helped things on the business side.

It was the same story with the Colorado Rockies, who had nine owners. At the time, the Rockies were an expansion team, so everything was new. In this case, the owners left us alone, and as a result, success became instantaneous, including an all-time attendance record for any sports team anywhere in the world—4.48 million fans. That record has never been beaten and never will be.

Most of these people have had people telling them the wrong thing for years because that is what they thought they wanted to hear. But you must find a direction and go. Make the decision, get behind it, and see where it takes you.

What are the secrets to getting leaders to foster a culture of making decisions faster?

Leaders can foster a culture of making decisions faster by challenging the notion that everything must be perfect before action is taken. This mindset shift involves recognizing that perfection is often unattainable and that delays can be more detrimental than imperfect decisions. Leaders must communicate this perspective throughout the organization, emphasizing the importance of agility and taking calculated risks.

One effective strategy is to encourage a bias for action among team members. Instead of waiting for all variables to align perfectly, individuals should feel empowered to make decisions based on available information and their best judgment. This approach promotes proactive problem-solving and allows the organization to capitalize on opportunities swiftly.

Additionally, leaders should create an environment where mistakes are viewed as learning opportunities rather than failures. By normalizing experimentation and acknowledging that not all decisions will yield the desired outcome, leaders foster a culture of continuous improvement and innovation. Encouraging open dialogue about lessons learned from both successes and failures promotes transparency and helps build collective knowledge.

Leaders also can set clear expectations around decision-making processes, empowering teams to prioritize speed and responsiveness. This may involve streamlining approval workflows, delegating decision-making authority to frontline employees, or implementing agile methodologies that emphasize iterative progress over perfection.

Furthermore, leaders should lead by example, demonstrating a willingness to make decisions swiftly and adapt as needed. By modeling decisive behavior and showing resilience in the face of setbacks, leaders inspire confidence and trust within their teams.

In the end, fostering a culture for making decisions faster requires a combination of mindset shifts, structural changes, and leadership behaviors. By promoting agility, embracing experimentation, and empowering individuals to take action, leaders can create an environment where decisive decision-making is valued and embraced as a driver of organizational success.

What is the secret to establishing agility and responsiveness within your team?

The secret to establishing agility and responsiveness within your team lies in several key principles. First, it is crucial that you select individuals who naturally gravitate toward teamwork and collaboration. Team-oriented individuals who have experience in team sports often understand their role within a collective effort and the importance of collaboration for success.

In my experience, maintaining a consistent senior executive team at The Aspire Group has been our secret sauce. Our senior team members have all been with the company for at least a decade, fostering a deep understanding of our organization's goals and values.

It also is important to prioritize healthy debates and conflict resolution within your team. By encouraging open discussions and quickly settling on the right solutions, you create an environment where everyone feels heard and supported.

Consistency, both externally with consumers and internally within our team, is critical. Our core DNA revolves around an eight-point ticket marketing, sales, and service plan that emphasizes market and fan research as the foundation for all our initiatives.

Strategically, focus on retaining, growing, and acquiring customers, ensuring you prioritize existing relationships while expanding your reach. Capturing and utilizing contact information allows you to communicate effectively with your audience, personalized messaging, and follow-up efforts to foster conversion and closure.

Finally, analytics play a crucial role in evaluating the success of your strategies and tactics. By consistently analyzing data, you can ensure maximum responsiveness and efficiency in your approach.

Ultimately, success stems from cohesive team dynamics, consistent leadership, and unwavering commitment to a shared philosophy.

Talk about the importance of giving people room to learn and grow through their mistakes.

Learning and growth often stem from the freedom to make mistakes and the opportunity to learn from them. Reflecting on a recent experience at New York Pizza University, where our senior leadership team listened intently to a pizza-making expert, I realized the importance of hands-on learning. Despite the expert's knowledge, the session lacked impact because we were mere spectators, unable to engage with the dough ourselves.

Similarly, in professional settings, merely instructing individuals without allowing them to apply their learning firsthand yields limited results. People need the chance to experiment, make mistakes, learn from them, and, ultimately, refine their approach. It's a process of trial and error, where failures serve as valuable learning experiences, shaping future successes.

This principle applies across various domains, including sports. Coaches often hesitate to entrust critical moments to rookies or inexperienced players, fearing failure. However, as I learned from a seasoned coach during my soccer career, providing incremental opportunities for growth is key. By gradually expanding responsibilities and setting achievable goals, individuals can build confidence and competence over time.

In my own journey, starting as a right-backer for the Oxford City Football Club, I was entrusted with specific responsibilities: prevent the left-winger from advancing and distribute the ball efficiently. Through incremental adjustments and feedback, I gained confidence and competence, ultimately solidifying my role within the team.

Translating this approach to professional contexts involves understanding individuals' strengths, assigning tasks that align with their abilities, and offering guidance and support along the way. By breaking down complex tasks into manageable steps and celebrating small victories, we empower individuals to learn, grow, and thrive.

Ultimately, it is about fostering an environment where mistakes are viewed as opportunities for growth, and success is built upon a foundation of resilience, perseverance, and continuous improvement.

What do you want more of and/or less of in business?

You need more momentum. When I first started with the Pirates, I read everything that Zig Ziglar wrote. One of his stories was about the importance of just getting started. Ziglar used the analogy of sitting in a car and turning the steering wheel. You have to start somewhere; you need momentum. Even if you're going in the wrong direction, you have to turn the wheel. Momentum is everything. Doing something, even if it's slightly the wrong thing, is okay. You need to trust your judgment. So you might be five or seven degrees off, but that's not 100 degrees off.

Years later, when I worked with David Stern and the NBA, I really saw what Ziglar was saying. Stern believed that even if it's not perfect, even if it's not right now, you do it. Of course, he might have ended up ripping the hell out of you, but he respected the effort. Even if it is not the perfect decision, get started. That is how we built our culture—a culture that demanded that we try something, anything, to get going.

As for less, it would basically be less of everything I just said. You have to give people a chance. If you don't, what are you doing? When a coach looks down the end of his bench, he doesn't think, "Great, I have to put the rookie in." Well, if he doesn't, how will he know if that rookie can get the job done? We are all going to make a certain amount of mistakes.

The expectation of management should not bet that you will make mistakes, but if you will make fewer and fewer mistakes each time you get an opportunity.

Can you outline strategies for collaborating with people from diverse backgrounds and personalities? Why is that so important?

The essence of effectively collaborating with individuals from diverse backgrounds and personalities lies in fostering genuine connections, understanding, and mutual respect. My journey into this realm began with a pivotal mentorship experience early in my career as a marketing director for a metal tubing company. Despite initial doubts about my qualifications, I approached the role with a focus on building rapport and relationships with decision-makers, placing value on personal connection above product promotion.

In navigating complex situations, such as managing multiple ownership groups in the sports industry, it is important to listen. Whether you are engaging with entrepreneurs or seasoned executives, prioritize asking thoughtful questions, listen intently to their perspectives, and address their concerns with honesty and integrity.

Central to successful collaboration is your ability to recognize and appreciate the diversity of experiences and viewpoints present within a team or partnership. From navigating disputes among ownership groups to developing marketing strategies, I always tried to embrace the principle of inclusivity. It is important to leverage the strengths and insights of each person involved.

Furthermore, there should be a great amount of significance placed on aligning objectives and approaches with a shared vision. Rather than imposing your ideas or agendas, advocate for a collaborative approach grounded in consensus-building and strategic alignment. You can cultivate a culture of continuous improvement and innovation if you prioritize the retention of existing relationships, foster organic growth, and systematically capture and leverage data.

In the end, the secret to successful collaboration lies in embracing diversity, fostering meaningful connections, and aligning your efforts toward common goals. By valuing authenticity, empathy, and open communication, it is possible to harness the collective strength of their differences to achieve greater success and impact.

Bernie Mullin's journey is a testament to the power of ethical leadership and the profound impact that one individual can have on an industry and on the lives of many. His dedication to nurturing talent and his visionary approach to sports marketing continue to inspire and shape the industry, making his story not only about personal success but also about the enduring influence of genuine, values-driven leadership.

Up Next

Explore Trey Hinson's journey, principal at Goliath Sales Strategies and a healthcare sales leader. Known for his strategic thinking and empathy, Hinson's story offers insights into understanding customer needs, balancing commitments, and leading with resilience and foresight.

Chapter 16

Balancing Empathy and Action with Executive Sales Strategist, Trey Hinson

Empathy and strategic thinking are key to effective leadership.
Understanding and addressing needs drives growth and lasting partnerships.

Known for his adeptness at fostering growth and forging robust industry connections, Trey Hinson's career is a testament to the power of strategic thinking and deep industry knowledge in the competitive marketplace.

Beginning his career in the emotionally intense environment of healthcare customer service, Hinson was exposed to the complexities of healthcare systems and the nuanced needs of customers. His unique approach to his work—characterized by patience, understanding, and strategic acumen—allowed him to navigate this challenging landscape successfully and laid the groundwork for his future endeavors.

Trey's journey is a compelling illustration of how visionary leadership and strategic foresight can create enduring success and influence in the business world.

Working with retirees who were already dealing with extremely emotional situations, Trey Hinson quickly discovered he didn't know what he didn't know. When the phone rang, the people on the other end of the line needed help—and needed help fast.

The emotionally charged atmosphere and people Hinson was dealing with were an immensely productive teaching experience. Working with extremely regimented thinking, structured individuals who followed the chain of command approach to the letter helped shape his thinking. It also created in him a way to handle people dealing with complex and difficult situations.

Just out of college, Trey stepped into a work environment that demanded a skill set not always available for recent graduates. As part of his leadership training came a slew of medical terminology and intricacies related to the healthcare system. And, there he was, trying day by day to help deescalate situations for people who had seen more in their lifetimes than he could ever dream of.

"I was 21. I'd lost some friends over the years, but that type of situation-dealing with military people who had experienced the things they had experienced hit me square in the nose. What you have to learn is how to push yourself so that the person across the table or on the other end of the phone knows you care."

After twelve years as a pod manager for Blue Cross Blue Shield, Hinson's work did not go unnoticed. Working his way up the ladder, he eventually caught the attention of a company called Ocozzio, a small marketing firm that focused on healthcare benefits, technology, and cost containment.

After working as VP of marketing and learning under the tutelage of Ocozzio's CEO, Trey would go on to become COO, an experience that would lay the foundation for his newest venture, Goliath Sales Strategies. Through Goliath, Hinson continues to focus on sales strategies, partnership development, and sales enablement services to build relationships in the healthcare sector.

What was the toughest obstacle you faced when tackling a big challenge? How did you overcome it?

Without question, it is balancing the challenges of being an executive, a husband, and a father. In the world I have served for more than twenty-three years, it is extremely demanding. There is no such thing as an off day, per se. When a partner needs you, the expectation is you are available to help and work through complex issues.

I encountered a personal obstacle due to this fact several years ago. I was like many business execs where I traveled for business whenever needed. My daughter was having a pre-school singing performance, and during the performance, she looked out in the audience for me, and I wasn't there. She knew it, of course. But when she sang the verse, "I love my daddy, and my daddy loves me" with my wife recording the performance for me, I literally saw her melt. At that time, I said I would do everything in my power as a father to never let my daughter down again.

While I would love to say I have made every performance since that isn't true. Business sometimes requires me to be gone, but I can promise you I have been sitting in the audience at every possible moment cheering on my children, so they know they come first in my life along with my wife.

This taught me the value of balance between family and work. It hurt when it occurred, but it was one of those pivotal moments in life that taught me what was truly important and better ways to communicate in balance. My daughter to this day has become an accountability partner just like the mentors that I value in my life. Time is the one resource that we can't replace, and I am truly fortunate to have so many amazing friends and mentors who help me keep it all in perspective.

How can mentors recognize potential in the people they manage and help them navigate complex situations?

Throughout my twenty-three-year career, I've been fortunate to encounter numerous individuals who have provided me with invaluable opportunities I never thought possible. Reflecting on my journey, I recall the pivotal moment I went to work for Blue Cross Blue Shield of South Carolina at twenty-one. Despite my youth, armed with an insurance and risk management degree from UFC, I was entrusted with the role of a pods manager, where I was tasked with overseeing claims processing, membership, and billing. Little did I know, that this experience would shape the trajectory of my career, equipping me with a profound understanding of the intricacies within the healthcare benefit space.

What set the stage for my growth and development was my unwavering curiosity and willingness to seek guidance. I was never afraid to ask questions, to inquire about what I did right or wrong, and how I could improve. Some mentors approached coaching with a firm hand, while others adopted a gentler approach, but all shared a commitment to providing honest feedback, regardless of how uncomfortable it might have been for me to hear.

While there were moments when my ego took a hit and I found myself grappling with self-doubt, each setback served as a valuable lesson that propelled my growth. The pivotal lesson I learned is the importance of actively seeking guidance and mentorship. While mentors play a crucial role in providing direction and support, it's equally essential for individuals to take ownership of their learning journey. By initiating conversations, asking questions, and expressing a genuine desire to improve, individuals can unlock a wealth of knowledge and insights from their mentors.

Today, as I find myself in a position to mentor others, I strive to pay forward the guidance and support that was bestowed upon me. Drawing from my own experiences, I aim to create a nurturing environment where individuals feel empowered to seek guidance, ask questions, and embrace continuous growth.

While I acknowledge that I am far from perfect, I remain committed to the journey of self-improvement and endeavor to support others in their quest for personal and professional development.

What do you wish was easier when tackling a challenge head-on? Why can it be so hard?

Personally, I have a tendency to gravitate toward the easiest problems first. I have had to train myself to embrace difficult problems. I don't know if this will ever become comfortable per se, but through diving in, I have found that my productivity and value to organizations have increased exponentially.

In long-term challenges, I break issues into categories and create action lists for each deliverable stage to keep myself moving in the right direction.

For larger issues, this can be extremely detailed and long. The key is to be willing to adjust as deliverables and challenges move to ensure that I keep the intended outcome at the forefront. The game changer for me is daily journaling, as it gives me the ability to look back at my day and determine what I would have done differently if I encountered the situation again in the future.

Sometimes, the strategies I thought would be the most effective didn't produce the optimal results, and I have had to learn that it is okay as long as I land the desired end results.

Why is it important to face head-on the tasks that seem difficult at first?

Facing difficult tasks head-on is not just about addressing problems; it's about embracing them as opportunities for growth and development. Throughout my career, I've learned that challenges often serve as springboards for success. When confronted with a problem, the most effective approach is to acknowledge it, take ownership, and devise a plan of action to address it.

While it may be tempting to avoid difficult conversations or shy away from daunting tasks, doing so only perpetuates the problem. Instead, by tackling challenges head-on, we demonstrate resilience, integrity, and leadership. It is not about seeking comfort or avoiding discomfort; it is about doing what needs to be done, even when it's hard.

One example that comes to mind is when I encountered misprocessed claims or difficult client situations in past roles. Rather than shying away from these issues, I confronted them directly. I initiated difficult conversations, listened to concerns, and communicated openly and honestly about my plan to address the issue. While the conversations may have been uncomfortable, they ultimately strengthened relationships and earned respect from those involved.

In essence, facing challenges head-on is not just a matter of problem-solving; it's a demonstration of leadership. Leaders do not shy away from adversity; they embrace it as an opportunity to demonstrate their capabilities and lead their teams through uncertainty. By confronting challenges with courage and conviction, we not only overcome obstacles but also pave the way for personal and professional growth.

How does taking a service-oriented approach help turn a challenging situation around? Give an example of a strategy you used to align your team's commitment with your business partner's needs.

In navigating challenging client relationships, I've found that adopting a service-oriented approach can be transformative. One memorable example involves a technology company based in New York, with whom we were experiencing significant communication barriers and misunderstandings. Despite initial frustrations, I recognized the importance of fostering a deeper understanding and alignment between our teams. With the support of my executive leadership team, I made the decision to personally visit the client in New York.

This gesture of commitment demonstrated our willingness to go above and beyond to address their concerns and find common ground. Despite the challenges of travel and adverse weather conditions, the face-to-face meeting proved invaluable. During our discussions, we broke bread and engaged in open dialogue, which fostered a sense of partnership and mutual respect. By truly listening to their perspective and articulating our own, we were able to bridge the communication gap and gain clarity on their needs and expectations. It became evident that we were not as far apart as initially thought; we simply needed to adjust our approach and communication style.

Through this collaborative effort, we developed a clear plan of action that aligned with their objectives. By demonstrating our commitment to understanding and addressing their concerns, we were able to salvage the client relationship and ultimately maintain their business for several years.

This experience underscored the importance of proactive communication, empathy, and a willingness to go the extra mile to meet client needs. By approaching challenging situations with a service-oriented mindset and a focus on building trust and understanding, it is possible to turn even the most difficult circumstances into opportunities for growth and partnership.

Define the importance of candidness and honest feedback in business. Is there a situation that led to a positive change that stands out?

Candidness and honest feedback are fundamental principles. In business, there's simply no time for sugar-coating. Consultants, in particular, often fall into the trap of telling clients what they want to hear. But true growth comes from having the courage to offer candid perspectives, even if they diverge from the client's expectations.

Throughout my career, working closely with numerous CEOs in the healthcare benefit space, I've learned the value of candidness firsthand. CEOs reach their positions for a reason—they possess exceptional judgment and are unafraid to provide feedback when necessary. I've internalized this candid approach not as personal criticism, but as an opportunity for personal and professional growth.

I extend this principle of candidness to my interactions with my teams and clients alike. If I perceive that we're heading down the wrong path, I don't hesitate to voice my concerns and offer alternative perspectives. While it can be challenging to push back, especially when met with resistance, I've found that presenting well-thought-out alternatives facilitates constructive dialogue and fosters mutual understanding.

In many Southern cultures, including my upbringing in South Carolina, there often is a preference for politeness over candidness. But I've come to realize that honest conversations, conducted either in person or over the phone, are essential for effective communication. Delivering difficult news through text or email can obscure intentions and undermine trust.

One memorable instance where candid feedback led to significant positive changes occurred about eighteen years ago. A leader imparted the wisdom that delivering bad news should always be done in person or over the phone, rather than through electronic communication. This lesson stuck with me, emphasizing the importance of conveying thoughts and concerns directly, with sincerity and empathy.

Ultimately, cultivating an environment of candidness requires courage and sincerity. By prioritizing open communication and embracing honest feedback, individuals and organizations can navigate challenges more effectively and foster deeper connections built on trust and mutual respect.

How can a technique like journaling be a valuable ally in managing challenges?

Journaling has emerged as a pivotal tool in my leadership journey, offering invaluable insights and clarity amid challenging situations. Initially, I perceived journaling as akin to keeping a personal diary—a practice reserved for documenting trivial details. However, I soon realized its profound relevance to business executives like myself.

Utilizing an electronic journal equipped with prompts, I jump into the core of my challenges, adopting what I term the "me perspective." This entails reflecting on my own perceptions and interpretations of the situation at hand. Subsequently, the journal prompts me to consider the viewpoint of the individuals I'm engaging with—what lens are they viewing the situation through? This shift in perspective allows me to grasp the broader context and empathize with their standpoint.

Equally crucial is the exploration of the opposite perspective, where I challenge my initial assumptions and consider alternative viewpoints. Initially skeptical of this approach, I've come to recognize its merit in fostering a deeper understanding of complex issues. By examining the situation from opposing angles, I unearth fresh insights and uncover hidden solutions.

The journal encourages me to envision the optimal perspective—the shared goal or aspiration that both parties strive toward. This forward-looking approach guides my decision-making process, ensuring alignment with overarching objectives.

Journaling has empowered me to navigate challenging decisions with confidence and clarity. For example, when faced with the realization that a particular career opportunity was not aligned with my aspirations, journaling provided the clarity I needed to step away and pursue a different path. By articulating my thoughts and examining the situation from multiple angles, I was able to make a well-informed decision that ultimately proved beneficial for my professional growth.

Incorporating journaling into my daily routine has become second nature, serving as a constant companion in my quest for effective leadership. I encourage fellow business leaders and aspiring professionals alike to embrace this practice, as it offers a transformative means of gaining perspective, fostering empathy, and unlocking innovative solutions to complex challenges.

What are some of the strategies or communication techniques you've developed to expedite the decision-making process?

One of the key strategies I use is to reach a definitive yes or no as quickly as possible. I've found it's essential to convey to stakeholders that a no is not necessarily a negative outcome. While it's certainly preferable to receive a positive response, it is equally as important to respect when a particular opportunity or solution is not the right fit at the present time.

By creating an environment where individuals feel comfortable expressing their honest opinions and preferences, we can avoid unnecessary delays and streamline the decision-making process. I often emphasize to stakeholders that it's perfectly acceptable to decline or reject a proposal if it doesn't align with their needs or priorities. This open and candid approach helps to remove any apprehension or hesitation about delivering a negative response.

In my experience, some of the most successful sales professionals are those who are able to swiftly discern whether a prospect is genuinely interested or not. Instead of prolonging the engagement with prospects who are indecisive or uncertain, I encourage a direct and straightforward dialogue. I make it clear that I value efficiency and respect their time, and I invite them to provide a clear yes or no answer based on their assessment.

I believe in embracing candor and transparency because it leads to a more efficient and effective decision-making process. By fostering an environment where individuals feel empowered to express their preferences and make informed choices, we can expedite progress and achieve better outcomes for all parties involved.

Share some strategies or tools you've used to ensure you maintain a balance in your decision-making.

One is to prioritize personal commitments alongside professional responsibilities. Initially, it felt uncomfortable for me as an executive to decline business trips or meetings due to family commitments. But I quickly realized the importance of being honest and transparent about my personal obligations.

By sharing glimpses of my personal life with colleagues and business partners, I discovered it fostered a deeper level of understanding and empathy. When I explained that I couldn't attend a meeting because of my daughter's dance performance or my son's soccer game, most people were understanding and supportive. This approach humanized me in their eyes and allowed them to relate to my experiences as a parent.

I've observed that younger generations, particularly millennials, often prioritize work-life balance more effectively. Their example has inspired me to strike a better equilibrium between professional aspirations and personal well-being. While work is undoubtedly important, I've come to recognize that family time and personal fulfillment are equally valuable.

The pandemic served as a catalyst for reevaluating priorities and spending more quality time with family. I've made a conscious effort to honor my commitments to my children's events and activities, and I've been fortunate to receive understanding and support from colleagues and superiors.

Moreover, I've cultivated a culture within my team that values work-life balance and respects personal commitments. I encourage team members to prioritize their families and personal well-being, knowing that a fulfilled and happy workforce leads to greater productivity and job satisfaction.

Becoming a parent was a transformative experience for me, prompting a shift in perspective and priorities. I've learned the importance of being present for my children's milestones and cherishing those moments. As a leader, I strive to instill this mindset within my organization, fostering a culture of empathy, understanding, and mutual respect for work and personal life commitments.

Trey Hinson's career highlights the transformative power of empathy, strategic thinking, and resilient leadership in navigating the complex and high-stakes world of healthcare sales and customer service. His story offers valuable insights into effective leadership and strategic sales practices, while also inspiring current and future leaders to prioritize empathy and strategic foresight in their professional journeys.

Chapter 17

Turning Decisions into Momentum

Success doesn't come from what you do occasionally.
It comes from what you do consistently.

In this chapter, the key theme is taking decisive action. The stories shared in this part of the book highlighted that leaders don't just face challenges—they act on them. While identifying a problem is crucial, success is defined by the actions you take to resolve it.

Action builds progress. Whether in real estate, healthcare, sports marketing, or trade shows, the leaders I talked with understood that standing still never solves problems. Even when the road ahead is uncertain, progress begins with a single, purposeful step.

The lessons from these stories emphasize that success comes from moving forward, even in the face of uncertainty. Taking small, deliberate actions is often the key to breaking through stagnation and creating momentum.

Key Takeaways

1. **Start Small, Move Fast.** Taking the first step—whether launching a new initiative or pursuing a passion—creates momentum. Identify one small action today to start moving toward your goal.
2. **Build Systems of Accountability.** Create clear accountability structures to ensure follow-through. Establish a simple system where tasks are clear, and accountability is embedded. Regularly review this system to maintain progress and refine it as needed.
3. **Execute the Plan.** Having a plan is just the beginning—execution is key. Pick one element of a stalled plan and commit to taking

action on it this week.

4. **Empower Your Team.** Empowering others leads to greater innovation and results. Delegate a decision to your team or encourage creative problem-solving in an area they can take ownership of.

5. **Balance Empathy with Action.** Effective leadership balances understanding team needs with decisive actions that drive results. Reflect on how well you balance empathy and results and adjust where necessary to ensure both are present in your leadership approach.

Leadership in Practice

- **For Emerging Leaders:** Simplify one area of your leadership today—whether communication, task delegation, or decision-making. Take immediate action to move from thought to action.
- **For Seasoned Leaders:** Audit your current processes. Where has complexity slowed you down? Simplify these areas to create space for decisive action.

Before moving onto the next stories, think about these three questions.

1. **Where have you delayed action?**
   Identify one area in your leadership where you've hesitated. What bold step can you take today to create momentum?

2. **How can you empower your team?**
   What barriers are preventing your team from taking decisive action? How can you support them to act with confidence?

3. **What's your next move?**
   Consider your current challenges. Where can you simplify your approach to create immediate impact?

Action is the defining factor between those who dream and those who achieve. Leadership isn't just about identifying problems—it's about taking bold, decisive steps to create solutions.

Simplifying your approach and focusing on action will lead to better outcomes, for both you and your team. The next move is yours—make it count.

Up Next: Zoom Out to Zoom In

Explore how keeping the big picture in mind leads to success, starting with José Perez. His dedication to detail and client satisfaction, paired with an entrepreneurial spirit, offers key lessons on overcoming challenges with resilience and creativity.

BONUS RESOURCES

By now, you've gained incredible insights
from the leaders featured in
Obstacles to Opportunity.

Want even more?

You'll also find exclusive tools
and resources to help accelerate your growth.

Create your free account today at
PatAlacqua.com/bonus-resources
and take the next step in your business journey!

PAT
ALACQUA
BUSINESS GROWTH
STRATEGIST

PART 3:
ZOOM OUT TO ZOOM IN

Through each growth phase of business, it's important to keep the big picture in mind. Challenges, however, often require a much more micro focus. The following leaders recognized that by first looking at the greater problem and then breaking things down into smaller, achievable milestones they could develop solutions that were both impactful and sustainable.

Chapter 18

Crafting Success One Stitch at a Time with Master Haberdasher, José Perez

True craftsmanship is about empowering clients through attention to detail, personalized service, and a commitment to excellence.

The illustrious career of master haberdasher José Perez reflects a compelling model of ambition, precision, and entrepreneurial spirit, one that has shaped the luxury custom clothing industry over the past few decades. Jose's approach to custom clothing goes beyond mere aesthetics; he sees his craft as a means to empower and elevate, turning each client interaction into an opportunity for personal transformation.

Throughout his career, Perez has faced challenges head-on, adapting to changes in the fashion industry and consumer preferences with agility and foresight. His resilience was particularly tested during the global pandemic, a period during which he skillfully pivoted his business model to continue providing exceptional service against all odds.

Now, Jose continues to innovate in the art of tailoring, blending traditional techniques with modern technology to create garments that are both timeless and contemporary. His leadership not only drives the success of his company but also inspires a new generation of designers and entrepreneurs.

Reflecting on his path to success, Perez emphasizes the values of hard work, dedication, and ethical business practices. His story is a testament to the power of nurturing relationships and staying true to one's vision, principles that have made him a revered figure in the world of fashion and beyond.

In 1985, fresh into his role at the Tom James Company, Jose embarked on a journey of self-discovery and ambition. Armed with a golden notebook, he dove deep into his aspirations, crafting a blueprint for his future success. Despite the myriad goals swirling around in his mind, Jose dedicated hours to distilling his dreams into tangible targets.

Over the next thirty-seven years, Perez transformed his aspirations into reality, generating over $50 million in revenue through his expertise in custom clothing. His dedication to his craft and his clients earned him a reputation as one of the nation's premier haberdashers. Guided by a desire for success and a relentless work ethic, Jose navigated challenges with resilience and determination.

Amid the upheaval of a once-in-a-lifetime global pandemic, Jose pivoted his business model, adapting to new realities while maintaining his commitment to personalized service. As a partner at Tom James, he continued to provide tailored solutions to business professionals, leveraging his experience and insight to meet the evolving needs of his clientele.

Reflecting on his journey, Jose emphasizes the importance of perseverance and dedication in achieving one's goals. Despite initial setbacks and doubts from others, he remained steadfast in his pursuit of success, ultimately becoming a top performer in his field, guided by the principles of deciding what to do, counting the cost of what it takes to do it, and determining the willingness it takes to pay the price.

Describe a problem or opportunity you tackled.

I sell a lot of clothing to successful men and women. One time, I was contacted by a very high-level executive who wanted to upgrade his wardrobe. He had been buying suits from a very inexpensive suit company, which basically cheaply sews the pieces together. His boss told him he had a "big boy" job now and that he needed to buy some "big boy" suits.

I met with him, and he picked out four handmade suits, three handmade sports coats, seven pants, and a dozen or so shirts. The order came to about $35,000. And while he had a very hard-to-fit physique, that was not his biggest problem. The biggest was the difference he had been paying for a suit, which typically ran him around $300. We have different price points for our suits, but he bought our $5,000 suit.

A handmade suit has puckers in it. Think of it as brushstrokes on the canvas of a painting by Michelangelo. Less expensive made suits do not have this. They are basically glued together with a piece of felt attached to the cloth by heated glue. When the clothes came in, he did not like the puckers and nuances of a custom-made suit. He did not understand it. It was one of the few times in my career I had someone who was dissatisfied. Because he was not happy, I decided to refund him the entire purchase price. That decision cost me personally thousands of dollars—a loss that hit my P&L. It took me six months to dig out of the hole.

But I felt it was the right thing to do—to save my good name and our company's good name. All he could ever say was that the experience didn't work out for him. I have run my business by the principle of doing to others as I would have them do to me. It has been an important principle to live by.

What do you wish was easier when tackling challenges?

I think it's a misconception to expect things to become easier over time. In my thirty-seven years at Tom James, selling more than $50 million worth of clothing, I've realized that challenges don't diminish with age; they evolve. As we grow older, we encounter new and greater challenges, demanding us to continually adapt and overcome. While I once hoped for tasks to become simpler, I now understand that true growth lies in confronting these challenges head-on.

Success isn't about the absence of challenges but rather about navigating them with skill and determination. Each obstacle presents an opportunity for growth and learning. By setting higher goals, I continuously push myself to new limits, accepting that this path comes with its share of fears and uncertainties.

Fear is a natural part of the journey, but it should never paralyze us into inaction. Instead, it should serve as a reminder of the importance of caution and respect for the forces at play. Like electricity, challenges can either power our progress or shock us into complacency. It's up to us to wield them wisely and channel their energy toward our goals.

The journey toward success is a dynamic and ever-changing one. While challenges may not get easier, our ability to navigate them with courage and determination is what defines our path forward.

What are the best ways to learn from the problems you face?

The best way to learn from the problems we face is to approach them with a structured and strategic mindset. One of the most influential books in this regard is Stephen Covey's *The Seven Habits of Highly Effective People*, which emphasizes starting with the end in mind.

Much like finding your way in a mall—where you locate your current position before charting a path to your destination, or the countdown to a rocket launch that begins with higher numbers and counts down to zero—tackling problems requires a systematic approach.

Breaking down complex issues into their least common denominators is key. By deconstructing problems into manageable components, we can address them one step at a time. It's crucial to not just identify problems but also propose potential solutions. Companies value individuals who can offer solutions that contribute to growth and profitability.

When facing challenges, it is essential to focus on finding the path forward rather than dwelling solely on the obstacles. This approach involves setting clear goals and systematically working backward to determine the necessary steps to achieve them. Just as putting a man on the moon required meticulous planning and countless incremental steps, building a successful business demands a methodical approach to problem-solving.

By breaking problems down into smaller, actionable tasks, we can navigate challenges effectively without becoming overwhelmed. I believe that success lies in our ability to approach problems with determination, strategy, and a forward-thinking mindset.

What strategies worked for you?

It's easy to find a problem. It's hard to find a solution. I try to begin, as Stephen Covey says, with the end in mind. What is the end result I want and then backtrack? I find it is easier to go to the end of a maze and work my way back to where I am.

It also is important to surround yourself with people who can find the answers. Everyone is my superior in some way, so I try to be a sponge. And while I come up with my own ideas, I like to draw from the resources available to me. I don't think you always have to try to reinvent the wheel. Certainly, there are things that change. Adaptation and resourcefulness are also very important.

I try to break problems down to the lowest common denominator, and then figure out what I want to achieve and what I need to do. It is important not to get distracted with complex problems, but to break them down. An ant can eat an elephant with enough time. The amount of time is always going to be an issue, so if you take one bite, you can handle just about anything.

Many times, problems seemingly come out of nowhere and seem insurmountable. But if you can break them down, you can handle them one at a time. I've used this in selling, too. When there's an objection, I try to break it down to individual objections, rather than one big objection. People will make a big decision by making very small ones, which eventually lead to a big decision.

Why is it important not to recreate the wheel when tackling challenges?

It boils down to the fundamental principle of being teachable. While it is tempting to believe we have a better way or a shortcut to success, most established methods and processes are time-tested and proven to work. Companies invest significant resources in developing and refining these methods, ensuring they yield consistent results when followed diligently.

When you attempt to deviate from established processes prematurely, you risk undermining the effectiveness of those methods. Just as baking a cake requires following a recipe with precision, success in any endeavor often hinges on adhering to a well-defined process. Each step in the process contributes to the desired outcome, and attempting to skip or modify steps can lead to suboptimal results.

While innovation and outside-the-box thinking are valuable, they should be built upon a foundation of established practices. Alexander Graham Bell didn't invent the telephone by immediately envisioning wireless technology. He followed a systematic process of experimentation and refinement.

Similarly, professionals in all fields must first master the basics before they can effectively innovate and improve upon existing methods.

The key comes down to recognizing the value of proven processes and embracing a mindset of continual improvement. By diligently following established methods and remaining open to learning and refinement, individuals can maximize their chances of achieving success in their endeavors.

Talk a little about the importance of mentoring.

Mentoring is a cornerstone of personal and professional growth, and its importance cannot be overstated. Reflecting on my own journey, I owe much of my success to the guidance and encouragement of my mentor, Carl Ham. When I joined Tom James, Carl believed in me and invested his time and expertise to help me navigate the complexities of the business. His unwavering support laid a solid foundation for my success.

Mentoring is akin to nurturing a child into adulthood. Just as children rely on guidance to develop essential skills, mentees depend on mentors to navigate challenges and unlock their full potential. Through mentorship, individuals gain the confidence and skills needed to thrive independently. It's a process of empowerment that transcends professional realms and fosters personal growth.

I feel a profound obligation to pay it forward. I strive to be a source of encouragement and support for others, just as Carl was for me. Mentoring isn't just about imparting knowledge; it's about instilling belief and nurturing resilience. By investing in others, we create a ripple effect of success that enriches not only their lives but also our own.

For me, mentoring is more than a duty; it's a source of joy and fulfillment. Witnessing the growth and achievements of mentees is immensely rewarding and reaffirms the purpose behind my efforts.

In the end, mentorship is about fostering human connection, inspiring growth, and leaving a lasting legacy of positivity and empowerment.

What keeps you up at night?

It's the fear of failure; it has been a constant companion throughout my career. Unlike idealists who believe in the inevitability of success, I approach challenges with a pragmatic mindset. Action, I've learned, is the antidote to fear. Instead of being paralyzed by daunting goals, I break them down into manageable tasks. Whether it's aiming for the President's Club or growing my business, I focus on what needs to be done each day, each hour, and each moment.

This principle of breaking down goals into their smallest components has been instrumental in my success. By tackling challenges incrementally, I've been able to overcome my fears and achieve my objectives. It's not about hoping for the best; it's about taking deliberate action and adjusting course when needed. Every small step forward builds momentum, gradually eroding the barriers of fear and doubt.

Benjamin Franklin's wisdom rings true in this approach. Just as taking care of the pennies leads to the care of dollars, addressing the minutiae of daily tasks paves the way for larger accomplishments. It is a cyclical process of setting goals, taking action, and reassessing, each iteration bringing me closer to my aspirations.

While the fear of failure may never completely dissipate, I've learned to confront it head-on by focusing on the actionable steps within my control. By embracing a pragmatic approach and cultivating resilience, I continue to push past my fears and strive for greater heights in both my personal and professional endeavors.

José Perez's story is a celebration of how passion, when paired with discipline and creativity, can weave the fabric of a fulfilling and prosperous career. His story is a testament to the idea that true craftsmanship involves not only skill and attention to detail but also an unwavering commitment to the client's experience, and that with hard work, dedication, and a focus on service, one can achieve extraordinary personal success and make a lasting impact in their industry.

Up Next

Discover the journey of Dez Thornton, a renowned speech coach, writer, and Vistage speaker. Thornton's career highlights the power of clear, impactful communication to inspire action and bridge understanding. Learn how his dedication to the art of speech helps professionals deliver precise, powerful messages. Gain insights on the importance of words, mentorship, and overcoming challenges.

Chapter 19

Putting Words into Action with
Messaging Mastermind, Dez Thornton

*Effective communication is about clarity and connection—finding the
right words to bridge understanding and inspire action.
It transforms how we speak and relate to one another.*

Through a multifaceted career as a masterful speech coach, writer, and communications consultant, Dez Thornton's journey is a testament to the transformative power of words.

His story is about the continuous journey of learning, adapting, and embracing one's potential, and his life's work underscores the importance of persistence, ethical integrity, and the relentless pursuit of excellence.

Dez's passion for words has not only shaped his career but also transformed the lives of those he has worked with, making him a revered figure in the realm of speech and communication.

His journey is a compelling reminder of the profound influence that one person can have, armed with the right words and the determination to use them wisely. Dez remembers the words his fourth-grade teacher spoke like they were yesterday:

"Class, take out your math books. Today we learn word problems."

When he thought of the worlds of math and words colliding in on him in one fell swoop, he did what most fourth graders would do, he panicked. With a love of words and a hate for math, Dez was a bit perplexed as to how they were being presented together to him in a class assignment all at once.

The words of his teacher would ring forever in his ears—going on to shape the rest of his life:

"Words are your friends. Get clear on the words and
you can solve any problem."

To say that Dez took those words literally may be the mother of all communication understatements. Thornton became obsessed with words and their clarity. To pass the time, he would manipulate word combinations just to see how many different ways he could say the same thing. It wasn't till an Easter play as a nine-year-old when his love of words failed him that he came face-to-face with his destiny.

His mother, understanding his plight, decided to put him in front of audiences so he could get comfortable with how important it was to communicate. Twenty-five-plus years down the road and Dez's love for all things words is what drives him.

As a speech coach and speechwriter, he works with professionals from myriad industries, helping craft the presentations that deliver their messages—thoughts and words that carry the meanings they need to make an impact.

What is one of the toughest situations you ever faced?

The toughest for me was when it came time to increase my company's fees. I was fortunate to come into the business under a person who already had his fees established at a certain level. So any work that I did was in conjunction with him or for him. It was working at a level much higher than I should have been at that particular time, so I was forced to be comfortable.

So when my client base started to grow, I didn't have any capacity or way to leverage myself. The alternative was to increase my fees. But because of my background, I struggled with the situation. Just raising my fees beyond what I thought I was already getting was hard to wrap my mind around. I had to process it all internally. It meant doing a lot of soul-searching and shaking off the ghosts of my past. That wasn't an easy thing to do. Honestly, it was more emotional than tactical.

When it came to my business, one of my coaches actually helped me with the process. He talked about value-based fees, where you basically are compensated for the value you provide. I was more comfortable with the mindset that you trade time for money, so this would take some time to process.

Ultimately, I ended up having to set a deadline, as an example, this is the date that I am going to raise my fees. I went with that. It was uncomfortable for a while, but ultimately, I dealt with it.

Another challenge I faced in my business was to what extent I would engage in social media. My colleagues, as well as conventional wisdom at the time, suggested that social media was something I needed to be doing. The issue for me was I'm just not a social media person. It just didn't feel right, so I wanted to follow my instincts. That was a challenge. I preferred a more referral-type business. I know that this process of building a business can take time to build, so I really had to give all of it considerable thought.

The first thing was to find if there was a middle ground. Was there a blueprint or strategy that I could use to solve this problem? I did what I always do in that I tried to find different perspectives. With social media, you are operating in a cluttered, messy field—one that can be very overwhelming. It was not something I necessarily wanted to deal with. That was the known—or spoken—part of it.

Next was the known—unspoken—part. A lot of my colleagues who were trying to help me suggested that I absolutely needed to be on every social media platform in order to be successful. All of this is impacted by energy and my spirit. Instinctively, I felt like it was something I should fully engage in. That became abundantly clear to me.

I ultimately took the slower route—to build my business through referrals. It was a more solid approach, at least from my perspective.

When it comes to facing challenges, share a few strategies that have worked for you.

If I'm dealing with a problem, I try my best to identify what all the issues are and if there are other people involved. If so, what are their interests? What is the problem? What is the opportunity? Personally, I try to strive so that everyone's interests are addressed.

There's a mutual sense that everyone benefits from the opportunity, so let's identify the issues and try to understand everyone's interests or perspectives. I make a short list of maybe three to five possible solutions. Then, I spend some time evaluating the particular options. In some instances, I can eliminate things very quickly. In others, there may be overlap, so I can kind of combine one or two of the particular options available to me. Ultimately, I try to choose the best option to help move the needle forward.

I try not to overwhelm myself. With doing too many things, how can I do something that will move me closer to success? If this is a group issue, then I try my best to document what everyone has agreed upon.

What is it that I'm committed to doing for myself so I can go back and look at it? And as I mentioned previously, it's all about monitoring and evaluations. You have to see how things are going throughout the course of the process. One of the things I think is important is the barriers. What are they? There are always going to be obstacles to progress, so you have to be clear about what those things are and have a plan to deal with them.

The last thing is to come up with a time frame. When should things happen? I think that's ultimately something that's important to consider.

Where do you turn to for support, answers, and guidance? What piece of advice can you offer?

When seeking support, answers, and guidance, I rely on two main approaches. First, I prioritize self-education by seeking out relevant literature or resources on the topic at hand. For example, I am currently into the literature on brevity to enhance communication effectiveness, considering the shortened attention spans of modern audiences.

Second, I turn to individuals with prior experience, whether through personal connections or a business coach, who may offer insights from their own decision-making processes. I value the perspectives of these trusted individuals and often seek input from multiple sources to inform my own decision-making.

Ultimately, I see myself as the tiebreaker in situations where advice may differ, using my judgment to determine the best course of action. This approach allows me to leverage both external expertise and personal knowledge to navigate challenges effectively.

As for advice, there are two things I would suggest. First, try to gain perspective by stepping back and looking at the big picture. Whether it's imagining yourself from an outsider's viewpoint or simply zooming out mentally, understanding the broader context can help when working through the details.

Second, don't hesitate to seek help from someone qualified to assist you. Whether it's a mentor, coach, or experienced professional, having a thought partner can provide valuable insights and guidance to overcome obstacles. Remember, it's okay to reach out for support when facing challenges.

What's the best piece of advice you've ever received?

The best advice I've received over the years is the 80/20 rule. Now, there are various interpretations of this rule, but for me, it's about launching or taking action when you've reached about 80 percent completion or readiness.

This advice came from a mentor who understood my tendency to overanalyze and seek perfection before moving forward. It's proved helpful because it pushes me out of my comfort zone into the unknown territory of the last 20 percent.

Now, determining when you've reached that 80 percent mark can be subjective. For me, it's often signaled by a sense of frustration, indicating that I've exhausted my options and it's time to take the leap. Interestingly, as I approach the 60 percent mark, I start preparing mentally for the final push. This conceptual framework has helped me sharpen my instincts and intuition, ultimately guiding me to know when it's time to make a move.

So, my advice would be to trust your gut and recognize when you're nearing that 80 percent threshold—it's often the signal that it's time to take action.

What are the things that keep you stuck?

It is my tendency to want to see down the road before taking action. As a left-brain thinker, I'm accustomed to linear problem-solving and struggle when outcomes aren't clear. This can lead to paralysis, where I freeze or hesitate to make a move if I can't foresee the future.

I've learned to overcome this by shifting my perspective. Instead of focusing solely on the big picture, which can be fuzzy, I shift to the micro-level and concentrate on the immediate steps ahead. By breaking the challenge down into smaller, more manageable tasks, I gain momentum and clarity.

I liken it to driving at night—my headlights only illuminate what's directly in front of me, but as I keep moving forward, more of the path becomes visible. This shift in perspective helps me navigate challenges more effectively and overcome the paralysis of indecision.

How do you make sure everyone's interests are addressed to arrive at alignment versus a compromise path that may not actually work?

It is crucial to foster an environment where everyone can contribute their input from the beginning. I believe in allowing people to make "deposits" upfront, meaning giving them the opportunity to express what's important to them. When individuals feel involved in shaping the mission and goals, they are more likely to be committed to seeing them through.

It is essential to gain clarity on each individual's position early on. However, it's equally important to separate personal opinions from the overarching goal. For example, as the chair of a nonprofit, I emphasize to our board that the best idea should win based on what serves the organization's mission, not personal agendas. While everyone's input is considered and valued, decisions are ultimately guided by what is best for the organization or the goal at hand.

Leadership and executive presence play a significant role in reinforcing this perspective and ensuring that everyone understands the importance of aligning with the overarching goal. By addressing issues upfront and constantly referring back to the main goal, we can ensure that every decision made contributes to achieving that goal.

Every person's opinion or question should be evaluated based on how it aligns with the main goal, rather than pitting one individual's opinion against another's. Ultimately, decisions should be guided by what best serves the purpose or mission, ensuring that the best idea wins.

Talk about the classic battle of thinking things through versus acting on emotion. What is the best approach?

I believe it is essential to understand your personal bias. As someone inclined toward thinking, I tend to analyze situations rather than immediately react emotionally. For individuals like me, it's crucial to acknowledge this bias and work on incorporating emotions into decision-making processes.

One effective approach is self-talk, where you ask yourself questions to bring emotion into your thinking process. Questions like, "How do I feel about this?" and "Why do I feel this way?" can help address the emotional component of decision-making. This is particularly important when trying to influence others, as decisions often involve emotions.

Addressing emotions is vital because failing to do so can lead to a lack of connection or understanding. When individuals feel their emotions are not being acknowledged, they may respond with uncertainty or reluctance. By incorporating emotions into your thinking process, you can increase the likelihood of connecting with others and influencing their behavior or thoughts positively.

On the other hand, for individuals who are highly emotional, combining their emotional intelligence with a structured process can be beneficial. While emotions are valuable, integrating them with a sequential process can help manage and channel those emotions effectively.

For emotional individuals, breaking tasks down into small, manageable steps can help establish a rhythm or pattern of thinking. By identifying the next steps and focusing on one thing at a time, individuals can navigate challenges without feeling overwhelmed by their emotions. This approach encourages a balance between emotional responsiveness and strategic thinking, leading to more effective decision-making and problem-solving.

Why do you believe business leaders struggle when dealing with challenges? What perplexes them?

I believe leaders struggle because they lack a clear process or framework for addressing them. With the fast pace of business and numerous responsibilities, leaders can find themselves reacting to problems rather than approaching them strategically. This reactive mode can lead to a feeling of constantly putting out fires rather than making meaningful progress.

To address challenges effectively, I view them as existing on three levels: the known spoken, the known unspoken, and the unknown. By considering these levels, I can gain a comprehensive perspective on the challenge and develop a strategy for tackling it. However, clarity on the end goal is crucial.

I follow Stephen Covey's principle of "beginning with the end in mind" and ask fundamental questions such as what I want to achieve, how I want others to feel, what I want them to believe, and what action I want them to take.

While it is essential to have clarity on the end goal, I also recognize the importance of flexibility. Sometimes, waiting to have all the details or reaching 100 percent clarity before taking action can lead to paralysis. Instead, I aim to reach about 80 percent clarity and then move forward. This acceptance of uncertainty allows for adjustment and refinement along the way, ensuring progress even in the face of incomplete information.

Ultimately, by combining strategic thinking with emotional intelligence and a willingness to adapt, business leaders can effectively navigate challenges and drive meaningful results.

Dez Thornton is a testament to the importance of adaptability and continuous learning, and the significance of understanding one's strengths and potential for growth, particularly in high-stakes environments that demand excellence. His story is one of overcoming personal and professional challenges through resilience, strategic thinking, and a deep-seated passion for the power of words.

Thorton serves as an inspiring example for current and aspiring professionals in any field, demonstrating that with perseverance, clear values, and a focus on personal growth, one can navigate any challenge and achieve lasting success.

Up Next

Meet Cara Roach, COO at Lancaster Management. Discover how her collaborative leadership turns failure into a stepping stone for success, fostering personal growth and team unity. Gain insights on overcoming obstacles, pushing past goals, and avoiding complacency.

Chapter 20

Navigating New Frontiers with Operations Pioneer, Cara Roach

Effective implementation involves sacrifice and hard work.
This process requires acknowledging when something doesn't work
and being willing to reassess and adapt.

Cara Roach's journey from community organizing to executive management is a testament to the transformative power of strategic thinking and its essential role in achieving sustained organizational success. As the chief operating officer of Lancaster Management Services, Cara has redefined traditional leadership methods, proving that an innovative approach can guide teams through challenges with dedication and strategic insight.

Her ascent to the COO position was a remarkable one, marked by her unwavering commitment to her team and the ability to adapt to unprecedented challenges. Transitioning from the director of account and marketing to COO just before the COVID-19 pandemic, Cara faced a global crisis head-on and emerged as a beacon of effective leadership.

Initially joining Lancaster Management in 2015 as an account manager, despite having no prior experience in the trade show industry, Cara's dedication and methodical approach propelled her to senior management. Her involvement in the local community and her sons' activities led her to meet Patrick Lancaster, the company's president, and discover the job opening.

During the seven years leading up to her appointment as COO, Cara witnessed significant company growth, necessitating more structured management. Her role involved overseeing daily operations and implementing policies and procedures to support this expansion. The onset of the COVID-19 pandemic brought everything to a halt, forcing immediate and drastic changes.

Facing a situation with no established playbook, Cara and the Lancaster Management team had to adapt swiftly. This involved canceling up to fifty jobs a day and implementing salary reductions to keep everyone employed. Thanks to Patrick Lancaster's entrepreneurial insight and some Paycheck Protection Program funding, the company pivoted to selling and installing Plexiglas shields, securing a lifeline during the crisis. Cara's strategic networking with the local chamber and the National Bowling Association proved crucial, leading to substantial orders from bowling alleys across the country. The move kept the company afloat.

Cara attributes the company's successful pivot to her methodical approach to problem-solving. She believes you must look at a challenge from every angle. What does the market need? What could you do to help? What do you already have in place that can work?

The experience reinforced Cara's belief in the importance of resilience and adaptability in leadership. She learned to embrace trial and error, understanding that failure is a part of the journey. Ultimately, Cara's leadership philosophy centers on execution and understanding her team, i.e., knowing your audience. The employees are the ones who are going to implement what you want to get done, so the key is making sure everyone is on the same page.

Cara's ability to mentor and lead her team through adversity and growth is a testament to her strategic mindset and empathetic leadership style. Her journey is a powerful reminder that effective leadership is about more than making decisions—it's about fostering a collaborative environment where every team member is empowered to contribute to collective success.

What typically frustrates you when taking on a challenge and how do you go about finding a remedy?

Honestly, I am never frustrated when I take on a challenge—I thrive on it. My frustration comes from the implementation of the solution to the challenge with other people. One way I lower my frustration is to introduce the solution slowly and ensure that the reason behind the solution and what challenges it solves are thoroughly explained to the employees impacted by the solution. When everyone feels a part of the solution to the challenge, there is less resistance to the implementation.

When looking at challenges from every angle, can you share more about this approach and how it leads to a breakthrough in decision-making?

Also, what tools or techniques do you recommend for others to adopt this methodical approach effectively?

When challenges arise, I adopt a team approach by examining the issue from every angle, considering perspectives from all departments and roles involved. This ensures that the solution benefits everyone and garners mutual buy-in. I focus on identifying the root cause and understanding its impact on different roles to develop an effective solution.

To adopt this methodical approach, I recommend breaking down the problem with these key questions: What is the root cause? How does it affect everyone involved? By answering these questions, you can develop a comprehensive solution that ensures team-wide support and effectiveness.

Could you provide an example of a strategy that effectively sped up implementation despite initial resistance?

About five years ago, we faced initial resistance when updating our system from using Excel and email to a cloud-based program for ordering and information transfer. As a twenty-year-old company, changing a fifteen-year-old process was challenging, but necessary for improved efficiency as we grew.

To ease the transition, we adopted a team approach, consulting with our operations, finance, and sales teams to minimize resistance. Instead of a rapid, drastic switch, we aimed to make the new system resemble the old one in appearance. Although the underlying technology was different, the familiar interface reduced pushback.

This strategy of maintaining a similar look while enhancing functionality helped decrease resistance significantly. By ensuring the change felt gradual and familiar, we avoided the shock factor and achieved smoother implementation.

Given your emphasis on efficiency and productivity, what metrics or indicators do you primarily focus on to assess the effectiveness of new policies and strategies?

When assessing the effectiveness of new policies and strategies, the primary metric I focus on is the feedback from our people.

If our employees are using the new systems without complaints and finding them efficient, that indicates success to me. Additionally, client satisfaction is crucial—if they're happy, it means our strategies are effective.

Over the past two years, our significant growth without a corresponding increase in issues or concerns highlights the effectiveness of our policies. The reduction in mistakes and customer service problems, even as we've doubled in size, speaks volumes about the success of our implementations. Ultimately, happy and efficient employees and satisfied clients are the best indicators of our success.

Given the challenges you face in identifying where to start, can you share some specific strategies or tools you found helpful in determining the initial steps? How do you ensure these first steps align with the overall strategic goals and capacities of your team?

When determining the initial steps to address challenges, I always begin with active listening. This means truly understanding the issue at hand without any preconceived judgments based on past information. Being present and fully engaged helps me grasp the core of the problem.

Next, I align potential solutions with our core values, which I keep visible at my desk: employees, clients, innovation, success, and excellence. I evaluate whether each proposed solution benefits our employees and clients, fosters innovation for the future, ensures long-term success, and enhances the excellence of our services.

I aim to address problems comprehensively rather than applying temporary fixes. This involves considering the future implications of the issue and ensuring that the solution effectively addresses it from the outset.

By consistently reminding myself of our core values and ensuring that any proposed solution aligns with these principles, I can confidently suggest procedural changes that support our overall strategic goals and the capacities of our team. Our employees are our most valuable asset, so solutions must benefit them and, by extension, our clients, ultimately driving the company's success.

What do you wish was easier when tackling challenges and why do you find it so hard?

When taking on a challenge, I wish finding the start was easier. I find it hard when solving a challenge is figuring out what is the best path to start. I have an ability to identify solutions to challenges efficiently but for me knowing where to start the solution is challenging to me.

As I want to tackle the challenge the right way first, without several attempts, this creates me to really examine each piece of the challenge, so I can implement the solution in the best way for my team the first time.

Describe a time when you successfully overcame roadblocks to change and expedited the implementation process. What specific strategies or

techniques did you employ to reduce fears and encourage acceptance among your team?

In my leadership role, overcoming roadblocks to change has been a significant challenge, both from employees and my own self-doubt regarding my capabilities. My natural inclination is to fix issues immediately, but I've learned that true leadership involves creating roadmaps for others to solve problems independently, ensuring long-term solutions.

To reduce fears and encourage acceptance among my team, I emphasize active involvement and collaboration. This means dedicating countless hours to brainstorming solutions, consulting with other executives for feedback, and ensuring that everyone feels included in the process. Quick fixes rarely succeed, so I've realized the importance of thorough preparation and patience.

Effective implementation involves sacrifice and hard work. I listen actively to feedback, address concerns, and iterate on solutions. This process requires acknowledging when something doesn't work and being willing to reassess and adapt. Encouraging an environment where team members can voice their concerns and contribute ideas helps build a culture of continuous improvement.

Ultimately, successful change management is about constant evolution, staying reflective, and using teamwork to refine strategies. By doing so, we can overcome roadblocks and implement changes that are beneficial and sustainable for the long term.

What do you wish would occur faster in business? Why?

The implementation of the solution should occur faster. Once a great challenge has been overcome, the time it takes to fully implement the plan seems to take a lifetime. I think any solution should be embraced but people in general are fearful of change of any kind, even if it is good. This fear puts up a lot of roadblocks to full implementation and I have seen it really just slows progress.

Leadership growth often requires reflection. What have been your key learnings from transitioning to a higher leadership role And how have they shaped your approach to business challenges?

Transitioning to a higher leadership role has taught me several key lessons. One of the most significant is that leadership can often feel lonely. As a leader, you must make decisions that benefit the majority of the company, even if they may negatively impact a minority. This can be challenging, especially for someone like me who is empathetic and desires harmony and success for everyone.

Despite the loneliness, I've learned the importance of active listening and making decisions based on what's best for the company. Sometimes, you have to rely solely on your judgment after considering all perspectives, and that can feel isolating. However, this solitude has also taught me to lean on others and seek their input confidently. Asking for help isn't a sign of weakness, but a way to grow and gather valuable insights from peers.

Leadership is a constant cycle of ups and downs. There are moments of triumph when you feel on top, followed by challenges that make you question your previous understanding. This process of overcoming obstacles and climbing back up the mountain is incredibly rewarding, even though the valleys can be stressful and tiring. I've learned that being in a leadership position means continually striving to make sound, reasonable decisions that advance our goals and keep pushing the company forward.

What was the toughest obstacle you faced when tackling a big challenge in your career? How did you overcome it?

My toughest obstacle is the one I am in right now—transitioning into a leadership role with a new title for a growing company. The challenge is everything I am doing, have done, or will do is on-the-job training. There has never been any role like this at my company, so every day is a new challenge to create a path for myself that aligns with helping the company grow structurally, financially, and culturally.

On top of creating policies and procedures for every department, I am working on establishing a company organizational chart which before was a one-way street from the owner, straight down to each employee. This is still an evolution as egos and entitlements prevent a clear path forward to a fully efficient, thriving company. I still must overcome it, but tomorrow is another day to work on it.

What do you wish was easier when tackling challenges and why do you find it so hard?

When taking on a challenge, I wish finding the start was easier. I find it hard when solving a challenge is figuring out what is the best path to start. I have an ability to identify solutions to challenges efficiently but for me knowing where to start the solution is challenging to me.

As I want to tackle the challenge the right way first, without several attempts, this creates me to really examine each piece of the challenge, so I can implement the solution in the best way for my team the first time.

As you look through the windshield of your own leadership journey, what excites you as you move forward?

What excites me most as I look ahead in my leadership journey is witnessing the growth of our team in the coming years. The most rewarding part of being a leader is seeing others achieve their dreams. I'm also eager to continue learning about myself and discovering ways to improve my leadership skills to better support our team's growth.

For me, leadership is about constantly pushing the goalpost forward, never settling for complacency. I'm passionate about continuous learning and instilling that mindset within our team. Even when we achieve great results, I always ask, "How can we be just a little bit better?" I want this drive for improvement to become systemic within our organization, ensuring that we're always looking to improve not just for ourselves, but for future employees, clients, and our overall growth.

As I look through the windshield of my leadership journey, it feels small now, but I hope it expands with each passing year. Reflecting on our accomplishments is important, but I'm always excited about what comes next and how we can continue to grow and improve as a team.

––––––––––

Cara Roach's leadership journey highlights the transformative power of strategic thinking, resilience, and adaptability in the face of unprecedented challenges. Her ability to lead through change, implement innovative solutions, and cultivate a culture of collaboration underscores her dedication to the growth and success of her team and organization.

Cara's story is a reminder that effective leadership is not just about making decisions, but about fostering an environment where continuous improvement and collective progress are possible

---

Up Next

Meet Mitch Ried, global business development director, and sales and marketing thought leader. From NBA teams to global summits, Mitch's leadership centers on empowerment, innovation, and turning adversity into opportunity. Gain insights on building teams, embracing challenges, and creating lasting impact through collaboration.

Chapter 21

Pushing Limits and Finding Balance with Resilient Leader, Mitch Ried

Leadership isn't about having all the answers; it's about cultivating growth, empowering teams, and turning challenges into opportunities for collective success.

In one of the exercises Mitch Ried likes to do with the teams he manages, he takes a sheet of paper and divides it down the middle. On the left side, he puts the team members' names. On the right, he adds a label that reads, "Strengths & Weaknesses."

The exercise is simple. Each person is tasked with labeling the strengths and weaknesses of every member of the team, themselves included. Ried wasn't sure what to expect when he used the process in his first leadership position as the senior director of new business and membership development for the Cleveland Cavaliers. It was 2014, and the Cavs were in the first of their non-LeBron James stages in the 2010s. The NBA star was finishing up a championship run with the Miami Heat and eyeing another jump into free agency.

Ried's timing with the Cavs culminated in the perfect storm of his career. Coming off consecutive seasons of having the No. 1 pick (Kyrie Irving, 2011; Anthony Davis, 2012; Anthony Bennett, 2013; and Andrew Wiggins, 2014), the Cavs were a model of ticket sales and promotions efficiency. "Everything I had ever learned was about building a cohesive team. I understood what it was like to have everything clicking. So, when I pulled everyone together and asked them to tell me what they needed everyone in the group to do better so they could get better individually, I knew it was a bold move."

Every second of every minute that Ried spent learning how to lead, how to motivate, and how to strengthen the weakest links in the chain went into constructing the exercise. Not bad for a person whose journey into the world of sports was inspired by the words every sports fan can recite by heart today, "Show me the money." It was the movie *Jerry Maguire* that set his sports-oriented career into motion. Heading to Ball State University, he created a path for sports management studies when none existed, taking a variety of classes in marketing, athletic administration, and accounting (which he admits he didn't last long in) to round out his experience.

By the time Mitch landed his dream job with the Atlanta Spirit in 2004, he was ready to elevate his career. He eventually became director of group sales and services, where he recruited, trained, and developed the group sales staff. Ried's contributions left behind a trail of sales and promotions that still exist today.

In 2006, he was named the "Group Sales and Service Executive of the Year" and consistently finished each sales campaign in the top five in the ticket sales and service department's weekly sales report. Ried generated over $2.5 million in revenue in personal sales and set an all-time NBA record for a single-game group sales gate receipt of $801,465. He also led the Atlanta Hawks to achieve a record $5.2 million in generated revenue during the 2012–2013 season, ranking No. 1 in the NBA for overall group sales revenue. And the list of his achievements goes on.

Leaving the Spirit for the Cavs after multiple recruiting pitches from then Executive VP of Franchise Operations and Chief Revenue Officer Brad Sims (the no that turned into a yes), he landed shortly before James returned in 2014. "I fell in love with everything about the Cavs and the city. It was the right opportunity at the right time for me. I wanted to be known as a leader and it was the perfect place to allow me to grow."

Using the same playbook, skill set, and passion he had with the Atlanta Spirit, Ried excelled in his new role, moving the team to No. 2 overall in NBA sales, and watching as James made good on his promise to deliver a championship to the city of Cleveland. "I like to think I was instrumental in him coming back to the Cavs."

Today, as the global director of business development for the Global Silicon Valley (GSV) Summit, Ried is again moving the needle forward, where he manages the world's leading education innovation summit from PreK–grade. GSV, a collaboration between Arizona State University and GSV, helps to connect startups, investors, educators, and more.

What typically frustrates you when taking on a challenge and how do you go about finding a remedy?

Tackling challenges is a part of life, and I've learned the importance of staying level-headed in the face of adversity. During my time with the Cleveland Cavaliers, we had a phrase that summed this up: "@#$% will break." It's a reminder that things often go wrong, and the key is to set emotions aside to find a practical solution. While it's not always easy, once the emotional element is removed, the path to a solution becomes much clearer.

Early in my career, I tended to react immediately when things went wrong, often without taking a step back to assess the situation calmly. Over time, I realized the value of pausing, taking a deep breath, and thinking strategically. Once I learned to manage my emotional response, I was able to make better, more thought-out decisions, both professionally and personally.

The first step is always to take a breath and accept that problems will arise—things won't always go smoothly, but that's part of building something great. Once you can see the situation clearly, you can map out the necessary steps to tackle the challenge and consider ways to prevent it in the future.

It is all about progress and moving forward. The sun will come up tomorrow with a new challenge, so there's no use dwelling on yesterday. The goal is always to keep pushing ahead.

What do you want more of and/or less of in business?

I would love to see more people supporting each other and humanizing business interactions. I have worked in sales for over twenty years. In sales, there's often a lot of discussion around whether something is business-to-business (B2B) or business-to-consumer (B2C). But as Lance Tyson pointed out in his book, it's really H2H—human to human. At the end of the day, there's always a person on the other side of any transaction, and it's crucial to approach every interaction with respect and the best intentions.

If I had a magic wand, I would love to see less corporate greed and bureaucracy. Rather than focusing on closing sales, it's more important to build genuine, meaningful relationships. Even if a sale doesn't happen immediately, maintaining those connections often leads to opportunities later on.

The key is to recognize the power of human connections. Throughout my career, I've always valued treating everyone with respect, regardless of their title or the outcome of the interaction. Ultimately, it's about being a good person—an approach that, in my experience, pays dividends in both business and life.

What do you wish was easier when tackling challenges and why do you find it so hard?

I wish every problem came with a Staples easy button. Challenges arise no matter how hard you try to avoid them, and many require significant personal sacrifice to overcome. They are called challenges for a reason.

To make tackling challenges easier, I always return to the mindset of removing emotion from the situation and thinking it through clearly. If you have analyzed the possible outcomes, it's important to trust your gut and commit to the direction you choose. You will fail sometimes, but it's through those uncomfortable times that growth happens.

When faced with a stressful decision, stepping away, if time allows, can be incredibly beneficial. Walking outside, getting some fresh air, or grabbing a coffee can help to clear your mind, regain perspective, and reduce the influence of immediate emotions on decision-making.

However, if an immediate decision is necessary, taking a deep breath and quickly evaluating the situation can also be effective. It's about giving yourself a moment, however brief, to refocus and approach the problem with a clearer, calmer mindset. Even briefly setting the issue aside, when feasible, and returning to it with fresh eyes can lead to more thoughtful and less reactive decisions.

What do you wish would occur faster in business? Why?

I wish businesses would adapt to a sustainable culture more quickly. How do we better engage with our front lines and hire the best talent in the world? The mindset of "this is the way we have always done it" is slowly fading.

There's been a lot of discussion about whether it's better to work remotely or return to the office. In my career, particularly in sports, I was always interacting with people—whether in the office, at events, or at games. So, I was initially nervous about transitioning to a remote work environment. Surprisingly, it's been better for me in several ways, particularly for managing stress. For example, if a call doesn't go well, I can take a step back, reset, and then return with a clear head. I've also set up structured office hours and created a designated workspace at home, which helps me maintain boundaries between work and home life, even though they're in the same place.

While it's not always as easy as physically leaving the office, I make it a priority to set clear boundaries. As Scott O'Neill writes in his book *Be Where Your Feet Are*, staying present is key. When I'm at work, I'm focused on the business and when I'm with my family, I'm fully present and engaged with them.

Though remote work has been productive for me, building rapport and relationships without face-to-face interaction is indeed more challenging. To address this, we set up virtual social times, like Zoom happy hours, where we can connect and get to know each other beyond work. When we do meet in person, it's even more energizing because we don't get that opportunity often.

Fortunately, I work with a fantastic team committed to a shared mission, which makes remote work both productive and fulfilling. Despite the challenges, remote work has allowed me to achieve a better work-life balance, while still fostering meaningful relationships.

Building a cohesive team has been a recurring theme in your career. Can you dive deeper into methods you've used to cultivate team cohesiveness beyond the initial strengths and weaknesses exercise?

I had a leader in Atlanta who emphasized the importance of managing with both grace and truth. There are times when you need to deliver direct feedback that might be difficult to hear, but it's crucial. As a leader, you can't shy away from tough conversations—they're inevitable. However, those conversations must always come from a place of trust and respect.

For instance, I once worked with a team member who had immense potential but was settling by comparing themselves to the average instead of striving for greatness. We had a candid conversation where I acknowledged their accomplishments but also encouraged them to see that they were capable of achieving three times as much. I shared with them how their peers in the industry were performing, and that was an eye-opening moment for them.

The key was helping them see their own potential before they fully believed it themselves. By presenting the reality of their situation with grace and encouraging them to aim higher, we unlocked growth they didn't know they had.

Today, that person has gone from being an individual contributor to a leader. I hope they look back on that conversation and remember how much more they had in the tank than they initially thought and settled for.

How do you handle situations where team members might feel defensive or discouraged by feedback, and how do you turn those feelings into positive outcomes?

I've inherited a variety of teams throughout my career, from young groups to more established ones. One key approach to fostering cohesiveness is a two-step process: building trust with individuals first, then uniting the team as a whole. It's essential to establish trust with each individual, learning what motivates them both personally and professionally, and helping them work toward their goals.

Once individual trust is established, I focus on building team cohesiveness.

One effective exercise I use is designed to help the team grow together. I start by telling everyone to check their egos at the door— it's a learning moment and a safe space. Importantly, I participate fully, showing that I'm not asking them to do anything I wouldn't do myself.

For the exercise, I list everyone's name on a sheet with columns for strengths, weaknesses, and one thing that might be holding the team back from reaching its goals. We spend a whole day going through this as a group, and I always go first. I ask them to give me honest feedback—how I can be a better leader and where I can improve.

Through this process, two significant things typically happen: first, team members realize that the things they've been trying to hide are already visible to others. This acknowledgment motivates them to address those areas for the good of the team. Second, openly sharing vulnerabilities creates a strong bond among the group. It builds trust, accountability, and mutual support as they work toward shared goals.

This exercise, paired with maintaining a supportive environment, helps the team handle the inevitable challenges that arise. With a foundation of trust and shared commitment to improvement, we're able to achieve aggressive goals together as a cohesive unit.

What are some actionable tips you recommend they implement to improve their leadership and problem-solving skills?

Leaders should focus on empowering their team to solve problems independently rather than acting as the chief problem solver for every issue. This can be achieved by using coaching techniques to develop problem-solving skills within the team. When team members present challenges, leaders should ask guiding questions such as, "What would you do?" or "What's your recommendation?" instead of providing immediate answers.

Resisting the urge to offer direct solutions helps team members develop their own critical thinking skills, making them more self-sufficient and capable. As the team becomes more adept at handling day-to-day challenges, leaders can dedicate more time to strategic planning and forward-thinking.

This shift allows leaders to focus on working on the business, anticipating potential future roadblocks, and adopting a proactive, long-term perspective. By empowering the team and encouraging individual problem-solving, leaders can create a more efficient and cohesive team, while freeing up their time to concentrate on higher-level strategic planning and business development.

What was the toughest obstacle you faced when tackling a big challenge in your career? How did you overcome it?

My biggest challenges have been balancing my career with my personal and family life. The toughest decision I faced was leaving the sports industry after twenty years of being a decorated industry leader. Ultimately, I chose to prioritize time with my kids and my health over the demands and sacrifices of working on the team side.

Managing the balance between work and personal life, especially in a remote setting, is an ongoing challenge. I've learned the importance of being fully present, whether I'm at work or spending time with my family. It wasn't always like this; that path to progress started with small steps gradually building toward larger goals.

Running has become a part of my routine for maintaining balance. I prefer running outdoors rather than on a treadmill, so I make time for it and stick to that commitment. It didn't happen overnight. I began with short distances and gradually increased them, treating it like any other important task that requires consistency. In the same way, I make sure I'm present and involved in my kids' activities, sports, and daily lives.

In my past role in sports, I struggled with guilt over taking personal time—whether it was a thirty-minute workout or leaving early to pick up my kids from school. I've since realized that there's no need for guilt when making time for what truly matters. Time flies, and children grow up fast, so prioritizing family is essential. It starts with small steps, staying consistent, and building toward larger goals. The key is taking that first step and committing to it.

As you reflect on your professional journey and look forward, what excites you about the future?

It's been a bumpy road, but I couldn't be more excited about where I am today. From my mindset to my physical and mental health, I've been able to prioritize what's important to me. I've worked hard to maintain a balance between home and work, giving 100 percent in both areas. I'm proud of the progress I've made over the last few years, even though it wasn't easy.

At times, it felt like there was no light at the end of the tunnel. Now, as I look ahead, I see things clearly. I'm in a much stronger place—professionally, mentally, and physically—and I'm excited about what's to come.

Mitch Ried's leadership journey exemplifies the power of collaboration, resilience, and thoughtful guidance. His dedication to building cohesive teams, coupled with his ability to balance both professional and personal priorities, showcases a path of sustainable leadership.

As he continues to forge new connections and push boundaries, Mitch's story is a testament to the impact of empowering others and consistently striving for growth in both business and life.

Up Next

In Chapter 21, dive into the journey of Jeff Hannah, founder of Global Exhibitor and an international business strategist. Hannah's career is a showcase of cultural intelligence, strategic vision, and resourceful problem-solving. Learn how his relentless pursuit of excellence has helped him bridge cultural gaps, align global teams, and navigate complex business landscapes with precision and creativity.

Chapter 22

Captaining a Collaborative Crew with Global Business Leader, Jeff Hannah

International business success hinges on cultural intelligence,
strategic foresight, and effective resource use, as well as bridging divides,
aligning teams, and navigating complexities with precision.

Let's explore the career of Jeff Hannah, an international business strategist, visionary, and connector whose influence spans the globe. With over thirty years of experience Jeff's approach to business is characterized by a deep commitment to practicality and the strategic use of resources, and his narrative is a compelling testament to the power of strategic foresight, cultural intelligence, and relentless pursuit of excellence.

Through Jeff's journey, we gain insights into the intricacies of international business strategies, the ability to effectively navigate multicultural environments, and the profound impact of cultural competence and visionary leadership.

Jeff's career is soaked in a variety of influences—thirty-plus years' worth. But if you ask him, he will admit that one influence reins above all others—his own pragmatism. His business realm is ruled by facts and the practical application of business ideals. An exhibit and trade show industry influencer since 1994, he is apt to ask lots of questions to accurately define or solve a challenge or problem. To get the job done, Jeff considers every resource at his disposal, carefully researching and strategizing every strategy to win a job.

This is how Jeff believes you succeed.

Jeff started in the exhibit and trade show industry in 1994, working for twelve years with the I&D Group (today, named Nth Degree) focusing on design, project management, and creative direction. The '90s was an era of face-to-face marketing, and nobody did it better than Jeff, who traveled the world gaining exposure to global brands and cultures.

"Having worked so closely with people all around the world, I learned that people have extremely varied viewpoints and philosophical approaches to life, morality, and business," Hannah says. "So, having alignment is very important. If you don't have alignment, people will be trying all sorts of ways to get to the finish line. Some ways may be okay, but many are not. This makes the journey just as important, if not more so, than the final destination."

His travels and worldview allowed him to start his own company, Nuance International, which was based in Atlanta. Nuance concentrated on design and project management globally for trade shows and high-end permanent interior environments. The business grew to include offices in London and Abu Dhabi.

In 2011, Jeff sold Nuance International to a Dutch holding company, Gielissen Interiors & Exhibitions, and continued to lead the US operation for five years. In 2016, he was hired as VP of creative, interiors, and international for Exhibit Concepts in Dayton, Ohio, where he focused on developing overall strategies, providing industry representation and thought leadership. He drove strategies, and sponsored the development of new initiatives such as ECI University, which helped to double overall revenues within his three years there.

When facing a big challenge, what keeps you stuck?

The administrative stuff. I'm slow at it, and it can bog me down. These are things such as scheduling meetings, booking travel, etc.

For most of my career, I have relied on the help of a strong administrative assistant. It seems like in some business circles, having an administrative assistant is frowned upon these days. And, often, that kind of position is seen as merely a stepping stone to something more important in their career. This is a critical role in my opinion. If you find the right fit with someone who really enjoys this type of work, it can be exceptionally effective.

I always tried to find someone who could run alongside me at a fast pace. This way, I could easily hand stuff over to them for help getting it done. They can do it much faster and more efficiently than I can anyway. It's a win/win.

What typically frustrates you?

Recurring, systemic problems. People sometimes make mistakes. I understand that—and I make them myself on a regular basis. But, when systems are not organized correctly, and people who are part of those systems are not empowered to change them or fix them, then you just continue to see mistakes produced by those broken systems.

When organizations fail to allow people to play to their strengths, they are missing huge opportunities for growth and success.

Another thing that typically frustrates me is the failure to recognize and reward creativity. In some organizations, people with new ideas and suggestions are quickly shut down and silenced. I believe all humans are creative. That doesn't mean all humans are artistic. There is a big difference. I think that people often fail to distinguish between the two.

We don't always need someone to be artistic per se, but we *do* need them to think creatively! Good, creative ideas can come from anyone—or from anywhere within an organization. So, be open to that—and don't shut people out just because they are not part of the management team or part of the design/creative team. A statement that I have popularized in the past few years within our organization is, "Creativity doesn't reside *just* in one department."

What are some things you do to ensure people can play to their strengths in their role?

Understanding people's strengths and weaknesses is crucial. In his book, *Good to Great*, Jim Collins emphasizes the importance of getting the right people on the bus. Many people fail to recognize the second part of his recommendation, which is ensuring they're in the right seats. This means aligning individuals with roles that leverage their strengths. Various tests, such as temperament and personality inventories, can help in this regard, but observation and working with people over time also provide valuable insights into their capabilities.

While it is possible to work on weaknesses, studies suggest that it's more effective to complement weaknesses by bringing in others who excel in those areas. Individuals should be allowed to focus on areas where they thrive, provided their weaknesses don't outweigh their strengths.

Ultimately, the goal is to have everyone in the organization playing to their strengths, maximizing their potential, and contributing effectively to the team's success.

How do you define the difference between artistic and creative people?

Artistic and creative often are used interchangeably, but they represent different aspects of human expression. Artistic people typically excel in traditional art forms like drawing, sculpting, or painting. They possess skills in artistic expression that are visually or aesthetically focused.

On the other hand, creativity is a broader concept that encompasses various forms of expression and problem-solving. All humans possess creativity, which can manifest in diverse ways, such as writing poetry, engaging in conversation, planning daily activities, or finding innovative solutions to problems. Creativity is not limited to artistic endeavors but encompasses a wide range of activities and ideas.

It's essential not to conflate artistic ability with creativity. While someone may not be particularly artistic, they can still be highly creative. Recognizing this distinction allows us to appreciate the creative potential in everyone, irrespective of their artistic talents.

Empowering individuals to recognize their inherent creativity fosters an environment where diverse perspectives and innovative ideas can flourish, enriching problem-solving processes and fostering a culture of collaboration and innovation.

How do you guard against the ready, fire, aim mentality?

Guarding against this is crucial in any organization. Sometimes, individuals may feel compelled to take action quickly, leading to hasty decision-making and ineffective use of resources. To prevent this, it is essential to prioritize thoughtful planning and strategic alignment.

Starting with the end goal in mind, as Stephen Covey suggests, is a fundamental approach. By clearly defining the desired outcome and purpose, you provide a guiding direction for your actions. This allows you to focus on activities that directly contribute to achieving the intended goal, rather than engaging in busy work for the sake of appearing active.

Additionally, it's important to consider multiple paths to reach your objective. By exploring various strategies and evaluating their potential outcomes, you can identify the most effective approach. This approach involves careful consideration and analysis before taking action, ensuring that your efforts are aligned with the overarching goal.

Rather than impulsively jumping into action, take a step back to assess the situation and develop a well-thought-out plan. By prioritizing strategy over activity, you can avoid wasteful endeavors and maximize the efficiency and effectiveness of your efforts. This approach fosters intentional decision-making and ultimately leads to better outcomes for the organization.

Working with people from all over the world, how do you ensure you have alignment for big initiatives? What are the keys to doing this effectively?

Working with people from diverse backgrounds and cultures requires careful attention to communication, cultural awareness, and strategic planning. One key challenge is the potential for misinterpretation of words and actions due to cultural differences. To address this, it is essential to take additional steps to establish foundational alignment and ensure that everyone involved shares a common understanding of goals and values.

Cultural awareness plays a significant role in navigating these challenges. Understanding the cultural norms, values, and communication styles of team members from different regions can help prevent misunderstandings and promote effective collaboration. For example, recognizing differences in power, distance (hierarchy) individualism versus collectivism, and concepts of respect can help avoid conflicts and build stronger working relationships.

Strategic communication is also essential for maintaining alignment across diverse teams. Clearly defining goals, expectations, and responsibilities ensures that everyone understands their role in the initiative and how their contributions fit into the broader strategy. This may involve using multiple communication channels, such as written documentation, verbal discussions, and visual aids to accommodate different learning styles and preferences.

Collaborating with local experts and native speakers can further enhance communication and alignment. Working with individuals who have a deep understanding of the local language, culture, and business practices can help ensure that messages are effectively communicated and received by all stakeholders.

Overall, achieving alignment for big initiatives in a global context requires a combination of cultural sensitivity, strategic communication, and collaboration with local experts. By fostering an environment of mutual respect, open communication, and shared purpose, teams can overcome cultural barriers and work together effectively toward common goals.

How do you ensure an approach or process is the right one in any given situation?

This involves several key steps. The first is to understand the culture of the group or organization involved, including identifying cultural values and norms that will influence decision-making and implementation.

One effective strategy is to establish *guiding principles* for the initiative. These guiding principles should align with the cultural values of the organization and serve as a framework for decision-making throughout the process. They provide clarity on what is essential and nonnegotiable, helping to keep the initiative on track and aligned with organizational goals. Guiding principles are not intended to solve the problem at hand, but help employees know how to think about (or approach) solving the problem at hand, or others that may arise.

Branding (naming) the initiative also can be helpful in promoting understanding and buy-in among stakeholders across an organization.. Giving the initiative a memorable name (i.e. Operation New Day) and identity helps to more clearly define it, make it easier to refer to it in conversation, and can help create a shared sense of purpose and direction.

It is crucial to remember that *processes* exist to support people in their work, not the other way around. Guiding principles should emphasize the importance of flexibility and critical thinking, allowing individuals to make decisions that best serve the organization's goals and objectives.

By establishing guiding principles that reflect the organization's cultural values and priorities, leaders can ensure that their approach or process is the right one for the situation. These principles provide a solid foundation for decision-making and help keep the initiative focused on achieving its objectives, even in the face of uncertainty or complexity.

How do you know when you're getting at the root cause of an issue versus the symptoms of that root?

The process requires a strategic approach, especially when it comes to leadership roles. One effective strategy is to engage with frontline workers directly, seeking their insights and perspectives. This direct interaction allows you to gather firsthand information and perspectives, bypassing potential filtering that might occur as information moves up the chain of command.

To ensure openness and honesty during these interactions, create a comfortable and non-threatening environment. This involves approaching conversations casually, visiting the frontline workers in their space rather than summoning them to the leader's office. By cultivating relationships and maintaining regular communication with frontline workers, you can establish trust and rapport, making it easier for employees to share their thoughts and concerns openly.

Encouraging a culture of open communication throughout the organization is crucial. Advocate for an environment where anyone can speak to anyone else, regardless of hierarchical boundaries. While certain decisions and assignments may need to follow the chain of command, communication should not be restricted or overly controlled.

By fostering open communication and engaging directly with frontline workers, you can gain valuable insights into the root causes of issues within the organization. This approach allows you to address underlying problems effectively, rather than merely treating the symptoms. Additionally, it promotes a culture of transparency, trust, and collaboration, which are essential for organizational success.

What type of approach can you use to break overwhelming situations into manageable chunks?

The process entails a strategic approach of prioritization and focus. Rather than trying to tackle everything at once, break down tasks and prioritize them based on urgency and importance.

Here's my approach:

- Review the entirety – Take some time to review all the tasks or components of the project at hand. This allows you to gain an overview of what needs to be done and helps in prioritizing.
- Prioritize – Identify the two or three most critical tasks or aspects of the project that require immediate attention. These are the top priorities that you need to focus on initially.
- Reprioritize – If necessary, reassess and reprioritize tasks based on changing circumstances or new information. Ensure that you allocate your time and resources effectively to address the most urgent and important tasks first.
- Focus on critical tasks – Concentrate your efforts on completing the top-priority tasks while temporarily setting aside less urgent or less important ones. By focusing on a few critical tasks at a time, you can prevent yourself from feeling overwhelmed.
- Maintain flexibility – Stay flexible and adaptable as you work through the project. Be prepared to adjust your priorities and plans as needed to address new challenges or opportunities that arise.

By breaking overwhelming situations into smaller, manageable chunks and focusing on the most critical tasks at hand, you can maintain a sense of control and progress, ultimately leading to successful outcomes.

What's the best way to use someone as a sounding board?

The key is to choose someone with relevant background or expertise in the situation or industry you're dealing with. This ensures this person has a frame of reference to understand your challenges and can provide meaningful insights.

Whether it is a coach, mentor, or adviser, they should be aware of your circumstances and able to ask probing questions to fill in any gaps in their understanding. Provide enough information about your situation to enable them to offer valuable advice and perspective.

Additionally, be open to their feedback and suggestions, even if it challenges your initial thoughts or assumptions. A good sounding board will ask questions, push you to consider alternative viewpoints, and help you approach the situation from different angles. This kind of constructive dialogue can lead to better decision-making and problem-solving.

Jeff Hannah's journey underscores a fundamental business and life philosophy: success is seldom a product of chance. It is the harvest of thoughtful planning, cultural attunement, and the empowerment of every individual's unique strengths. His narrative invites us to reflect on our approach to challenges, urging us to prioritize strategy over haste, alignment over solitary pursuits, and creativity over conventionalism.

Let it act as a roadmap for those who aim to craft a future by design, not by default.

Up Next

Join us as we explore the remarkable journey of Brendan Donohue, former president of the NBA 2K League and senior leadership executive. Known for his transformative leadership, Donohue consistently turns challenges into opportunities, empowering teams to achieve success. His story offers deep insights into the world of sports management, highlighting the importance of mentorship, adaptability, and innovation. Discover Donohue's strategic approach to leadership and decision-making, and learn how empowerment drives extraordinary outcomes in the ever-evolving sports and entertainment industry.

Chapter 23

Leading Through Adversity with
Strategic Sports Executive, Brendan Donohue

Leadership seizes opportunities to innovate, turning challenges into stepping stones,
and empowering every team member to succeed.

Brendan Donohue is a visionary leader whose strategic acumen has significantly impacted the sports industry, particularly within the NBA and its 2K League. His journey is marked by his ability to navigate and overcome profound challenges by transforming obstacles into stepping stones for innovation and leadership. Through a leadership style focused on empowerment and strategic growth, Brendan emphasizes the importance of mentorship, strategic foresight, and the ability to adapt to the ever-changing landscape of sports and entertainment.

Brendan recalls the buses on the day before Hurricane Katrina swept through New Orleans. He was sitting down for lunch and watched a line of coaches glide through downtown. It was a subtle warning, a signal that the storm was imminent, urging residents to evacuate while they still could. Little did anyone know that August 26, 2005, would mark the calm before a devastating storm. When Katrina made landfall the following day, it unleashed destruction, claiming lives and leaving behind a wake of devastation.

At the time, Brendan was the director of ticket sales for the New Orleans Hornets (now the Pelicans). He had transitioned to the role after stints in corporate and suite sales with the Detroit Pistons and Milwaukee Bucks. The opportunity in New Orleans was part of his strategy to diversify his experience in the realm of professional sports. Just over a year and a half into his role with the Hornets, he received a life-changing call from mentors Lou DePaoli and Bernie Mullin, inviting him to Atlanta to oversee sales for the Hawks.

That call marked a pivotal moment in Brendan's career. He ventured to Atlanta only five weeks after Hurricane Katrina struck. For Brendan, sports was not just about team records; it was about seizing opportunities, particularly in turning around struggling organizations. His tenure in Atlanta exemplified this ethos, transforming the Hawks' sales and operations and leaving an indelible mark on the franchise.

Atlanta was just the beginning of his journey. He would join the NBA, where he held roles such as VP of team marketing and business operations and Senior VP of team marketing and business operations. Here, he played a crucial role in shaping the strategic direction of NBA teams, fostering innovation in sales, marketing, and digital initiatives. His goal was clear: to position himself for a future role as a team president.

That opportunity arrived when he was appointed president of the NBA 2K League in 2017. Leading the esports league, co-founded by the NBA and Take-Two Interactive, Brendan oversaw its remarkable growth over six seasons. Under his leadership, the league expanded to twenty-five teams, including international franchises, and forged partnerships with major platforms like YouTube and Twitch, driving significant fan engagement.

Navigating the uncharted waters of esports presented Brendan with new challenges and experiences. From drafting players to brokering sponsorships, he immersed himself in every facet of the league's operations. But perhaps the most rewarding aspect was his role as a mentor to young gamers thrust into the spotlight. His leadership philosophy emphasized empowerment and talent development, instilling confidence in his team to navigate obstacles and seize opportunities.

In October 2022, he announced his departure from the NBA 2K League, a decision he describes as "brutally hard." Throughout his tenure, he viewed his team as family, nurturing a culture of trust and accountability. As he reflects on his journey, Brendan cherishes the impact he's had on the lives of those he's mentored, knowing that true leadership lies in empowering others to reach their full potential.

For Brendan, the path to success has been marked by resilience, adaptability, and a steadfast commitment to empowering others. As he embarks on the next chapter of his career, his legacy as a thought leader and mentor in the world of esports will continue to inspire future generations.

What recommendations can you offer leaders looking to revitalize their businesses?

Transformations are exhilarating experiences. They allow you to leverage your skill sets and past experiences while rallying your team around a common vision. One key aspect of successful transformation is recognizing the potential of employees. They are not merely clocking in; they crave purpose and desire to contribute to something meaningful. Employees want to be part of a movement, to achieve extraordinary goals, and to make a difference. As a leader, it is essential to acknowledge and tap into this intrinsic motivation.

Building trust is paramount in initiating and sustaining a revitalization effort. This begins with active listening—understanding employees' perspectives, concerns, and aspirations. By taking the time to comprehend individual goals, both personal and professional, you can tailor your approach to inspire and motivate each team member effectively.

Identifying individual motivators is crucial. For some, it may involve the prospect of embarking on an unforgettable vacation with their family. Others may be driven by the opportunity to take a well-deserved second honeymoon. And for others, financial incentives may serve as the primary motivator. Whatever the case, you must incorporate these motivators into your strategy, aligning them with broader organizational objectives.

In the end, successful revitalization hinges on collaboration and partnership between leaders and their teams. By fostering an environment of trust, understanding, and shared purpose, leaders can harness the collective energy and passion of their employees to achieve remarkable results.

How did the past experiences you had define your leadership style and the strategic decisions you have made?

My journey through team marketing and business operations at the NBA was pivotal in shaping my leadership style and strategic decision-making process. Initially conceived by David Stern in the late 90s, this initiative aimed to foster collaboration among NBA teams by sharing best practices and insights. Each week, I immersed myself in different markets, meeting with team leaders to understand their challenges, preferences, and areas for improvement.

This experience broadened my perspective on leadership. While my background was rooted in sales, team marketing, and business operations exposed me to diverse organizational structures and leadership styles. I realized that successful leadership transcends a one-size-fits-all approach; it requires a deep understanding of individuals' motivations and unique organizational DNA.

Transitioning from a sales-focused role to an organizational leader demanded adaptability and versatility. I learned to tailor my leadership approach to accommodate the distinct needs and preferences of each team member. Just as a diverse menu caters to various tastes, effective leadership necessitates a multifaceted approach that resonates with individuals on a personal level.

Moreover, my time spent observing and learning from different teams served as a comprehensive education in the sports business. It was akin to earning a PhD in organizational dynamics and success principles. By studying successful teams and identifying their key practices, I gained invaluable insights into what drives excellence across the industry.

As I ventured into leading the NBA 2K League, I drew upon these lessons to build a thriving organization. I leveraged the knowledge gained from observing various teams to implement strategies tailored to our unique context. Whether it was emulating Toronto's innovative approach or adopting Denver's collaborative culture, I applied these learnings to cultivate a high-performing team.

My experience in team marketing and business operations underscored the importance of adaptive leadership and continuous learning. By embracing diverse perspectives and remaining open to new ideas, I was able to navigate complex challenges and drive meaningful change.

What are some specific tactics or methodologies you've used to effectively empower and develop less experienced team members?

In terms of empowering and developing less experienced team members, I've employed several tactics that have proven to be effective, particularly during my tenure leading the NBA 2K League.

One of the most important is that I embraced an "ask, don't tell" approach. Instead of immediately providing solutions to challenges brought forth by team members, I encouraged them to articulate their thoughts and proposed solutions first. This allowed them to exercise critical thinking and problem-solving skills while fostering a sense of ownership over their work. I refrained from imposing my own ideas and instead guided them through the process, offering gentle nudges or suggestions to steer them in the right direction.

This approach not only empowered them to find their own solutions but also encouraged them to develop their unique style of handling tasks and challenges.

Another crucial aspect of my leadership style was prioritizing one-on-one meetings with team members. I cannot overstate the importance of these meetings in fostering individual growth and alignment with organizational goals. Despite the demands of a busy schedule, I consistently upheld these one-on-one sessions, recognizing them as invaluable opportunities to provide personalized guidance, address concerns, and align personal and professional goals with the overarching objectives of the organization. These meetings served as a platform for open communication, feedback, and mentorship, allowing me to offer support and guidance tailored to each team member's needs.

Furthermore, I emphasized the significance of ongoing feedback and performance discussions throughout the year. Rather than waiting for formal mid-year or year-end reviews, I prioritized continuous dialogue and feedback to ensure that team members were aware of their progress, areas for improvement, and alignment with organizational goals. By maintaining regular communication and setting clear expectations, I aimed to eliminate surprises during formal performance evaluations and ensure that team members were actively engaged in their development journey.

My approach revolves around fostering a culture of trust, autonomy, and continuous learning. By encouraging independent thinking, providing personalized support, and facilitating open communication, I wanted each member of my team to reach their full potential and contribute meaningfully to the organization's success.

Share the secrets to building a cohesive and caring team environment.

Building a team environment is rooted in fostering emotional connections and creating a culture of trust and authenticity. When I took on the leadership role at the NBA 2K League, I quickly realized the significance of nurturing a supportive and inclusive culture. One of the key ingredients was allowing team members to let their guard down, be themselves, and show vulnerability. I am a big believer in wearing my emotions on my sleeve, which sets the tone for open and honest communication within the team.

Creating a safe space where team members feel comfortable admitting their struggles or asking for help is paramount. I encouraged individuals to raise their hands and seek assistance when needed, emphasizing that we are all in this together. This sense of camaraderie extended beyond individual departments, with team members rooting for each other's success and offering support whenever necessary. As a servant leader, I led by example, demonstrating respect, understanding, and a genuine willingness to assist others in achieving their goals.

Effective leadership in a diverse team requires recognizing and leveraging the unique talents and expertise of each individual. While I may not have been the expert in every area, I focused on establishing clear goals and guiding principles that applied across the organization. By empowering team members to take ownership of their respective domains and celebrating their successes along the way, I cultivated a sense of collective achievement and unity.

Delivering difficult news or constructive feedback was approached with honesty and empathy. I trusted my team to handle tough situations with maturity and professionalism, knowing that they appreciated transparency and authenticity. Through clear communication and mutual respect, we navigated challenges together, emerging stronger and more resilient as a team.

What typically frustrates you when taking on a challenge? How do you go about finding a remedy?

When taking on a new challenge, oftentimes, there is a sentiment of "we have tried this before" or a lack of belief in what's possible. In those instances, as you are building trust with your team, I attempt to communicate a North Star—create intermediate mileposts that will get us on the path to success. And when you achieve those mileposts, you begin to celebrate wins and create a "new normal." As time moves you, you start to sway some of the non-believers and hopefully, before you know it, you have a team galvanized and excited to pursue that North Star goal.

Elaborate on how you identify and communicate reaching those North Star, milepost achievements. Why does recognizing and celebrating these wins foster a culture of belief and enthusiasm?

When I step into a leadership role within an organization, I often find myself envisioning ambitious goals that may seem daunting to others. However, I firmly believe in the potential of my team and their ability to achieve remarkable outcomes.

To ensure your team embraces these lofty objectives, it is essential to break them down into smaller, achievable milestones or mileposts. These intermediate wins serve as checkpoints along the journey toward the North Star goal, providing the team with tangible evidence of progress and success. By setting clear mileposts, I prevent the overarching goal from feeling unattainable and make it more manageable for the team to digest and execute.

Celebrating milestones is equally important in nurturing a culture of belief and enthusiasm. Each milestone achieved represents a victory, which demonstrates their collective capability and potential. Celebration can take various forms, from team outings and happy hours to public recognition during meetings or gatherings. What matters most is the acknowledgment of individual contributions and achievements.

I make it a point to highlight the specific efforts and successes of team members, regardless of their position or seniority. Recognizing the contributions of every individual, especially those who may not typically receive recognition, reinforces a sense of belonging and motivates others to strive for excellence. Whether it's praising a junior team member for their innovative approach or commending a seasoned professional for their leadership, each acknowledgment reinforces the idea that everyone's efforts are valued and essential to the team's success.

Moreover, celebrating wins serves as a morale booster and inspires the team to continue pushing toward the next milestone. It fosters a positive and supportive environment where team members feel appreciated, motivated, and empowered to go above and beyond. By shining a spotlight on achievements and creating opportunities for recognition and celebration, I reinforce a culture where belief in the team's capabilities is unwavering, and enthusiasm for future endeavors remains high.

In the end, all of this serves as a roadmap for transformational success. It provides the team with a clear direction, instills confidence in their abilities, and fuels their passion for achieving greatness.

How do you cultivate an environment that encourages quick, yet informed decision-making aligned with core values?

This is essential for fostering agility and adaptability within the team. Initially, I observed that my team was relying on me for every decision, seeking guidance and approval even for routine matters. While I supported them initially, I soon realized that this approach was highly inefficient and hindered our ability to respond swiftly to challenges.

To address this, I shifted toward empowering team members to make decisions autonomously within the framework of our core values. I communicated the importance of aligning decisions with our organizational values and provided clear guidelines on decision-making criteria. I emphasized that unless a decision posed significant risks, I trusted them to exercise judgment and take action independently.

To reinforce this autonomy, I encouraged open communication and feedback during our regular one-on-one meetings. These sessions became opportunities for reflection and learning, where team members could discuss their decisions, rationale, and outcomes. Instead of critiquing decisions after the fact, I focused on understanding their thought processes and offering constructive feedback for improvement.

This approach not only empowered team members to act decisively but also facilitated a culture of continuous learning and improvement. Team members became more adept at evaluating situations, weighing options, and making informed decisions aligned with our core values. As a result, they gained confidence in their abilities and felt motivated to take ownership of their work.

The benefits of this approach became evident during the COVID-19 pandemic when the sports industry faced unprecedented challenges. With live sports events canceled, our team had to pivot quickly to adapt to the new reality. Thanks to their autonomy and decision-making skills, they responded swiftly, conceptualizing and executing a virtual experience that garnered widespread attention, including coverage on ESPN 2.

This success underscored the importance of cultivating a culture that values quick yet informed decision-making. By empowering team members to act autonomously and aligning their decisions with core values, we fostered a nimble and resilient organization capable of navigating uncertainty and seizing opportunities.

What advice would you give to leaders needing to earn the respect and trust of an established team?

I have always found that it is crucial to balance humility, respect, and leadership. When I was president of the NBA 2K League, I understood that my expertise might be questioned. Instead of imposing my ideas, I focused on showing respect for their skills and a genuine commitment to their success.

Acknowledging the expertise of team members in their respective areas was vital. For example, I recognized that the head of the broadcast team had more knowledge of esports broadcasting than I did. Rather than giving orders, I collaborated with them to enhance their capabilities and achieve better outcomes. I shared leadership insights and encouraged creative thinking tailored to esports, such as considering real-time fan feedback.

Listening was key to building rapport. I actively sought to understand their challenges, perspectives, and goals. Engaging in open dialogue and showing a willingness to learn from them earned their trust and positioned me as a partner, not just an authority figure.

Embracing a collaborative leadership style was essential. I emphasized the importance of working together toward shared objectives and encouraged team members to contribute their ideas. By empowering them to take ownership of their work and decisions, I fostered a sense of accountability and ownership within the team. Consistent actions and genuine efforts to support their success were crucial. Over time, I bridged the credibility gap and earned the respect of the team.

Brendan's narrative is one of impactful leadership, marked by a continuous thread of overcoming challenges and leveraging opportunities for growth. As he moves forward, the lessons drawn from his experiences will undoubtedly continue to influence his approach in future endeavors, enriching whatever roles he assumes next in his ongoing career journey.

Up Next

Leigh Ann Alacqua's healthcare staffing journey highlights resilience, strategic thinking, and mentorship. From solo recruiter to talent acquisition leader, she navigated growth with foresight and determination. Learn how her leadership and dedication to learning led to success and gain insights to help you tackle challenges in your own leadership journey.

Chapter 24

Scaling New Heights with
Staffing Expert, Leigh Ann Alacqua

*Leadership aligns business needs with team growth, fostering continuous learning
and strategic foresight to drive organizational success.*

Leigh Ann Alacqua exemplifies resilience, strategic thinking, and relentless commitment to growth in the competitive healthcare staffing industry. Leigh Ann has laid her own foundation for success on a journey marked by a time of significant transition, from handling the entire recruitment process to strategizing for a burgeoning company in need of scaling its operations efficiently.

Her professional efforts are characterized by a deep understanding of the importance of aligning business needs with the growth and satisfaction of her team, and her journey underscores the importance of adaptability, strategic foresight, and the power of mentorship in navigating the complex landscape of healthcare staffing.

Leigh Ann remembers it as a time of great learning. On any given week, her time in the office could range anywhere from sixty to eighty hours. It wasn't so much her ever-present, always-growing to-do list that forced the long hours as it was there's only so much time in a week.

Admittedly, in 2014, when she joined the healthcare staffing firm of Jackson + Coker (J+C) as a corporate recruiter, the resources or bandwidth needed to keep up with the company's growing stature were not there. Somewhere in those exhaustive hours, seemingly endless retracing her steps from Point A to Point B, she knew the answers were there. But until she could figure it out, Leigh Ann's one-person team (her) would need to carry the load.

Here's where she contributed to the growth of J+C's reputation for helping healthcare providers find work. As locum tenens (Latin for "to hold the place of, to substitute for"), J+C connects healthcare organizations, big and small, with providers and practitioners who share the mission to transform lives. The company simplifies the locum tenen process by combining concierge-level service, responsive communication, innovative tools, and customized, scalable solutions built for its customers.

And as the demand for its services grew, Leigh Ann was at the center of the action trying to bolster its internal team. But with this great promise came great expectations. "I learned that you don't always have the resources, and you don't always have the bandwidth, but when you're solving a problem, the key is to push forward. I was in a situation where it was just me—I was recruiting for the entire organization."

Her strategy, along with all the hours and workload, was to prove her value—to show that at the peak of what she was capable of doing on her own could be tenfold if she could replicate her role. "I had to show them that this is the value. If you had five more of me, this is what we could do. So even though it was hard and in the short-term, the long play seemed longer, that's what I had to do."

To say that her strategy worked is the easy way to tell the story. That today she is the Division VP of Talent Acquisition with a team of five people working with her is not the only lesson to Leigh Ann's story. The lesson, as she tells it, is that her rise was the culmination of the people she leaned on and learned from. The lesson is the lessons she learned along the way—ones that she not only uses every day but passes along to other willing colleagues.

Take the objectives and key results (OKR) approach she learned from J+C President Tim Fischer. OKR is the goal-setting and leadership tool Fischer shared with his team for communicating what you want to accomplish and what milestones you'll need to meet in order to accomplish them. As a mentor, Fischer fits the bill. Serving in leadership roles at RCG Global Services and IMI Systems before joining J+C, he also is a member of the Illinois High School Basketball Hall of Fame.

Leigh Ann recalls that upon Fischer's arrival, he made a point to sit down with every person in the company to get their insights on their jobs and the company. What she saw was that leadership on any level is not only about understanding the mission, purpose, and vision of the company but the people who drive it.

The recruiting and talent acquisition part of her job was instilled early on. Leigh Ann's first job was with Heatcraft Worldwide Refrigeration, where as a human resources specialist she helped find the right fit for the global leader in commercial refrigeration. Learning the ins and outs of recruiting and talent acquisition, she eventually landed at J+C.

Peeking into the rearview mirror at the journey she has taken to date, Leigh Ann believes there are more lessons and challenges to experience. And, as the road has taught her, there will be scores more opportunities to lean on her network and colleagues to keep learning the ropes.

What typically frustrates you when taking on a challenge and how do you go about finding a remedy?

What can frustrate me when taking on a challenge is the time it may take to not only create a solution but to implement that solution and to have all the key players fully adopt it. I am a driver and have an extreme sense of urgency, sometimes that can translate to being impatient. I like to move quickly and see results follow.

When a problem arises that I must solve, and it entails making changes that an entire organization must follow, the implementation and adoption process can be frustrating. You can solve all day but if you don't have your key stakeholders' buy-in, that solution will not be adopted, and you will be unable to overcome that challenge. I have learned to remedy an organizational challenge by first pinpointing each problem that has created the challenge.

After that, I come up with solutions that are backed by data. From there it's important to pilot these solutions with a pilot group. Once I flush out any challenges that the pilot group uncovers and hopefully see success from the pilot group, I move forward with gaining the buy-in from the key stakeholders. I start at the top by presenting to the president the challenge, the solutions, the results of the pilot group, how I plan to implement the changes, and what I need from them to make it happen.

Once I receive buy-in from the president, I move to our executives and follow that same process all the way down to associates. If people feel a part of the solution and understand how they will benefit from implementing the changes, the time it takes for these changes to be adopted becomes much quicker.

What do you wish was easier when tackling challenges and why do you find it so hard?

What I wish was easier when tackling challenges is the implementation of the solutions and the adoption by the key stakeholders. I find this difficult when you are working on a challenge that affects a lot of people.

Creating solutions that touch every part of the business means there are many things to consider and there are many people you must loop in to ensure you have thought things through from all perspectives. Doing everything you can to poke holes in your solutions and make certain that you have not left any stone unturned can be hard because it's time-consuming.

I feel another level of difficulty is having the knowledge and the expertise to make the decision of what will work best for the organization even if it's not ideal for every single person that may be affected by it. However, if you execute everything I spoke about above, making that decision becomes a lot easier.

How do you balance organizational needs with individual concerns when implementing new solutions?

I try to be as detailed as possible during the gap analysis processes. For example, when implementing a new interview and hiring process across all divisions, the gap analysis stage has to be very detailed. The emphasis on a thorough gap analysis is pivotal. I engaged with leaders across all divisions to solicit feedback on the current interview and hiring process. It is important to get diverse perspectives. This approach ensures you are capturing a broad spectrum of organizational needs and individual concerns.

The meticulous collection of data enables you to make informed decisions. By delving into what's working, what's not, and why, you gain insights into the underlying issues. Also, by understanding the desired changes and success factors, you can get clarity on the expectations of both the organization and its members.

After collecting the data, I worked to find solutions and create a process that could address the needs of my internal customers and my team. Piloting the proposed solutions with several teams serves are a crucial validation step. Hands-on testing enables you to identify potential challenges and refine the processes accordingly. Involving various stakeholders in this phase helps to foster a sense of ownership and increase the likelihood of successful adoption.

Once we worked out all the kinks, I presented the finalized solution to the appropriate channels for approval, which signifies accountability and transparency. Once approved, the implementation process can proceed with confidence, knowing that the solution has undergone rigorous testing and refinement. Continuous monitoring and feedback loops during implementation ensure that any emerging concerns are addressed promptly.

What do you wish would occur faster in business? Why?

I wish the decision to move forward with an initiative, process, or project would move faster. I feel it is important to think things through and make the time to plan and ensure that the solution you are implementing is the right one.

But I feel like the red tape you sometimes must get through to receive the approvals to then move forward with implementing changes/solutions can take a long time. This can cause you to lose momentum and can lead to other priorities taking precedence and the project/process etc. falls to the side and doesn't get accomplished.

Navigating red tape can be challenging. However, if you follow a strategic approach, you can effectively overcome barriers and gain buy-in for your initiatives. It starts with understanding who holds the decision-making power and who the key stakeholders are. This allows you to target your efforts toward those who have the authority to enact change and those who will be impacted by it.

If you present the facts on why something is a problem, a proven way to solve it, and articulate the benefits, you can get stakeholder buy-in. People want to know what's in it for them. Clearly communicating the benefits and demonstrating how the proposed changes align with their interests and objectives is the key.

What was the toughest obstacle you faced when tackling a big challenge in your career? How did you overcome it?

It was when I introduced a structured interview and hiring process to my organization that had never followed such procedures before. Overcoming this required a strategic approach focused on gaining leadership buy-in and effectively implementing the changes across the organization.

I began by seeking to understand the current state of interviewing and hiring practices within the organization. I met with each leadership team to assess their processes, gathering insights into what was working well and what needed improvement. This thorough assessment provided a foundation for developing tailored solutions that aligned with the organization's needs and goals.

Utilizing my expertise and drawing upon proven best practices, I formulated solutions to enhance the existing processes. Before presenting these solutions for approval, I conducted pilot groups to test their effectiveness. This allowed me to gather data and demonstrate the potential benefits of the proposed changes.

When presenting my recommendations to the president and senior executive team, I emphasized how these changes would benefit them and the organization as a whole. By presenting the data and information in a clear and compelling manner, I effectively secured their buy-in, which facilitated support from the next level of leadership.

Educating leadership on the shortcomings of the current processes and highlighting the successes of the pilot groups were crucial steps in driving the process forward. Additionally, I enlisted their help in implementing the changes by pairing each division's leadership team with a talent acquisition member to create the necessary materials and facilitate adoption.

By fostering collaboration and making key stakeholders integral parts of the process from the outset, we were able to smoothly implement and adopt the new process. This approach instilled confidence in the changes and motivated leaders to follow the process to reap the benefits. Ultimately, partnering with leadership teams and establishing a collaborative environment proved instrumental in overcoming the obstacle and achieving success in implementing the new interview and hiring process.

Can you describe a breakthrough moment when you were carrying the load solo that other leaders might learn from?

Early in my career at J+C, I was eager to prove myself and make a significant impact on the company's growth. Despite being relatively inexperienced with only two years in recruiting, I was entrusted with starting a new division in an unfamiliar industry. Determined not to falter, I threw myself into the role, determined to overcome any obstacles.

As the company expanded and hiring demands increased, I shouldered the workload alone, hesitant to ask for assistance. My dedication and ability to deliver results led the company to perceive me as someone who could handle it all. But behind the scenes, I was struggling and sacrificing more than I let on. I lacked the confidence to admit that I needed help to sustain the pace and scale the company as a team of one.

My breakthrough came when our new president, Tim Fischer, joined the company. He took the time to understand each team member's contributions, including mine. Upon learning about the immense workload I was managing solo, he immediately intervened, offering support and resources to lighten the burden. His recognition of my efforts and willingness to provide assistance was a turning point.

This experience taught me valuable lessons. First, I learned the importance of advocating for oneself and recognizing the value one brings to the table. It's crucial to have the confidence to ask for help when needed and to prioritize working smart over working hard alone. Second, I realized the significance of internal networking, especially with senior leadership. Building relationships with influential stakeholders not only provides support but also facilitates advocacy for important initiatives.

How did you identify and prioritize the tasks that would demonstrate your value most effectively?

I identified and prioritized tasks that effectively demonstrated my value by aligning them with the organization's goals. Recognizing that hiring the right people quickly while maintaining thorough vetting processes and cultural fit was crucial, I focused on this priority. I emphasized the significance of hiring individuals who aligned with our core values and contributed to low turnover, echoing the belief of our president that our people are our greatest asset.

By showcasing the importance of strategic hiring and the consequences of poor staffing decisions, I underscored my value to company leaders. Through my efforts, I contributed to the growth of the organization, as evidenced by its tripling in size since my tenure began. Additionally, I prioritized solution-oriented approaches that addressed broader organizational challenges, rather than solely focusing on individual or team issues.

Understanding the company's overarching goals and aligning personal and team objectives with them allowed me to effectively demonstrate my value. By successfully achieving these aligned goals, I showcased my contributions to the organization's success.

What specific lesson did you learn from a colleague that you find invaluable, and how have you applied it?

One of the most invaluable lessons was from my first boss at J+C, Christa Scollard. She taught me the importance of embracing failure and taking risks. Previously, I was overly focused on avoiding failure and being perfect, which limited my growth. Christa showed me that failure is a part of learning and that taking risks is essential for innovation and success.

By creating a safe environment for experimentation and learning, Christa encouraged me to step outside my comfort zone and try new things. This shift in mindset enabled me to develop significantly in my career. Now, as a leader, I consistently emphasize the importance of embracing failure and taking calculated risks with my team.

This lesson has become ingrained in my approach to leadership, and I believe that creating a safe space for failure is crucial for individuals to reach their full potential.

How do you incorporate the company's mission and core values into your recruiting process?

Incorporating the company's mission and core values into our recruiting process is integral from the outset. Rather than leading with position details or benefits, we emphasize how J+C positively impacts lives and fosters an exceptional culture guided by our core values.

During the interview process, we prioritize behavioral and situational questions to assess candidates' alignment with our values and commitment to our mission. Additionally, candidates shadow current employees in their potential roles, allowing them to experience firsthand our culture and values in action.

Our recent recognition as the No. 1 best staffing firm in North America for 2024 by Staffing Industry Analysts serves as external validation of our culture, people, and mission, reinforcing our commitment to these principles throughout the recruiting process.

Leigh Ann's story is a vivid illustration of how dedication, strategic foresight, and a commitment to personal and professional development can drive significant growth in high-pressure environments. Her narrative serves as a beacon for current and aspiring leaders, illustrating the profound impact of resilience, strategic planning, and a commitment to personal and professional development in building a successful career in any dynamic industry.

Up Next

Get inspired by 'Deji Ayoade, a cyber security specialist and author who rose from humble beginnings in Nigeria to become the first African immigrant nuclear missile operator in the US Air Force. Overcoming hardship and loss, Ayoade's resilience and faith fueled his success in the US military, earning him prestigious recognitions. His story is a powerful testament to perseverance, purpose, and embracing life's opportunities.

Chapter 25

Turning Challenges into Triumphs with Military Leader and Author, Deji Ayoade

In silence, we often find the strength to rise above our greatest challenges, and in perseverance, we discover the path to our greatest triumphs.

'Deji Ayoade loves the quiet. It was not always that way. Growing up in Nigeria, his life was once filled with impoverishment and loss. Born in 1980, at a time when his native country had made significant strides following a brutal civil war and military dictatorship, he watched as it slowly slipped back into economic hardship, wrought with corruption and religious violence.

'Deji remembers rocking back and forth between the seemingly endless challenges his family endured. His father lost his job. His mother's business was going bankrupt. In the emotional and physical toll it took on everyone, 'Deji dreamed of a better life. One day, in the aftermath of what would be another in a series of emotionally complicated scenes playing out in his life, he promised to take his mother away from the madness.

His journey—from being a gifted student in a broken-down world to the hero in one of the most inspiring stories you may have never heard of—is worth embracing. 'Deji used to hitchhike on the back of petrol tankers to get to his exam center. He went on to become the first African immigrant nuclear missile operator in the US Air Force, where he would end up serving in three US military branches, including the US Space Force Department of Defense Civilian at the Pentagon.

But as remarkable as the ride has been, it is only part of 'Deji's story. The spaces that strategically fit in between those duties are equal parts impressive ever since he left Nigeria on July 4, 2008 (his own independence day). "It has been a journey, which for the most part, has been moving from one challenge to the next until all those visions I had finally became realities. When I look back and see myself going from one phase to the next, it almost seems inconceivable. I grew up in Nigeria. I finished my primary and second-level school there. I received my doctorate in veterinary medicine degree and practiced for a few years there. And then I realized I could not go any further."

It was in the silence, those times he could steal away, that he plotted the next steps in his journey. After studying veterinary medicine and getting an opportunity to come to America, he did, until he realized again that there was more. So, after getting married, he sat down with his wife, Tolu, and said he was joining the military. Enlisting in the US Navy, he became a combat medic, until he was commissioned into the US Air Force. After his active duty career ended in the Air Force, he transitioned to civilian life and was offered a position by the Air Force at the Pentagon.

In January 2021, 'Deji received a notification from his general that he had been selected for the secretary of the Air Force recognition. Nearly a year later, in October 2022, he was selected as a "Space Force Guardian of the Year" at the Pentagon level. Every move, every rung on the ladder, was more than he ever expected.

In his book, *UNDERGROUND: A Memoir of Hope, Faith, and the American Dream*, 'Deji recounts how each step led him to places of remarkable pride and valor. "Ever since I was seven years old, I dreamed of America. I knew the sacrifices I had to make, and the faith and hope it would take to get here. And while there has been a little wind from time to time, it happened. And it has taken me to a place where I believe anything can happen. That's the one thing this country has not denied me; it has shown me that if I keep going at a hard pace and put in the hard work and commitment, dreams can come true."

'Deji's book, which complements other poetic writings he has published, is an ode to the heartfelt moral tenets and emotional moments he has endured. Interestingly, the title, *UNDERGROUND*, speaks almost poetically to Ayoade's love of the silence and quiet times he so often relies on. As a nuclear operations officer working on classified assignments some seventy feet below the Earth's surface in bunkers where he did his work, 'Deji has learned to further appreciate the wisdom that silence offers.

"It takes a different kind of person to do what we do. Each of us has a talent, a gift that we can excel at. For me, it's important that my principles are true. If you are a combat medic, you have to be physically able to do that. If you're a nuclear missile operator, you have to be mentally strong enough to handle the silence and precision. But as solo as the job can be, the military is built on teamwork. We value each other and what we are each supposed to do. I strongly believe our success—each of us—depends on each other."

'Deji recalls one of the first encounters he had with his team in an underground bunker, where a bit of tension lingered in the air. Gathering everyone together, he spoke of his efforts to try and understand the different personalities, dialects, and cultural differences among the unit. As it turned out, each of them had the same struggles. "The key to anything is communication. You have to be able to communicate with people, be straightforward."

If 'Deji has learned one thing in his journey, it is that the world is filled with imperfect people trying to do perfect things—an equation that while it doesn't always add up to perfection, he believes it is worth the time spent to strive for.

"None of us are perfect. For me, it's about finding balance. I can question my actions, like we all do. I have my weaknesses and other people have theirs, so I can set any level of expectation for anyone else that I'm not able to meet up to myself. From what I have seen and experienced, behind any bad occurrence or bad behavior, there's always a story. It is in that history that you have to figure out the present. What do you want to be in the present? I truly believe that there's something good about every single one of us. Sometimes, it just takes patience to find it."

In a journey that has seen its share of complicated people working through even more complicated situations, his own family included, 'Deji understands that patience is a virtue well suited, yet underutilized. "I know people have made assumptions about me, whether they were positive or negative. But you hope that if they spend enough time with you, they can find what they are looking for. I'm always going to try to find that one good thing I can focus on in someone. Mine has been a long journey through a lot of different experiences, whether it was political or racial. I have no issues talking to people when I want to learn. If something is bothering me, I have to talk about how we learn, so that we can make the changes needed to succeed. It is about finding that balance. In the end, I want to find the balance to be the best teammate I can—the best husband—the best father."

What typically frustrates you when taking on a challenge and how do you go about finding a remedy?

I don't get frustrated when taking on a challenge. If anything, I enjoy taking on new challenges consistently. When I face a new challenge, I often ask myself: Why this a challenge? What's the end result? What would it take? What research is needed? What is the execution plan? How long would it take? What expertise do I need? Once I have the answers to these questions, I follow through to execute as smoothly as possible.

It is important to define your goals and objectives, and then take that first step forward. With every plan, you need to have a way to get from Point A to Point B. And in doing so, your actions must be consistent. Even if your strategy fails, you will be able to go back to where it does and try a different course of action.

Too many times, people head for Points A and B without any clear plan on how to get there. Sometimes, the hardest part is getting started. There is too much pressure put on the risks and making mistakes. But making mistakes is fine. These are the times when you go walk it back and see where they were made.

What do you want more of and/or less of in business?

More action and cooperation, less talking and bureaucracy.

What do you wish was easier when tackling challenges? Why do you find it so hard?

Leading people, especially those who have different and complex personalities. I don't find it so hard because I have the patience to adapt. It's not often the same when the coin is flipped.

As an immigrant, I have a different background and experience from most of my leaders, and the people I lead or work with. I often see and process challenges and solutions differently. It makes it difficult when there's impatience and group thinking prevails.

When it comes to challenges, I believe you have to start with the *why*. This means clearly understanding the reason or purpose behind what you're doing. This helps provide clarity and conviction when explaining it to others. If you can identify the end goal, you can break down the steps you will need to achieve or accomplish your goal.

Break down the end goal into specific, measurable goals and objectives—a roadmap. Too often, failing to plan is planning to fail. By developing a step-by-step plan, even if it's quick, you can begin. Once you have a plan, start executing it consistently, taking one step at a time toward the end goal.

Along the way, you can adapt if needed. If your initial strategy/plan fails, be flexible and adaptable. Go back, assess where it failed, and try a different course of action. Sometimes, you just need to commit and start, despite the risks or fears of making mistakes. You can always learn from your mistakes.

What do you wish would occur faster in business? Why?

Decision-making. Because there is no perfect solution to any challenge in life. We must be bold enough to take reasonable risks, make mistakes, learn from them, and move forward toward better results.

What was the toughest obstacle you faced when tackling a big challenge in your career? How did you overcome it?

Leading multidisciplinary teams and organizations. I overcame it through transparency in communication, collaborative exercises, assigning tasks based on expertise, mutual respect for subject matter expertise and experts, and acknowledgment of excellence.

How did your early experiences in Nigeria shape your resilience and determination? And how do these qualities continue to influence your work today?

My experiences significantly strengthened my resilience and determination. From a young age, the environment and circumstances around me shaped my resolve. I witnessed and processed many things as a child, understanding that life could be better than what I saw. Watching TV and movies exposed me to different possibilities, which fueled my desire to change my situation.

Growing up, I constantly thought about the opportunities available and what I could do to improve our circumstances. The challenges I faced, and the efforts required to overcome them became crucial steps toward progress. These experiences are detailed in my book but suffice it to say that every stage—from primary school through high school and veterinary school, and ultimately moving to the United States—prepared me for the obstacles I would encounter.

By the time I left Nigeria, I believed that no challenge was insurmountable if I was willing to put in the necessary time, perseverance, and hard work. I had reached a point where I was convinced that my life's meaning was intertwined with the challenges I faced. Each obstacle was a stepping stone toward my goals, and I was always focused on where I was headed.

The trials of my primary and secondary education, family hardships, and financial struggles all contributed to my readiness when I arrived in the United States. It was just a matter of reminding myself why I was here, what I wanted to achieve, and what my American Dream entailed. The qualities and experiences I gained in Nigeria prepared me to face challenges that others might find daunting. To me, these were opportunities to climb higher and find my way.

What was the transition like from active military service to a civilian role at the Pentagon? What challenges did you face during this period?

My transition was a multifaceted journey. While it wasn't particularly hard, it certainly wasn't without its challenges. Before making the transition, I did my homework thoroughly. My wife and I had several conversations about our future plans, and I started preparing early. I took advantage of the resources the military offers to those transitioning to civilian life, including training programs and extensive research.

The specific shift from active duty to a role at the Pentagon presented unique challenges. Initially, my plan was to return to practicing medicine after leaving the military. However, moving from a background in nuclear arms to practicing medicine, especially after several years in the military, was a significant transition. While I loved my time in the military, I knew I had to make a compromise for the well-being of my family and myself.

In the first three months after my transition, I tried practicing medicine, but I quickly realized that it wasn't fulfilling enough. I missed the structure and purpose I found in the Department of Defense (DoD). I decided to return to the DoD, knowing that I wouldn't be satisfied spending the rest of my life in a clinic performing surgeries. Practicing medicine would remain a personal endeavor, something I could do on my own terms, but it wasn't something I wanted to commit to daily.

I updated and circulated my resumé, and it didn't take long to receive responses, including from the Pentagon. The interview process went smoothly, and I was selected for a role. During my terminal leave—a period where you use your accumulated leave before your final day of active duty—I began in-processing at the Pentagon as a contractor. This transition was seamless because of my thorough planning. I eventually completed my paperwork and transitioned to a civilian role.

Overall, while the transition involved significant decisions, such as whether to continue my career within DoD or return to private practice, it was smooth thanks to meticulous planning and preparation. The challenges were primarily about making the right choice for my career and family, but ultimately, it was a well-executed process.

Tell us what the recognitions you received from the Secretary of the Air Force and Space Force meant to you.

The secretary of the Air Force holds the highest position within the Department of the Air Force, which encompasses both the US Air Force and the

US Space Force. This department includes hundreds of thousands of members, both civilians and active duty personnel, and numerous agencies and offices. Receiving recognition from the secretary is a significant honor, highlighting one's contributions to the mission and the decisions that help propel the department forward.

The awards and recognitions were an acknowledgment of my efforts to support the mission of defending Americans both at home and abroad. Though our work may not always be on the ground in places like Iraq or Afghanistan, the contributions we make from within the department are crucial. These recognitions signify that the secretary appreciates the work I've done in advancing our objectives and ensuring the safety and security of our nation.

One of the most memorable moments was receiving an unexpected email from a three-star general informing me I had been selected for Air Force recognition. It was a humbling experience, and I was honored to be acknowledged in such a significant way. The Guardian of the Year Award, a Space Force-level recognition at the Pentagon, was another highlight. This award showed that my efforts had been noticed at the highest levels, further emphasizing the importance of the work I was doing.

Winning a service-level award in the military is a tremendous honor, indicating that you've made significant contributions to the nation. While these awards are gratifying, they are not what drives me. My motivation comes from personal fulfillment and a sense of purpose. I believe in making the most of every opportunity and giving my best in everything I do. This dedication not only benefits my work but also has a positive impact on others around me.

Since winning the Secretary of the Air Force Award in 2022, I've received several more recognitions. In 2023, the new secretary of the Air Force honored me again, and recently, I received an award at the secretary of Defense level. These achievements are a culmination of my previous recognitions and efforts.

Ultimately, these awards remind me of the importance of continuous improvement. They encourage me to keep striving for excellence and to never take my opportunities or leadership for granted. The recognition from the secretary of the Air Force and the Space Force means that I am on the right path, and it motivates me to keep pushing forward and contributing to the mission of the Department of the Air Force and the DoD.

Talk a little about your book and why you wrote it.

My book is about demonstrating that no matter where you come from or the circumstances that surround you, you can turn your dreams and aspirations into reality. Through commitment, perseverance, integrity, honor, mutual respect, and hard work, dreams can indeed come true. The book is meant for people to experience and understand what it takes to achieve success.

Often, people see successful individuals and admire them without comprehending the amount of work that goes into their achievements. There is so much that happens behind the scenes, in the quiet moments, that people are unaware of. The book aims to reveal these efforts, showcasing the many untold stories and illustrating that no matter the challenges, you must keep going and believe in the possibility of success. Having faith means being convinced in your heart that what you believe will happen is indeed possible if you're ready to put in the work. This faith should be unwavering, and you must commit wholeheartedly to your goals.

Initially, I started writing the book as a record for my children. I didn't want a situation where I passed on and my kids, born here in America, wouldn't know the story of how we came to be here. I was the first in my family to come to the United States, and I wanted to ensure my children understood their heritage and the journey we undertook.

When my daughter was born, I began writing to keep a record of our family's history. Three years later, when my son was born, I picked up the project more aggressively. It was important for me to document how we built our life here in the United States, so my children would know their roots and be able to share these stories with their own children someday.

When my wife read the draft, she insisted that I had to publish it. Initially, I was reluctant because the content felt too personal. However, I decided to test the waters by sending out queries to literary agents. The positive response I received indicated that there was something powerful in my story. That was when I realized I needed to clean up the book and share it with the world.

The goal is to inspire confidence and courage in others, encouraging them to pursue their biggest dreams and achieve the greatness they envision for themselves.

Discuss the mental and physical toughness it takes to be a nuclear missile operator. What does the role of teamwork play in fostering collaboration and mutual respect within your teams?

In the military, roles like that of a nuclear missile operator require mental strength. The ability to handle silence and solitude is crucial. Teamwork also is vital to operational success. If you're not capable of teamwork, you won't make it through training. If the corporate world practiced the same level of teamwork as we do in the military, I believe organizations would perform better.

Team building doesn't happen overnight. The military spends a lot of time instilling its core values in its members, translating these values into their character. In the Air Force, one of the first things you learn in training is the Air Force's core values: integrity first, service before self, and excellence in all we do. These values provide a solid foundation for building teamwork.

When everyone in a team shares the same values, communication becomes more natural and efficient. This shared foundation facilitates a quick understanding of both verbal and non-verbal cues. It's similar to how Americans might quickly connect with each other when they meet in a foreign country because of their shared background.

Effective teamwork and fostering mutual respect hinge on good communication. It's important to keep communication lines open and ensure information flows up and down the chain of command in a timely manner. Understanding your team members and their expertise also matters. Tailoring your communication to what is meaningful to them helps in fostering transparency and mutual respect.

Respect is structured around ranks and grades, making it easier to maintain. Translating this into a civilian context, I focus on understanding my team members, communicating frequently and effectively, and showing genuine care for them. In the military, there's a saying: "Take care of your people, and they'll take care of the mission." This principle holds true in any setting. When you ensure your team members are in the right frame of mind, they are more likely to execute the mission successfully.

What tips can you offer for making decisions more effectively and confidently, especially in high-pressure situations?

It starts with being yourself. As a leader, you are in your position for a reason. Trust in your abilities and believe in yourself. You've earned the trust of others, so remember why you're there.

You also have to leverage your expertise and the expertise around you. Don't try to do everything on your own. You have a team for a reason. Delegate authority, prioritize tasks and assign them accordingly. Trust your team members to execute their tasks. Be available to guide them if necessary, but allow them to own their expertise and deliver results.

Make decisions confidently. That means not being afraid. Not every decision will be perfect, especially in a fast-paced environment. Trust your expertise and take informed risks. Gather the necessary information and data to back up your decisions, then make those decisions confidently. If they don't turn out as expected, be ready to pivot and try a different approach. It also is important to rely on your experience as a leader. People count on you and trust in your capability to make decisions. Confidence comes from recognizing that trust and experience.

One of the other keys is to avoid micromanaging. A common struggle for leaders is trying to do everything themselves. Trust the smart people you've hired to do their work. Micromanaging can hinder the effectiveness of your team and slow down decision-making processes.

How do you foster a culture of transparency and collaboration within multidisciplinary teams? And what advice do you have for leaders facing similar challenges?

First, it's crucial to recognize that multidisciplinary teams consist of individuals with diverse backgrounds and expertise. They process information differently and have unique perspectives. As a leader, you must be flexible and adaptable, tailoring your leadership style to meet the specific needs of each team. Understand the unique challenges and requirements of each team to make them feel valued and integral to the organization.

Consistent and open communication is critical to fostering transparency. When team members believe you are not withholding information from them, they are more likely to share information openly with you. This mutual trust is essential for effective collaboration. Regular updates and open channels for feedback help build this trust.

It also is important to give your team members visibility and recognition for their expertise. For example, if you need to brief a senior leader, bring along a subject matter expert from your team to present detailed information. This not only showcases their skills but also makes them feel respected and trusted. When team members see that their contributions are valued, they are more likely to invest in the success of the team and the organization.

If you're new to an organization, start by meeting with team leads or department heads. Understand their challenges and ask how you can best support them. This initial engagement helps open lines of communication and shows that you are invested in their success.

Based on the feedback you get, you can create actionable plans to address their challenges. Communicate your priorities clearly and understand their priorities in return. This two-way street of communication ensures that everyone is aligned and working toward common goals.

I have found that regularly delegating high-level tasks to your team members is important. This not only helps in their professional development but also builds their confidence. By making them points of contact for significant projects, you can foster a sense of ownership and accountability.

Internally, fostering collaboration provides opportunities for team members to showcase their work and take on new responsibilities. Externally, it builds relationships with other departments and agencies through effective communication and by demonstrating value. Be tactful and transparent in your interactions to build trust and ensure that collaboration leads to meaningful outcomes.

I always like to remember the military adage, "Take care of your people, and they will take care of the mission." Ensure your team is in the right frame of mind and has the resources they need. When they feel supported, they are better equipped to execute the mission successfully.

As you reflect on your journey through the rearview mirror, what excites you about moving forward?

What excites me most about moving forward is the realization that there are no limits to how far we can go in life. My journey, my American Dream, began with coming to the United States to provide my family with safety and opportunities. I wanted them to aspire to something greater, to pursue their dreams, and to achieve personal fulfillment. The same opportunities I had, I wanted them to have.

When I was seven, I promised my mom I would become a doctor, come to the United States, become an American, and build a new life for us. That promise was the foundation of my American Dream. For some, the American Dream might mean having a family, a pet, and financial security. For me, it was about fulfilling that promise and creating a better life. I achieved that within a few years of arriving in the United States.

Once I reached my initial goals, I asked myself if that was all there was for me. I realized I had barely scratched the surface of my potential. I began raising the bar for myself, setting new goals, and striving to achieve them. Each time I accomplished something, I set a higher goal. This continuous pursuit keeps the fire alive within me.

I've faced and survived incredibly difficult situations, both before and after coming to the United States. These experiences have shown me that I can handle even greater challenges. Why set the bar low when I know I can achieve more?

Every time I raise the bar and reach it, I feel more motivated to aim higher.

The key takeaway from my journey is there are no limits to what we can achieve in our lifetimes. The only thing holding us back is ourselves. Embracing challenges and accepting both the good and the bad in life is essential. The people we meet, the experiences we have, and even the hardships we endure all contribute to the richness of our stories.

I don't plan on slowing down. I will continue seeking new challenges and pushing myself as far as I can go. My goal is that when I reach the end of my journey, I can look back with a smile, proud of what I've accomplished. I want to live without regrets, knowing that I gave everything I had and never held back.

Deji Ayoade's journey from humble beginnings in Nigeria to a distinguished career in the US military is a story of resilience, adaptability, and unwavering perseverance. His ability to navigate personal and professional challenges, while staying grounded in his purpose, illustrates that with determination and discipline, even the most ambitious dreams can be realized. As Deji continues to inspire others through his leadership and writing, his journey shows how embracing life's challenges can lead to triumphs far beyond expectation.

Chapter 26

Widen Your Lens, Sharpen Your Focus

"The key is not to prioritize what's on your schedule but to schedule your priorities."

—STEPHEN COVEY

In this chapter, we explore the importance of balancing the big picture with focused execution. The leaders in the stories throughout Part Three demonstrated how stepping back to see the broader context allowed them to simplify challenges and take more effective action.

Effective leadership often requires stepping back from the details to gain perspective. These stories highlight how broadening your view can help identify new strategies and focus on the most important actions.

Key Takeaways

1. **Take a Step Back.** Challenges are often easier to solve when viewed in a broader context. Step back from a current challenge and assess the bigger picture. Adjust your priorities based on what truly matters.

2. **Simplify to Focus.** Simplifying complex tasks or processes leads to more efficient execution. Identify one area of your leadership that could benefit from simplification—whether decision-making or communication—and focus on what drives the most impact.

3. **Think Long-Term, Act Now.** Long-term success requires a balance of vision and action. Break down your long-term goals into smaller, actionable steps, and start on the first one today.

4. **Resilience Through Perspective.** Resilience is built by stepping

back to see the larger picture, especially when faced with setbacks. Reflect on a recent setback—how can a broader view help you find a better path forward?

Leadership in Practice

- **For Emerging Leaders:** Simplify your approach to challenges by taking a step back and gaining perspective. Identify one area where a broader view can clarify your next steps, then zoom in to take focused action.
- **For Seasoned Leaders:** Reassess your current strategies. Are you too focused on the details, losing sight of the bigger picture? Step back, evaluate, and adjust your approach to align with long-term goals.

Before moving on to the next group of stories, reflect on these questions to apply what you've learned.

1. **What's the bigger picture?**
   Consider a current challenge—have you been too focused on the details? Step back and assess the broader context. How does this change your approach?
2. **How can you simplify?**
   Look at a complex area of your leadership. What can you simplify to focus on what matters most? How will that improve your results?
3. **Where do you need to pivot?**
   Think about recent setbacks. How can stepping back and gaining perspective help you pivot and find a better way forward?

Leaders who balance perspective with focused execution are the most effective. The leader stories show that taking a step back to see the bigger picture allows for more deliberate and impactful actions. As you move forward, remember: the best leaders know when to step back and when to focus, ensuring their actions align with long-term success.

Up Next

In this final part, we explore how mastering the fundamentals of business propels leaders to success. We begin with Jane Gentry, founder of Jane Gentry & Company, and a renowned business consultant and executive coach.

Gentry's journey from the performing arts to corporate leadership demonstrates the power of resilience and adaptability. Her story highlights the importance of empathetic, visionary leadership and offers valuable insights on navigating challenges and leading with purpose.

PART 4:
PLANS, PERSPECTIVE, AND PEOPLE

It's important to remember that the fundamentals of business are often what helps propel you through challenges. Developing effective strategies, gaining a clear perspective on your goals, and relying on the team of people around you are imperative in moving through the inevitable growth roadblocks.

Chapter 27

Acting on Strategy with
Leadership Expert & CEO Adviser, Jane Gentry

Resilience and adaptability are key to effective leadership. By leveraging diverse experiences, we can navigate challenges and drive transformation in our personal and professional lives.

Jane Gentry's inspiring career arc from the world of performing arts to the echelons of corporate leadership encapsulates a profound narrative of transformation. As we explore her contributions to the world of business consulting, her story offers invaluable lessons on the power of resilience, the importance of adaptability, and the profound impacts of empathetic and visionary leadership.

Jane's journey is a compelling reminder that the paths to personal and professional fulfillment are often non-linear and that embracing one's entire story can lead to unexpected, rewarding destinations.

Jane wanted to be an actress. After getting her bachelor of fine arts from Kent State University, she went on to get a master's in fine arts in acting performance from the University of Pittsburgh. When she initially told her father about her decision to switch majors and pursue a career in the entertainment world, he was less than impressed.

Undeterred by his disapproval, Jane faced the harsh realities of the real world head-on. With mounting debt from her undergraduate studies, she seized an opportunity in sales, responding to a classified ad in the newspaper. Despite the initial skepticism of the VP of sales at an exhibit house in the tradeshow industry, her resilience shone through. Embracing the challenges of rejection, she honed her sales skills.

As Jane navigated the fast-paced world of sales, her journey took an unexpected turn when she was diagnosed with the first of several autoimmune diseases. Faced with the sobering question of her doctor—"Do you want to live a long time?"—she realized the demanding job path she chose was taking a toll on her health.

In 1999, Jane made the bold decision to quit her job and embark on a new path. Starting her consulting practice allowed her to leverage her expertise in sales and leadership development by helping guide high-growth organizations to improve company valuation, establish organizational clarity, and develop strong leadership cultures.

Armed with equal parts resilience, adaptability, and unwavering determination, Jane has spent the past two decades building Jane Gentry & Company, along the way becoming a trusted adviser to numerous prestigious organizations. Her clients include Assurant, The Home Depot, Milliken, Philips, Coca-Cola, Leidos Healthcare, Mercedes Benz, Stryker, and GlaxoSmithKline, among others.

"I have come to realize that small- and mid-size business owners typically don't start a business because they are great business people. They start it because they have a passion or a giftedness."

Today, Jane leverages her experience in both running companies and consulting in large enterprises to leaders in mid-market organizations, providing the resources needed to drive growth. Her toolkit includes rigorous, data-driven, validated diagnostics that help provide a clear strategy direction. She is a regular on the speaking circuit, lending her insights to high-profile meetings from Canada to the Czech Republic on topics like relational intelligence, inspirational leadership, and selling value.

How much pushback do you get from leaders who cannot change?

A CEO I was advising was working on the structure of his organization and he wanted to put a person in charge who I said wasn't the right fit. I told him it would hurt him in the long term. This person was just not capable of doing that job.

He looked at me and said, "It's not your job to tell me I'm wrong." No, but it is my job to tell you what I know to be true. The advice is yours to take or leave. Fast-forward six months and she admitted she couldn't do the job. She had the self-awareness to take herself out of the role.

Most leaders I work with have hired me because they value another perspective. That doesn't mean that they will always embrace the counsel or frankly, that I'm always right.

The key is understanding your culture. How are you going to align your organization if you do not? That's a leader issue. Do you know how to lead and empower your people? A CEO's job is to cast the vision for the organization, create the environment where people can succeed (that is culture), and give them the tools and training to be successful in their roles.

What was the toughest obstacle you faced when tackling a big challenge in your career? How did you overcome it?

The higher you get in an organization, the more you are responsible to the people in the organization who drive results daily for your customers. When I was misaligned around values with leadership in organizations that I ran, I found I was unable to deliver on that to the level of my satisfaction.

People and things change. I have to ask the questions that help people see what's changing and what needs to be changed. That's the biggest part of my job. Does the strategy need to change? How do we get your people aligned around that strategy? While I don't like the term executive coach or coach because it tends to put me in a box I don't belong to, it's what I end up doing. Executives cannot align their people and empower them to do what's needed without a strategy and organizational alignment around that strategy. It just doesn't happen.

Define the importance of data in making decisions.

The importance of data in decision-making cannot be overstated. As the saying goes, "You can't fix what you can't measure." This highlights the fundamental role data plays in driving effective business strategies. In today's increasingly complex and competitive landscape, leaders are inundated with countless metrics and indicators to track. However, the key lies in identifying and focusing on the most meaningful data points that provide actionable insights.

One crucial aspect of leveraging data effectively is to prioritize metrics that align with strategic objectives. For example, understanding where your customers come from is not only vital for day-to-day operations but also plays a significant role in long-term business sustainability and scalability. By analyzing customer acquisition channels and the composition of your client base, leaders can mitigate risks associated with over-reliance on a few key accounts or market segments.

Moreover, it is essential to differentiate between leading and lagging indicators when evaluating performance. Lagging indicators, such as end-of-month or end-of-quarter sales figures, provide historical insights but offer limited value in terms of proactive decision-making. Instead, leaders should focus on leading indicators—the activities and behaviors that drive desired outcomes.

By monitoring leading indicators, such as sales activities or customer engagement metrics, organizations can identify early warning signs, make informed adjustments, and course-correct in real time.

Furthermore, data-driven decision-making empowers leaders to establish clear cause-and-effect relationships within their organizations. By mapping out key drivers and dependencies, leaders can develop more accurate forecasts, allocate resources more effectively, and optimize processes for maximum efficiency. This approach transforms data from mere numbers into actionable intelligence, guiding strategic planning and operational execution.

It is essential to exercise caution and discernment when selecting and interpreting data. Not all metrics are created equal, and leaders must resist the temptation to drown in a sea of data without direction. Instead, they should adopt a thoughtful and strategic approach to data analysis, focusing on the metrics that truly matter and provide actionable insights.

What has sitting with a problem before acting on it taught you about patience? How does that help take a business to the next level?

It teaches invaluable lessons about patience and the power of discomfort. As someone with a natural bias toward action, I have often found myself inclined to rush into decisions, driven by a relentless desire to make things happen. However, I have come to realize that this inclination isn't always beneficial, particularly when faced with complex challenges that defy easy solutions.

In those moments of uncertainty, where the path forward isn't immediately clear, I've learned to embrace the discomfort of not knowing. Instead of succumbing to the pressure to act quickly, I've trained myself to sit with the problem, allowing myself the time and space to explore different perspectives and potential solutions. This process of patient inquiry often leads to insights and breakthroughs that wouldn't have been possible if I had rushed to a resolution.

Patience, in this context, is not about passivity or inaction—it's about cultivating a willingness to tolerate ambiguity and wrestle with complexity. It is about resisting the urge to seek quick fixes and instead leaning into the discomfort of uncertainty. By doing so, I have found that I'm able to engage more deeply with the problem at hand, uncovering hidden nuances and uncovering innovative solutions that might have otherwise remained hidden.

Moreover, sitting with a problem before acting on it has helped me develop a greater appreciation for the importance of patience in leadership. As the CEO, it's easy to feel the weight of responsibility and the pressure to have all the answers. However, I've come to understand that true leadership isn't about having all the answers—it's about having the humility to admit when you don't know and the patience to work through challenges collaboratively.

This approach to problem-solving has not only enriched my own decision-making process but has also had a transformative impact on my business. By resisting the impulse to act impulsively and instead taking the time to sit with problems, I've been able to uncover innovative solutions and foster a culture of thoughtful inquiry within my organization. This, in turn, has propelled us to new levels of growth and success, positioning us to tackle even bigger challenges with confidence and resilience.

In essence, patience isn't just a virtue—it is a strategic asset. By embracing the discomfort of uncertainty and sitting with problems before acting on them, leaders can unlock new possibilities and drive their businesses forward in meaningful ways.

What advice can you offer leaders who face challenges they might not have answers for?

The first piece of advice is to recognize the inherent loneliness of leadership. As the CEO, you often bear the weight of decision-making alone, which can be isolating. It's crucial to seek out trusted individuals with whom you can be vulnerable and share your uncertainties. Building a network of smart, diverse, and supportive individuals who genuinely care about your success can provide invaluable insights and guidance when navigating uncharted territory.

One effective approach is to assemble an informal advisory board composed of individuals from various industries and backgrounds. These individuals should possess qualities such as intelligence, diversity of thought, and a genuine interest in your success. By convening this group periodically, you create a safe space to discuss challenges openly and collaboratively explore potential solutions. Drawing on the collective wisdom of this advisory board can offer fresh perspectives and creative solutions to complex problems.

Furthermore, leaders must cultivate their professional network actively. Networking isn't just about collecting business cards or making superficial connections; it's about fostering genuine relationships built on trust and mutual respect. Take the time to engage with your network authentically, seeking opportunities to learn from others and share your own experiences. By nurturing these relationships, you expand your pool of resources and gain access to diverse perspectives that can help you navigate challenges more effectively.

They should also embrace qualities like vulnerability, teachability, and transparency in their leadership approach. Admitting mistakes, seeking feedback, and being open to new ideas are essential traits for effective leadership. It's okay not to have all the answers, but it's essential to be willing to learn and grow from every experience. By modeling vulnerability and transparency, you create a culture where others feel empowered to do the same, fostering a more collaborative and resilient organization.

It also is important not to overlook the value of seeking advice from individuals outside your industry or expertise. Sometimes, the most valuable insights come from those with entirely different perspectives. By engaging with individuals from diverse backgrounds, you expose yourself to fresh ideas and innovative approaches that you may not have considered otherwise. Be open to learning from everyone, regardless of their professional background, and be willing to adapt and evolve based on the insights you receive.

What can small- and medium-sized company leaders do to help their people build skills like empathy, situational awareness, and strategic and long-term thinking?

It is essential to recognize the growing need for these capabilities in today's workforce. Studies indicate a concerning decline in empathy among college students over the past two decades, highlighting a crucial gap in traditional education. With business schools focusing primarily on technical knowledge, employees often lack the interpersonal skills necessary for success in the workplace.

For leaders looking to address this issue within their organizations, investing in formal training programs may not always be feasible due to budget constraints. However, there are alternative approaches that can be just as effective. One of the most impactful methods is coaching and mentoring. Pairing employees with experienced leaders who embody the desired skills can provide invaluable learning opportunities. These relationships offer a personalized and hands-on approach to skill development, allowing individuals to learn from real-world experiences and receive tailored feedback.

Additionally, leaders can encourage participation in affordable training programs like Toastmasters or Dale Carnegie, which focus on communication, leadership, and interpersonal skills. While these programs may not delve deeply into empathy and situational awareness, they provide a solid foundation for enhancing overall soft skills.

Furthermore, fostering a culture of open communication and feedback within the organization can facilitate skill development. Encouraging employees to engage in constructive dialogue, share perspectives, and consider the impact of their actions on others promotes empathy and situational awareness. Leaders play a crucial role in modeling these behaviors and creating a supportive environment where employees feel empowered to express themselves openly.

Moreover, leaders should emphasize the importance of face-to-face communication over digital interactions like email or text messaging. While these tools serve practical purposes, they are not effective for building meaningful relationships. Encouraging employees to engage in direct conversations fosters deeper connections and strengthens interpersonal skills.

Finally, for organizations lacking internal resources to support skill development, outsourcing coaching services can be a worthwhile investment. Hiring external coaches or consultants to work with employees on a one-on-one basis provides a fresh perspective and specialized guidance tailored to individual needs.

Why is it important for leaders to value other perspectives?

I believe it offers them a broader understanding of their business landscape and challenges. Often, CEOs and leaders operate in what can feel like isolation, making it difficult to see beyond their own perspective. By embracing feedback and insights from others, leaders gain valuable perspectives that can lead to better decision-making and problem-solving.

Leadership roles come with their own set of strengths and blind spots. A visionary CEO may excel at strategic planning but struggle with operational processes, while a financial-minded CEO might overlook the importance of sales and marketing. Seeking input from individuals with diverse expertise allows leaders to fill these gaps and approach challenges from multiple angles.

Engaging in conversations with others who challenge their assumptions and offer alternative viewpoints encourages leaders to explore new ideas and possibilities. It fosters a culture of continuous learning and growth, where leaders are open to feedback and willing to consider different approaches.

Moreover, valuing other perspectives accelerates decision-making processes. When leaders collaborate with others to thoroughly analyze options and anticipate potential outcomes, they can confidently move forward with actionable plans. Rather than feeling stuck in indecision, they gain clarity and direction, leading to more efficient and effective execution.

I remember a meeting with a manufacturing company CEO where the discussion centered on reallocating accounts. The conversation led to a deeper exploration of the concept of house accounts. By challenging the CEO's initial decision and presenting alternative scenarios, a more strategic approach emerged. This collaborative process not only avoided potential pitfalls but also led to a clearer understanding of the company's priorities.

What do you see as the greatest value in impacting the customers you work with?

It lies in the ability to tailor methodologies, processes, and sales techniques to meet specific needs. While they have a structured approach, my role is not to dictate or criticize, but to facilitate a shift in perspective. By asking probing questions and encouraging clients to see their business from a different angle, I aim to uncover hidden opportunities and potential threats.

One person who has greatly influenced my approach is Seth Makowski, a mindset coach for professional athletes. Initially skeptical of the concept, I was intrigued when he introduced the idea of using chess as a tool for mental fitness. Through chess, athletes learn to protect their king, identify opportunities, and manage threats—all valuable lessons applicable to business.

In chess, protecting the king is paramount. Similarly, in business, it is essential to identify the core elements that must be safeguarded at all costs. Whether it's the integrity of a product, the reputation of a brand, or the security of sensitive data, understanding what constitutes the *king* is crucial.

Furthermore, recognizing opportunities requires a keen eye for potential moves. Just as each chess piece has unique abilities, every business possesses strengths that can be leveraged to seize opportunities. By homing in on these strengths and deploying them strategically, businesses can gain a competitive edge.

But it is not enough to focus solely on opportunities. Just as in chess, where players must also be vigilant of threats, businesses must be aware of potential risks that could undermine their success. By balancing the pursuit of opportunities with proactive threat management, businesses can navigate challenges while capitalizing on growth opportunities.

Ultimately, the goal is to help CEOs and business leaders develop a holistic understanding of their organization's landscape. By equipping them with the tools to protect their core assets, identify opportunities, and mitigate threats, they are empowered to make informed decisions that drive sustainable growth.

Jane Gentry's story highlights the power of resilience in the face of adversity and the profound impact of thoughtful, informed leadership on both personal and organizational levels. It inspires current and aspiring leaders to persist in their pursuits, invest in their continuous development, and remain adaptable to navigate the ever-changing business landscape.

Up Next

In the next chapter, we focus on Lou DePaoli, president of executive search at General Sports Worldwide. A C-level innovator and mentor, Lou has a strong track record in recruiting and developing top talent in sports and entertainment. His strategic thinking and open communication enable him to turn challenges into opportunities, driving organizational success. Lou's story offers essential insights for leaders navigating complexities while fostering growth, innovation, and trust.

Chapter 28

Building a Strategic Playbook with Sports Innovator, Lou DePaoli

True leadership is based on planning, trust, and innovation. Open communication and strategic thinking turn challenges into opportunities, driving organizations to new heights.

Lou DePaoli's career as a transformative leader in the sports and entertainment industries is marked by a robust strategic foundation and an unwavering commitment to innovation and effective communication.

As a visionary leader whose strategic acumen and innovative thinking have reshaped the landscape of management, Lou leads with the principles that guide him: belief, trust in leadership, the importance of a clear structured plan, the ability to think creatively under pressure, and the importance of combining rigorous strategic planning with a deep commitment to employee empowerment.

Lou's journey provides invaluable insights for leaders aiming to steer their organizations through complex challenges while maintaining a focus on growth, innovation, and the cultivation of trust. The secret to Lou's success is in the playbook. The first thing he asks of the clients he sits down with is to show him their plan. Not the budget. Not a few bullet points scribbled down on a piece of paper. He wants the business plan—the playbook, that when constructed and followed strategically, serves as the guiding principle for all things leadership.

If you don't quite follow what Lou wants, the president, executive search, and team consulting for General Sports Worldwide recommends you view it like the McDonald's book of franchising. In essence, your playbook should provide a structure where someone can come into the picture on the same day and be able to run everything, i.e., everyone and everything is on the same page. The secret, as Lou might openly admit, is really no secret at all. To succeed, you need to take planning to the next level.

Take listening, or more specifically, listening more than you talk. No plan, no matter how detailed, cannot be implemented without the ability to listen and follow. If you know what is going on, you can provide solutions. You find what is believable and what is not.

Driven by his ability to provide trust, guidance, and resources, Lou is what you might call an "executive whisperer" if such a moniker existed in the leadership realm. Known for his innovative and charismatic leadership, DePaoli offers the kind of guidance that instills confidence that the business plans and mission statements he helps create can work.

The results can be found in the proven track record of success he continues to rack up helping sports and entertainment franchises increase their values across multiple sports leagues, markets, and venues. Over the years, he has held roles as Executive VP for the New York Mets (Major League Baseball), Executive VP and CMO for the Pittsburgh Pirates (MLB), and Executive VP and CMO for the Atlanta Spirit, including the Atlanta Hawks (NBA), the then Atlanta Thrashers (National Hockey League) and State Farm Arena.

He also was an original member of the NBA's team marketing and business operations department, where as vice president of team marketing and business development, he helped create the in-house consulting group's philosophy of driving and sharing best practices and innovation across the NBA, WNBA, and NBA G League. It was Lou who was responsible for building the analytical infrastructure and reporting that still is used today. Before that, he worked with the Florida (now Miami) Marlins and Worcester IceCats in the American Hockey League.

What typically frustrates you when taking on a challenge and how do you go about finding a remedy?

One of the biggest items I look for when tackling a new challenge is ensuring the staff is not limited by their own thinking, a.k.a., wanting to do things the way they have always been done. This can be very frustrating and usually leads to a conversation about changing their mindset and how to do so.

Once we get through these types of exercises and retraining, it is amazing how much smoother the process of ideation and execution of ideas becomes. As the leader of the group, my role is to really help push them to think outside the box and let them know that it is all right to share their ideas. Nobody is going to be judged. This is a safe space to have a conversation. The process usually leads to me throwing out the first off-the-wall idea, which is designed to get shot down and show everyone how the safe space works. Original thinking is always encouraged.

Take my team with the New York Mets organization, which is in the media capital of the world. It can be daunting. The best approach is to figure out a way to try to leverage the media and make them an ally to help drive your business. One of the things we did was to spend time building relationships with the media—get to know them as people and to help them understand your thought process. Sometimes, maybe that is talking off the record. The key is that the first step in building relationships is getting people to trust you. We felt that within reason, we could trust them.

There are times when things don't go as planned and they would attack us on a certain story. It is their job to try to generate readership and get clicks, so you cannot take it personally. The key for us was to take a step back, take a deep breath, and figure out our game plan. Never react or overreact immediately. The knee-jerk reactions are where you run into problems. Inevitably, people say something that gets misconstrued.

We always took time to be prepared—to get our narrative in place. Getting all of the facts and making sure everyone knows what is needed to provide a cogent response. You are never going to walk away from potential negative stories. Nobody goes away unscathed, but if you can find a way to minimize them, you can use the media as an ally.

What do you want more of and/or less of in business?

More transparency and open communication from leaders with their teams and customers. People need to get back to trusting leadership, and not being so skeptical and cynical all the time. The less friction, the smoother the ride.

Also, I would like to see less self-promotion and grandstanding in business, as too many people manipulate the truth in order to drive followers/engagement with the hope of driving revenue. The falsity of their persona many times leaves lots of people drowning in their wake. We are all using social media to build awareness of ourselves personally as a businessperson. But that is not more important than actually driving results in building your career. Some people have put the cart before the horse. They spend too much exaggerating about what they've done and what they are doing all for the sake of getting that opportunity or next opportunity.

The key is to build your career. That is your professional and personal brand. Spend time building a true network and making sure you have the accomplishments to back up who you are and what you have done before you start bragging about them.

One of my favorite expressions is, "It's not about me." It is important to spend more time focusing on what your team has done, not what you have done. What have you helped build together? One of the biggest red flags I see in the executive recruiting space is people using the first-person so much. People spend too much time focusing on making sure everybody knows what they did, but organizations want to see what they have done collectively.

What do you wish was easier when tackling challenges? Why do you find it so hard?

Too many people don't have an open mind or more of a can-do attitude. Having belief is a powerful thing—just ask Ted Lasso.

Why is it so hard? Leaders have let many people down more and more recently, which has created a lack of trust in leadership. This is unfortunate. That said, questioning and transparency around leadership are needed, but there has to be a level of trust that goes both ways.

I always tell people believing is always the first step; you have to believe you can do it. Let's take Ted Lasso. It is what the show was all about. They had a big "Believe" sign as one of the backdrops. The Ted Lasso character made people believe in the impossible—break down barriers. As a leader, you have to get rid of the negativity; you have to make people see that they can reach XYZ goal.

After you get that buy-in, the second step is to make sure everyone understands there's a plan and that their job is part of that plan. Leaders cannot force the top-down process. Everyone must have the buy-in and want to be successful together.

Get the buy-in. Build the plan and get people excited about being involved and taking ownership. When people know their voices are going to be heard, and that what they contribute makes a difference, they will want to be part of the process. It's amazing how that belief button starts to go through when people believe it can be done.

The final step is setting benchmarks that people can understand. If we're trying to go from A to Z, there is going to be a B, C, and so forth. Hitting benchmarks are tangible things people can see.

One of my favorite expressions is about how you eat an elephant. It is one bite at a time. Most people don't quite get that today, so I translate it into, how do you eat a slice of pizza? One bite at a time. One bite, one slice at a time. It's believing in the process.

Questioning and transparency around leadership is needed, but there has to be a level of trust that goes both ways. Trust is one of the key elements of becoming a successful leader. It is imperative to build a culture of trust. That takes building relationships by having clear transparent communications with people, so they understand where they stand. Everybody can rally around an open environment.

What do you wish would occur faster in business?

Decision-making. Too many businesses and leaders suffer from paralysis by overanalysis. I'm not encouraging reckless decision-making in the name of speed, but rather reducing red tape and internal obstacles to get ideas to market sooner.

As Basketball Hall-of-Famer Earl "The Pearl" Monroe famously said, "Don't rush. Be quick, but don't hurry." The process is all about finding where you can improve. The key is not in rushing to a decision, but in taking the time to find out what is needed. Sometimes, they require thinking out of the box in areas you might have never imagined.

I lean on a system called the McKinsey 7-S Model, which was created by McKinsey & Company in the late 1970s. The process is a change framework based on a company's organizational design. The goal is to depict how change leaders can effectively manage organizational change by strategizing around the interactions of seven key elements: structure, strategy, system, shared values, skill, style, and staff.

Of the seven parts of the framework, I focus heavily on structure, systems, staffing, and shared values. These four steps are the ones I've found to have the largest immediate, and long-term, impact. If you build the structure and put the systems in place, find the right people, have them play to their strengths, and build a dynamic culture, you are going to grow your business. If the alignment is off, or systems are clunky, or people are playing out of position, or the culture is non-collaborative, the whole thing will not work properly.

What was the toughest obstacle you faced when tackling a big challenge in your career? How did you overcome it?

One of the bigger obstacles was just after the 1997 World Series with the Florida Marlins, my employer at the time. We won the World Series, and then immediately began to dismantle the on-field team in a manner that was unprecedented in North American sports. Dealing with the team being dismantled wasn't the obstacle; it was dealing with the staff. Everyone wanted to leave for other jobs.

My career started with the Marlins in 1996, and we completely remade the sales department by getting rid of most existing staff and recruiting all new members from all over the country to be part of what we were building. We had tremendous success that season and led MLB in attendance growth at +34 percent, which was largely driven by the great work the sales team put in. The staff had very low base salaries and aggressive commission incentives to drive revenue, and it worked. They worked incredibly long hours all season, especially during the World Series, where many volunteered for roles to assist MLB in a variety of roles without any additional compensation and very little sleep.

Most of the sales team departed within nine months of our World Series victory and we had to rebuild all over again. The key for me, as the leader, was to stay positive and keep the staff positive in a very tough environment. Both sets of sales teams contained people who have gone on to great heights in their careers—some in sports and some outside of sports. Almost all of us are still in contact twenty-six years later.

The staff understood I was empathetic toward their situation, and if they wanted to leave for other opportunities, I encouraged—and in many cases helped—them secure new roles. A valuable lesson for all involved as being a caring leader helped them become caring leaders in their own situations down the road.

Lou DePaoli's story is a compelling study of how visionary leadership, coupled with rigorous planning and a commitment to innovation, can create lasting change in any field. His journey underscores the importance of aligning team efforts with strategic objectives to achieve extraordinary results, making his story a vital read for anyone looking to elevate their organizational impact.

Up Next

Discover the journey of Stephanie J. Wong, a psychologist and advocate for work-life harmony. In her podcast, The Color of Success, she highlights the stories of Asian Americans and other minorities overcoming challenges in their careers.

In this chapter, learn how Stephanie's commitment to empathy and resilience inspires others to achieve balance in their personal and professional lives.

Chapter 29

Work-Life Harmony with Psychologist, Advocate, and Podcaster, Dr. Stephanie J. Wong

Work-life harmony is achieved by aligning purpose with passion, fostering resilience, and building meaningful connections through empathy and support.

In the first season of her celebrated podcast, *The Color of Success*, Dr. Stephanie J. Wong interviewed former American Idol contestant William Hung, whose off-key rendition of "She Bangs" catapulted him to unexpected fame. For Wong, this conversation, held during the early days of the pandemic, highlighted her ability to make guests feel at ease as they shared their challenges and triumphs.

Now in its sixth season, *The Color of Success* continues to explore the journeys of Asian/Asian Americans and underrepresented individuals as they build careers, businesses, and brands. Stephanie dives into the mental health strategies these individuals use to overcome self-doubt, anxiety, and other barriers.

Through her interviews, Stephanie skillfully blends her expertise in mental health, culture, and business to dissect the often chaotic paths to success, providing listeners with insights into the lives of her guests, including comedians/actors Margaret Cho and Andrew Phung, and author Abigail Hing Wen. The podcast, which began as a way to de-stigmatize mental health in the Asian American community, has evolved into a platform where Stephanie's empathy and curiosity create powerful connections, offering a unique perspective on resilience, success, and the human experience.

What typically frustrates you when taking on a challenge and how do you go about finding a remedy?

When facing challenges, common frustrations include not having enough time for thorough brainstorming, problem-solving, or building meaningful connections with others. Another difficulty is dealing with less open and inclusive individuals who may lack empathy or fail to validate your feelings.

I deal with these challenges by relying on my support network and asking for help to make time for entrepreneurial pursuits. I connect with supportive, welcoming individuals and commit to lifelong learning, drawing inspiration from the amazing people who share their unique perspectives and generously offer their time and resources.

What do you want to do more of and/or less of in business?

I want to diversify my sources of income, particularly through passive investments, and focus on exciting projects with high returns, helping me build genuine relationships and facilitating work-life harmony. I want to continue practicing values-based leadership and to work smarter, not harder.

What I want less of is involvement in projects that drain my energy or limit my opportunities to work with genuinely kind people. I also want to focus less on activities that don't contribute to my goal of early retirement and ultimately achieving inner peace.

What do you wish was easier when tackling challenges and why do you find it so difficult?

I wish it was easier to address challenges rooted in institutional and interpersonal bias. As a strong advocate for social justice, seeing these biases in action can lead to feelings of frustration and burnout. It is easy to go down the rabbit hole of, "Why do these challenges even exist? Why don't all people have equal access to resources to thrive?" Unfortunately, equitable treatment is not always the reality.

For many entrepreneurs from underrepresented groups, these obstacles can add even more complexity to the stressful (and joyful) entrepreneurial journey. Still, I remind myself that we have the power to be agents of change—setting positive examples and providing the resources others need to reach their goals.

What do you wish would occur faster in business? Why?

I wish that return on investment (ROI) could happen faster in business. Every entrepreneur wants to see their ideas come to fruition, quickly. Realistically, it takes a lot of hard work, luck, time, continuous learning, and building strong connections. It also means paying attention to mental and physical health and striving for work-life harmony. It is rare to enjoy an immediate payoff in your business.

What was the toughest obstacle you faced when tackling a big challenge in your career? How did you overcome it?

The toughest obstacle I faced was having my credibility questioned by people who felt threatened due to their limited understanding of an issue. To cope, I relied on my network for support and fortunately, my immediate supervisor was among those who were immensely supportive.

After presenting data on my processes, it became apparent that my methods of resource management resulted in cost savings for the organization. Having people to comfort me and help me problem-solve made a significant difference in overcoming the obstacle.

What inspired you to start your podcast, *The Color of Success*? And how did you overcome any initial challenges?

The Color of Success podcast was actually a happy accident. I took a free course by Dr. Melvin Varghese on starting a podcast and using it as a platform to share your message with the world. That got me thinking.

As someone who works with many Asian American clients who face stigma around mental health—and being part of a community where this stigma is still prevalent—I realized the need for open conversations. So, I began talking to others who were willing to share their mental health stories and how they navigated these challenges while building their businesses and brands. That idea has since grown into six seasons of the show.

How do you balance your roles as a psychologist, podcaster, and author while maintaining your mental health and productivity?

It's interesting that you ask because I recently discussed this on a mentor call with the Ascend Leadership team. One mentor mentioned that work-life balance is a myth, which I wholeheartedly agree with. Instead, I align more with the idea of work-life harmony.

As the CEO of Hybe mentioned, when we talk about work-life balance, we often see work as the villain. In reality, work is a significant part of our lives. That doesn't mean prioritizing work over family to the point of neglect, but rather recognizing that there are times when work requires more of our attention.

I'm fortunate to have a very supportive husband who takes on roles that I can't—or won't—like cooking, as well as handling pickups and drop-offs of our kids. Having a supportive family and partner allows me to focus on my roles as a psychologist, podcaster, and author.

Can you share some strategies you use to create a comfortable and open environment for your podcast guests?

The skills I use in podcasting are very similar to those I use in clinical interviewing. While I'm not trying to diagnose my guests, my initial goal is to build rapport and understand their stories. Early in my therapy career, a supervisor once told me, "Don't try to help someone." It seemed counterintuitive at first, but I eventually understood his meaning.

What he meant was to focus on truly *understanding* the person. That advice has stuck with me over the years. When you genuinely understand someone's story, you can validate their experiences, ask meaningful follow-up questions, and offer support. This approach has guided me in connecting with my podcast guests and providing them with a comfortable and open environment, both on- and off-camera.

What advice would you give to other business leaders about the importance of listening and being heard in their professional and personal lives?

I can't emphasize enough how vital listening and being heard are in both personal and professional settings. I strongly believe in fostering psychological safety. Many employees leave workplaces because of toxic environments, often stemming from managers who fail to listen, validate, or understand their team's challenges, both inside and outside the organization.

While it's important not to take on the role of a therapist, it's equally important to recognize that people can't simply leave their personal concerns at the door—especially with the rise of remote work, where home and work often blend together. Simple gestures like asking how someone is doing or offering help can make a significant difference.

Also, when leaders—especially those in positions of power—are transparent about their struggles and coping methods, it creates a powerful ripple effect. It encourages others to share their challenges, fostering a more supportive and understanding environment. I witnessed this firsthand during a mentorship call: one person's vulnerability led others to share, strengthening our sense of connection and support.

What are some effective ways to destigmatize mental health in the workplace?

Before addressing mental health with your staff, it's crucial to explain why it's important to you as a manager or business owner and to highlight the available resources. Psychological safety is key—without it, people won't feel comfortable being vulnerable. One of the most effective ways to destigmatize mental health is by genuinely asking your team how they're doing—specifically, regarding their mental well-being.

Acknowledging that work can be challenging helps create an environment where people feel supported. Especially when they are in roles involving helping others manage their well-being. It's also important to discuss self-care—not just in terms of taking time off, but by modeling it yourself. For example, when I take vacations, I ensure there are processes in place so the organization can continue to run smoothly in my absence.

This not only supports my own mental health but also demonstrates that self-care is a priority. By embodying these principles, you set an example, encouraging your team to prioritize their well-being without feeling guilty or apologetic.

How do you navigate and address the challenges of working with less open and inclusive individuals?

Working with less open and inclusive individuals can be incredibly challenging, often leading to frustration or burnout. One strategy that has helped me is leaning on a strong social support network—building relationships with allies and advocates who understand the unique challenges faced when working with underrepresented individuals and communities.

These supportive relationships offer non-judgmental listening, advice, and encouragement, which is invaluable. Additionally, collaborating with allies within the workplace to address issues like sexism, racism, and ableism is crucial. Having a community that can help call out and confront microaggressions or overt biases makes a significant difference. There's real power in finding and fostering this kind of support system.

What strategies do you recommend for maintaining motivation during the long wait for ROI in business?

To stay motivated during the long wait for ROI in business, I always return to my core values. Values are aspirational, guiding principles that we strive toward continuously, unlike goals, which are specific milestones we achieve and move past.

Your values should shape your goals. For instance, if your goal is to build your business to a certain level or retire at a specific age, it's important to remember that reaching a goal doesn't mean progress comes to an end.

Just as nurturing a relationship requires ongoing effort, so does building a successful business. If your value is connecting with people and growing your business to serve a larger purpose, it becomes easier to endure the wait because you're aligned with something meaningful.

Another helpful strategy is adopting a mindset of lifelong learning. Each phase of the journey offers valuable lessons, and being open to adjusting your approach based on lessons learned can make the long wait for ROI more manageable.

Can you share more about the importance of having a support network and overcoming professional challenges?

Having a support network is crucial for navigating professional challenges. I have a colleague who has become a close friend, and we regularly vent to each other, empathize, and provide mutual support. We understand how intersectionality shapes our workplace experiences, and we've formed a strategic partnership to handle challenging situations.

For example, if one of us is interrupted or the target of mansplaining during a meeting, the other steps in to amplify our voice. Support networks like these are essential for driving cultural change, though it's often an uphill battle that requires patience. It's also important to be honest about our limitations so we can work through them together. If one of us hesitates during a meeting, the other can provide guidance and support.

Ultimately, I can't emphasize enough how vital community and support networks are—not just professionally, but personally as well. You need allies and advocates who can empathize with your experiences and offer a broader perspective beyond your immediate environment.

What excites you when looking through the windshield for what is ahead on your professional journey?

What excites me most about my professional journey is the unknown. If someone had told me ten years ago that I'd be hosting a podcast, coauthoring a book like *Cancel the Filter: Realities of a Psychologist, Podcaster, and Working Mother of Color* with Charlie Munn at Munn Avenue Press, and engaging deeply with the community, I wouldn't have believed it.

I'm thrilled by the unexpected opportunities that continue to come my way.

What began as a passion project to destigmatize mental health has evolved into a platform for meaningful work and connection with like-minded people. I'm eager to see where this journey will take me next.

———————————

Stephanie Wong's journey illustrates the profound impact of empathy, resilience, and intentional connections in both personal and professional life. Her dedication to destigmatizing mental health, fostering open conversations, and balancing her multiple roles with grace is a powerful testament to the transformative power of vulnerability and purpose.

As Stephanie continues to inspire others through her podcast, advocacy, and leadership, she reminds us that success is not just about achieving goals, but about creating a life that aligns with our values and supports our well-being.

Chapter 30

Resilience Through Uncertainty

"In the middle of difficulty lies opportunity."

—ALBERT EINSTEIN

As leaders, we all face moments of uncertainty—times when the path forward is unclear, and challenges seem insurmountable. In these moments, great leaders are not defined by their ability to maintain the status quo but by their capacity to adapt, pivot, and grow through adversity.

In this chapter, we focus on the leaders you just read about and how they embraced resilience as an active choice, turning challenges into opportunities to rethink strategies, empower their teams, and remain focused on the bigger picture.

Key Takeaways

1. **Confront Challenges with Purpose.** Resilient leaders face challenges head-on. Addressing issues directly creates momentum, even when the solution isn't immediately clear. Is there a leadership challenge you've been avoiding? Take the first step today, no matter how small, and watch how confronting it shifts the energy forward.

2. **Simplify to Adapt.** In times of uncertainty, complex strategies can weigh leaders down. Simplifying your focus helps you cut through the noise and adapt to changing circumstances. Clear vision, decisive action, and empowering your team are essential. Where are you overcomplicating your leadership approach? Simplify and focus on what truly drives results.

3. **Pivot with Purpose.** Leaders who can pivot when circumstances

change are more resilient. Adjusting your strategy doesn't mean abandoning your vision—it means finding new ways to reach your goals. Where in your leadership could a pivot unlock new opportunities? Instead of doubling down on a failing strategy, explore how shifting direction could lead to success.

4. **Empower Your Team to Build Resilience.** Resilience is a team effort, not a solo pursuit. Empowering your team to take ownership cultivates resilience within the group. When team members feel trusted and responsible for decisions, they rise to the occasion during tough times. Reflect on your leadership—are you giving your team enough autonomy to manage challenges? Create space for them to take more ownership.

Leadership in Practice

- **For Emerging Leaders**: Start by simplifying one area of your leadership, whether it's communication, decision-making, or delegation. Take action today to streamline your approach and adapt to changing circumstances.
- **For Seasoned Leaders**: Reassess your strategies. Are you too focused on details and losing sight of the bigger picture? Step back, simplify, and create space for more decisive action by seeing the broader landscape.

Before moving on to the next chapter, reflect on these questions to apply what you've learned.

1. **Where are you stuck?**
   Identify one area in your leadership where you're feeling stagnant. What bold step can you take today to break through and create forward movement?

2. **How can you empower your team?**
   What barriers are preventing your team from taking decisive action? How can you shift responsibility and trust them with more autonomy?

3. **What's your next move?**
   Consider your current challenges. Where can you simplify your approach and take action today to create more immediate impact?

Resilience is not just a trait—it's a choice. The leaders in Part Four demonstrated that resilience comes from moving forward with clarity, simplifying approaches, and empowering teams to rise to challenges.

As you face your own uncertainties, remember that each step you take—no matter how small—builds the momentum to overcome adversity and achieve long-term success.

Up Next: Becoming Your Own Leader: The Ultimate Challenge Story

It's now time to shift the focus inward, as we explore *your* personal leadership journey. Get ready to turn obstacles into opportunities and become the star of your own challenge story.

SECTION 3

Becoming Your Own Leader:
The Ultimate Challenge Story

PAT
ALACQUA
BUSINESS GROWTH
STRATEGIST

Introduction

True leadership starts with self-awareness and courage. Documenting your journey, exploring strategies, and engaging in ongoing learning turn obstacles into opportunities for growth.

Now that you've learned important tools and valuable lessons from others who have overcome challenges in their career journey, it's time to focus on the most important leader of all...**you.**

As you have inevitably run into issues, setbacks, hardships, and unknowns, it's likely that you've wished for a set of skills and go-to steps to face these challenges so that you can confidently work through them with clear foresight and a concrete course of action.

In this section, I'd like to give you the opportunity to dive deeper into addressing a challenge (or challenges) that has plagued you and your company. Essentially, this gives you the chance to be the star of your own challenge story.

In the following chapters, you'll have an opportunity to:

Explore the Leadership Persona Pathway

We'll learn about the Leadership Persona Pathway. This will guide you on how to navigate your challenge of personal leadership development effectively. By understanding this pathway, you'll be better equipped to apply the insights, strategies, and processes you've learned earlier in this book.

Build Your Leadership Muscles Through Practical Exercises

First, I'll have you document your biggest challenge in detail. Reflect on what stage of development your company was in, why/how the challenge arose, the feelings that emerged when facing it, the steps you took to try and overcome it, what worked and didn't work, and where it ultimately led you.

I'll then have you engage in several exercises that will allow you to put my 3Cs To Faster Results method into action. These exercises are designed to give you

229

the opportunity to tackle a challenge like never before, using proven methods to achieve faster and more effective results.

Deep Dive Into Your Leadership Evolution

This deep dive into your leadership evolution is a structured self-assessment to guide you through various stages of your leadership growth, aligning with the Leader Persona Pathway. This exercise promotes introspection and disciplined thinking at each stage of a leader's development.

Up Next

Leadership demands self-awareness, strategy, and discipline. In this chapter, we'll explore the Leader Persona Pathway, focusing on navigating leadership roles and applying disciplined thinking to overcome challenges. Learn to align your personal growth with your organization's needs for continuous advancement.

Chapter 31

Leadership Persona Pathway

Leadership is a journey of evolving roles, requiring self-awareness, strategy, and discipline to drive sustainable success for yourself and your organization.

Let's now cover what I call the Leader Persona Pathway.

The leadership journey is filled with bumps. It's about navigating a team's internal dynamics or the market's external forces. Yet, it's also about who you are on this journey and who you aspire to become. This transformation from who you are to who you want to be is the essence of the Leader Persona Pathway.

The challenges that arise while growing your career and your company require you to not only take action, but to take an introspective look at your goals, the knowledge and skills you personally need to reach them, and the mindset required for successful problem-solving.

When it comes to this journey, people tend to talk a lot about the *where*— Where are you now? Where are you coming from? Where do you want to go? But it is just as important, if not more so, to talk about the *who*—Who are you now in your pursuit of moving both your career and company forward? Who do you want to become?

Why is this important? Because if you can define yourself and the role you need to play to be successful as a leader, you can determine the actionable changes required of you, the new knowledge you need to gain, and the specific tools you need to take your success to the next level.

Let's take a deeper dive into this concept, and as we do, think about who you identify with the strongest, and, who you ultimately aspire to be. This is what I mean by the Leader Persona Pathway.

To give you a clear understanding, we're going to visualize this concept as a set of circles, each one reflecting the role that we'll be exploring.

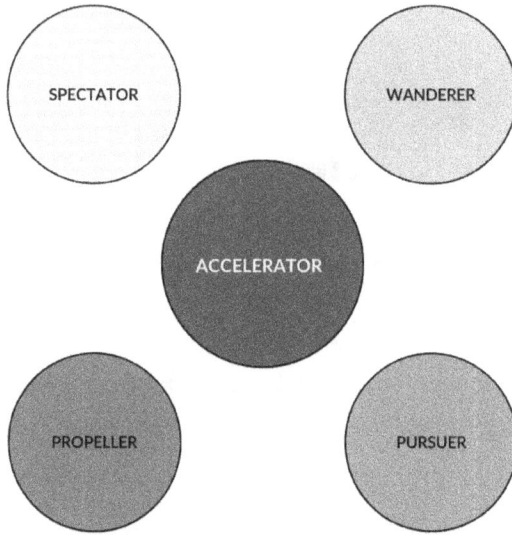

Consider what happens as we move from one to the next. Let's begin!

The Spectator

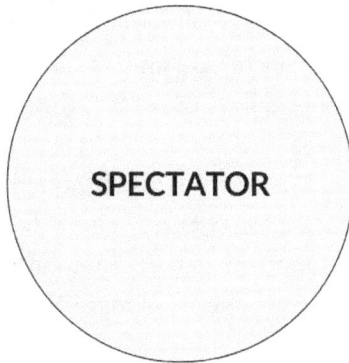

As a spectator, you have goals and dreams for your business; you can envision where you would like it to go but have no real plan for getting it there. You're perhaps feeling stuck, or even fearful, and you're sitting on the sidelines because you lack the tools needed to take real action in moving your business forward.

Spectators have a desire to learn what they need to know and are motivated to put their ideas into play but need that first push that will give them the knowledge—and confidence—to do so. Many people will stay spectators indefinitely, leading to a career and business that never quite takes off, despite the potential it has.

The Wanderer

As a wanderer, you've gotten in on the action but are lacking focus and vision. You perhaps have taken some small steps to get closer to reaching your desired outcomes when overcoming challenges but have done so without a well-thought-out or sustainable path to and through successful implementation.

This aimless approach can lead to a one-step forward, two-step back pattern, leaving you feeling frustrated and defeated before you've had the chance to see where your ideas could lead you. It's like taking a road trip without a map: you know where you'd like to end up, but without clear direction, you'll likely end up on a very long trip filled with wrong-turns and unknowns, ultimately taking a U-turn back to home base.

The Pursuer

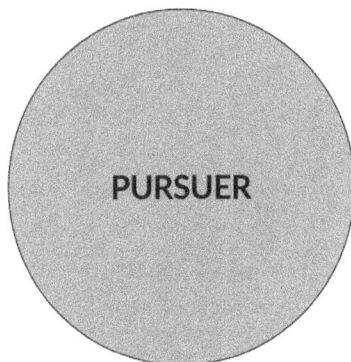

As a pursuer, you've figured out the path you need to be on, the groundwork has been strategically laid, and you're working hard to implement your ideas, but without any real approach to efficiency and effectiveness.

You are in the game and are clear on how to get to your end goals, but the moves you're making lack power, strength, and speed. You're inspired by the knowledge that you're on the right path and the desire to pursue your business goals is there, but you're having to work harder and longer to reach them. You haven't quite figured out the formula that will get you there...but you're close.

In other words, you've got the *working hard* down and are getting some results, you're just not quite there with *working smart*—and this is where you see true changes in your business.

The Propeller

PROPELLER

As a propeller, you are now actively on that path to driving your company forward. You have determined the right steps to take and are implementing them with clarity, efficiency, and some speed, and you've acquired some of the tools you need to make timely decisions, advancing your business steadily. You can even feel the momentum starting because those on your team are beginning to understand what they need to do to play their roles most effectively, leaving clues that real alignment could be possible.

Now, this is a place where you could easily stop, thinking it's enough to sustain. Business is doing well, and you feel confident. But your ultimate goal of putting things into high gear isn't being reached—all of the pieces are there but you're constantly needing to keep it all running in order to ensure they are fitting together properly.

What you're missing is leverage, the key strategy that creates an environment of real collaboration and alignment. The process that closes everyone's knowledge gaps and gets the team rowing in the same direction. The point in time when everything is in place and working without the need for your involvement in every component.

This is where building real sustainable momentum can catapult you and your company to the next level and improve your business infinitely.

The Accelerator

Your career and company are now moving forward at full speed! You've implemented the right tools to be on the fast track to reaching your desired outcomes. You've become a powerhouse leader, harnessing strategies that impact your company in the ways you need them to, and leading teams that are aligned and motivated.

The groundwork has been laid, the goal of *working smart* has been reached, and you're now able to leverage the skills and processes you've learned to create automated, limitless growth...at maximum speed.

This is the ultimate goal—or should I say role—for any entrepreneur or business leader—to get your company to a place of continual advancement, and into a constant state of moving forward...and upward.

Now, the big question you need to be asking is: How do I step into the role of the accelerator? Well, I have the answer for you. But first, let's summarize what we've learned.

We have now explored all the roles that you could be playing, past, present, and future. As we've learned, who you are is defined by a way of thinking and a mindset for how to take on your challenges.

Disciplined Thinking

But, no matter how you see yourself, there is one skill that is most effective in growing your career and company: that skill is disciplined thinking.

**YOUR MINDSET FOR TAKING ON CHALLENGES
+ THE WAY YOU THINK = WHO YOU ARE**

Disciplined thinking is a mental process of approaching problems using rational and objective reasoning and moving in a systematic, focused, and sequenced manner. By practicing disciplined thinking, you can make better decisions, solve problems more effectively, and reach the outcomes you desire with clarity and speed.

Now, are you ready for that answer for how you can step into the role of the accelerator?

You see, I help leaders like you become accelerators by teaching you the art of disciplined thinking, enabling you to apply the right decision-making skills to a set of actions that put you on the smartest and fastest track to your desired outcome, using my 3Cs Process Path to Fastest Results.

**DISCIPLINED THINKING + 3Cs PROCESS =
FASTER RESULTS**

The 3Cs is the most effective and powerful system to ignite your business-building skills, activate your ability to overcome challenges, and set your company and YOU in motion.

Let's now take a look at our graphic about the Leader Persona Pathway one last time.

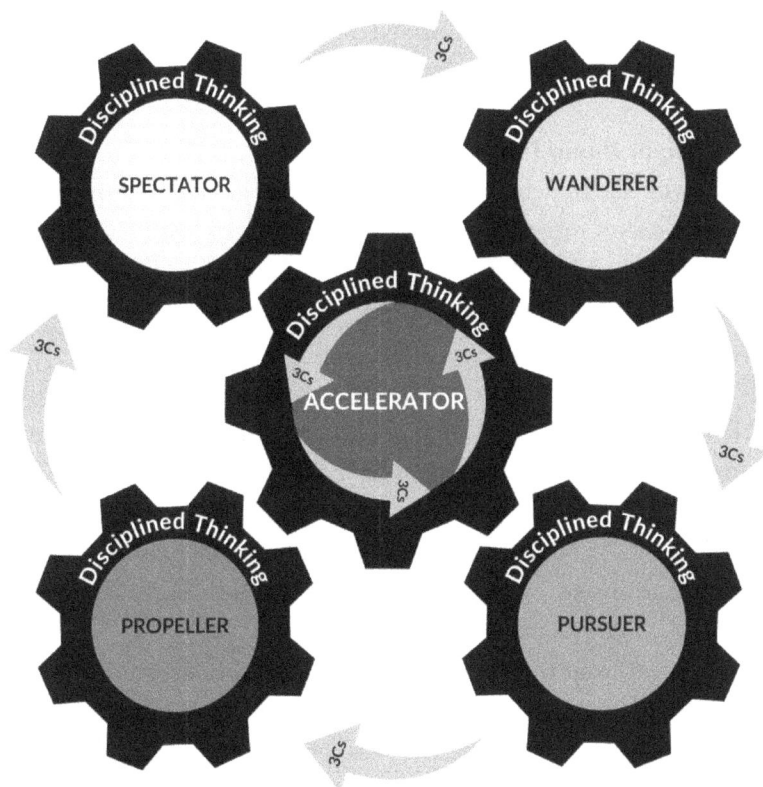

As you can see, we no longer have just a group of circles; we have a set of powerful gears, each one becoming a part of a bigger mechanism, one that inevitably leads you to and through your business-building goals.

The roles exist and are ready to be played, but in order for that to occur, they need the disciplined thinking that connects goals to action, and, most importantly, the 3Cs Process to put everything in motion.

You can progress in sequence or jump gears, take your time, or move through quickly–because with the right knowledge, tools, and guidance you'll remain confident that the gears will keep turning...and you will keep moving forward.

Now, you may be asking yourself, "What can I do right now to get the gears moving in my business?"

Well, I'll do a deep dive into that in the next chapter. Right now, let's give you an overview to get you started.

Get the Gears Moving On Your Leadership Pathway

Let's now talk about what you can do to get the gears moving on your Leader Persona Pathway so we can get you beyond the obstacles to moving your career and company forward and upward... faster!

What You Might Bump Into

Rolling with the punches and adapting to change is something we all need to keep finding ways to get better at doing. It all starts with CLARITY. As a spectator, you have visions but need the push to act. Begin by CLARIFYING your challenge: recognize the tools you lack and the knowledge you need to move forward.

When facing tough calls, as a wanderer, you're in motion but lack direction. CHART your course with intention. Lay down strategic steps toward your desired outcomes to prevent the aimless wandering that leads to frustration.

Keeping the peace within your team means shifting from the wanderer to the pursuer. You're taking action here, but now it's time to COALIGN your stakeholders. Ensure that everyone understands their role in the collective vision for it to translate into practical action.

Staying true to your roots and not burning out is about mindful growth. As you evolve from a pursuer to a propeller, you implement ideas clearly and efficiently. Still, you must maintain the balance that keeps your personal and professional life sustainable.

Your Toolkit for Getting Past the Bumps

Making the game plan means planning precisely, learning from those who have walked the path before you, and never ceasing to learn. This is how you move from the propeller, which has momentum, to the accelerator, which drives the company forward at full speed.

Remember when you face challenging times: it's a chance to build your leadership muscles. Each bump is an opportunity to CLARIFY, CHART, and COALIGN, transforming challenges into victories.

Embrace your current role and understand the actions needed to propel yourself forward. Apply the 3Cs as you grow through each persona on the Leader

Persona Pathway. These are not just steps but a powerful sequence that ensures the gears of your business and your professional growth are always turning, propelling you toward continuous advancement and upward movement.

By maintaining the Leader Persona Pathway as a backdrop for applying the 3Cs, you create a seamless integration of identity and action, ensuring you navigate your challenges and evolve through them. This is how you transform bumps in the road into a launchpad for growth, moving your career and company forward faster.

Up Next

In the next chapter, we'll explore practical exercises to strengthen your leadership skills. Learn to navigate challenges and turn them into growth opportunities by applying the 3Cs—CLARIFY, CHART, COALIGN—on your journey to success.

Chapter 32

Building *Your* Leadership Muscles

Great leaders are forged through the discipline of consistent growth, the strength of disciplined thinking, and the wisdom of aligning passion with purpose.

By embracing disciplined thinking and strategic action with the 3Cs—CLARIFY, CHART, COALIGN—you can transform obstacles into milestones, propelling yourself and your company toward sustainable success.

Your progress from spectator to accelerator on the Leader Persona Pathway is marked by key milestones: bouncing back stronger, thinking outside the box, earning trust, stretching your comfort zones, and achieving great success. It's a path defined by disciplined thinking and strategic action, driven by the engine of my 3Cs Process for Faster Results.

In this section, you will find a series of exercises designed to help you reflect on your leadership journey, plan for future challenges, and practice aligning your team. As you work through the upcoming exercises, you will begin creating a tailored action plan that not only aligns with your personal growth but also enhances your ability to lead others effectively.

The exercises below will help you gain deeper insights into your past experiences and prepare you to apply the strategies and methods shared in this book. This reflective practice will transform your insights into actionable strategies, propelling you forward on your leadership journey.

General Guidelines for Exercises
   1. *Prepare your Mindset*
      a. Take a moment to reflect before starting each exercise.
      b. Ensure you have a quiet space where you can focus.

3. *Be Intentional*
   a. Follow the specific points for each exercise.
   b. Write down your thoughts and plans clearly and concisely.
3. *Determine Action Steps*
   a. After completing each exercise, think about how you can apply the insights gained to your leadership practices.
   b. Consider what changes can be made in the short-term vs. long-term.

> **Take a moment to write down your responses. Remember, initiating this kind of thinking is more important than the final answers right now.**

EXERCISE 1: Identifying Your Leader Persona

Before you can grow, you must first understand who you are now and what has shaped your leadership journey. Reflect on your current leadership style and abilities by identifying your position within the Leader Persona Pathway.

Understanding your current position on the Leader Persona Pathway is essential for recognizing your strengths, challenges, and areas for growth. This exercise will help you identify where you stand and the key areas you need to focus on to progress on the pathway.

Instructions:
1. Assign a score to the questions below using a sliding scale of 1–6, with 1 meaning you "strongly disagree" and 6 meaning you "strongly agree."
2. Write down your score for each question.
3. Calculate your total score for each section. The highest-scored section indicates your current leader persona.

Reflection Questions:
  SPECTATOR
  • Do you frequently watch others succeed and wonder why you're not making the same progress?
  • Do you spend more time planning and dreaming than actually implementing your ideas?
  • Do you feel overwhelmed by the amount of information available, unsure where to begin or what to prioritize?

WANDERER

- Do you often start new projects or initiatives but struggle to see them through to completion?
- Do you find yourself frequently changing direction or priorities without a clear reason?
- Do you feel like you're working hard but not making significant progress toward your goals?

PURSUER

- Do you find yourself putting in long hours but not achieving the level of success you expected?
- Do you struggle with prioritizing tasks and often feel overwhelmed by your workload?
- Do you find it challenging to delegate or streamline processes, resulting in slower progress and growth?

PROPELLER

- Do you often feel that your business progress relies heavily on your constant involvement?
- Do you see areas where your team could be better aligned and more collaborative?
- Do you recognize the potential for greater efficiency and speed in your current strategies and processes?

ACCELERATOR

- Do you consistently seek new opportunities for growth and innovation to stay ahead?
- Do you focus on maintaining alignment and motivation within your team while managing rapid growth?
- Do you continuously adapt your strategies to stay relevant and effective in a changing market?

Action Steps:

Remember, understanding your current position on the Leader Persona Pathway is essential for recognizing your strengths, challenges, and areas for growth. Score each question honestly, then calculate the totals for each persona category.

Identify which persona category has the highest score—this represents your current position on the Leader Persona Pathway, who you are now. In the next exercise, we'll work on identifying who you want to be.

EXERCISE 2: Leader Persona Gap Analysis

Now that you have identified your current leader persona (who you are now), take some time to consider what your ideal leader persona is (who you want to be). The following exercise will guide you through a gap analysis of your leader persona and help you develop an action plan for addressing those gaps.

For the best results, be detailed and honest in your self-analysis. Acknowledging your shortcomings is not a sign of failure, but rather a sign of growth—recognizing your willingness to grow, your capacity for growth, as well as your fortitude.

Gap Analysis:
1. Write down some of the current leadership challenges you are facing.
2. Identify the gaps in your tools and/or knowledge that need to be filled to better navigate those challenges.
3. Acknowledge your strengths. List the tools and knowledge you bring to the table.
4. Now, list actionable steps you can take to fill the gaps.

Action Steps:
1. Using the matrix below, identify where addressing each gap falls in terms of effort required and potential impact.

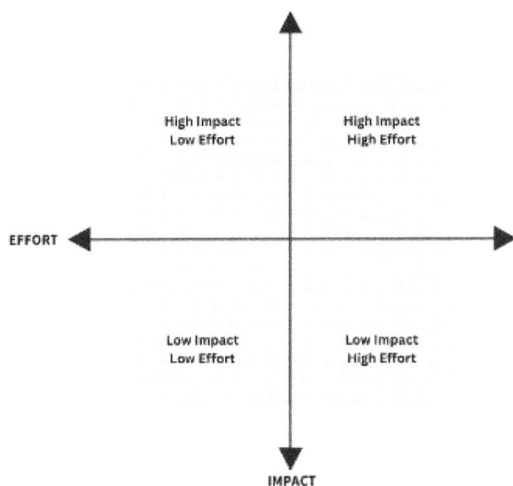

2. Then, list the efforts in priority order starting with High Impact/ Low Effort items (the low-hanging fruit). Anything that falls within the Low Impact/High Effort quadrant should be put on the back burner.

3. Outline up to three actionable steps you can take within the next thirty days to start closing some of the gaps.

EXERCISE 3: Reflecting on Your Leadership Challenges

To kickstart your journey, reflect on the most significant challenge you've faced in your leadership journey. Understanding how you overcame this challenge—or how you could have handled it better—will provide you with invaluable insights for future success.

Write down your responses to the questions listed below. For the best results, be detailed and honest in your analysis and interpretation of the events.

Reflection Questions:
1. The Challenge:
   - Think back to a significant challenge you've faced in your leadership journey. What was it, and how did you approach it?
   - Looking back on the Leader Persona Pathway, which role's traits best describe your involvement in tackling the challenge?
2. The Outcome:
   - What was the result of your approach?
   - Did it lead to success, or could it have been handled differently?
   - How would an accelerator have handled it?
3. The Lesson:
   - What one strategy, if applied earlier, could have transformed the outcome?

Action Steps:
1. Based on this reflection and considering the matrix from Exercise 1, write down one immediate change you can implement in your leadership approach to better navigate future challenges.
2. Now consider, will this change move you closer to your desired leader persona too? If not, are there other solutions that not only improve your outcome but also help you progress to a more effective leadership style?

EXERCISE 4: Scenario Planning

Applying the 3Cs framework (CLARIFY, CHART, COALIGN) to a specific challenge ensures disciplined thinking and strategic problem-solving. The goal of this exercise is to grease the wheels of your disciplined thinking skills. These are the gears that will move you forward in your leadership development journey.

This exercise guides you through a structured approach to tackling current business challenges. Follow the 3Cs process steps outlined below to describe a current challenge and plan your next steps.

3Cs Process to Faster Results:

1. CLARIFY the Challenge:
   - Briefly describe a current challenge you're facing.
   - Identify the core issue and the key stakeholders involved.

2. CHART Possible Actions:
   - State the desired outcome you seek when moving forward to tackle this challenge.
   - Identify any non-negotiables (what must happen and what cannot happen) in any path you take to reach your desired outcome.
   - List two potential actions you could take in your approach to address this challenge.
   - Evaluate the pros and cons of each option.

3. COALIGN Your Team:
   - Identify the key stakeholders who need to be aligned. Outline each of their roles and how you will engage and communicate with them to ensure alignment.
   - Develop a one-page communication and engagement plan to ensure everyone is on the same page.
   - Consider whether resources or context need to be provided, what decisions need to be agreed upon, and what needs to happen before the plan can progress into implementation.

Action Step:

Write down three specific actions you will take this week to begin integrating the 3Cs process to tackle upcoming challenges. It could be as simple as scheduling a meeting, emailing a stakeholder, or communicating with an accountability partner. Each step needs to happen to ensure everyone involved is working in harmony toward the desired outcome.

Your Leadership Evolution

Leadership is an evolving journey. Before we conclude this chapter, I encourage you to reflect on your progress, no matter who you are on the Leader Persona Pathway. Take the time to identify areas for improvement and plan your next steps.

Through introspection and disciplined thinking, you will begin creating a tailored action plan that not only aligns with your personal growth goals but also enhances your ability to lead others effectively. This is a reflective practice that transforms insights into actionable strategies.

Spectator Reflection: If you are a spectator, take some time to reflect on the goals and dreams you have for your company. Consider what tools or knowledge gaps are preventing you from taking action. Are there fears or obstacles keeping you on the sidelines? Self-awareness goes a long way in your leadership evolution.

Wanderer Strategy Development: If you are a wanderer, focus on your strategy development efforts. Outline some current, concrete short-term goals for your personal growth journey. Then identify a long-term vision to gain focus and direction. Are your short-term goals and long-term vision aligned?

Pursuer to Coaligner Transition: If you are a pursuer, create an action plan to enhance your efficiency and effectiveness in aligning your team. Make sure to identify which stakeholders need to be involved and how you plan to engage with them. Then consider what communication strategy or team-building efforts you plan to use to gain alignment within your team.

Propeller Action Plan: If you are a propeller, focus on driving your company forward with clarity, efficiency, and speed. List at least five steps you can take to improve your decision-making and implementation efforts. Consider what tools and resources you need to acquire to accomplish those improvements. Take action to acquire those tools or resources.

Accelerator Focus: If you are an accelerator, focus on maintaining sustainable growth. Continue to leverage collaboration and alignment to create momentum. Then, consider how you plan to capitalize on that momentum for additional growth. List at least three actionable strategies to do so.

By reading this book and engaging in these exercises, you've taken the first steps toward evolving your leader persona. As you continue to apply the 3Cs— CLARIFY, CHART, COALIGN—remember that each step forward on your Leader Persona Pathway brings you closer to your ultimate goal: becoming the accelerator who drives your company toward sustainable, scalable success.

Remember, the goal of these exercises is not to find the perfect answers but rather to hone some discipline in your thinking process. You are now equipped with a framework to continuously refine your approach through thoughtful reflection and actionable strategies.

Visit my website at www.PatAlacqua.com for additional resources, tools, and guidance to keep your leadership development on track.

Up Next

In the next chapter, we'll explore the transformative power of collaboration and facilitation. Learn to align visions, leverage diverse skills, and turn challenges into growth opportunities. Discover the blueprint for effective collaboration and how facilitation enhances personal and company performance.

SECTION 4

Key Insight Takeaways

**PAT
ALACQUA**
BUSINESS GROWTH
STRATEGIST

Chapter 33

Amplifying Your Performance

Collaboration and facilitation drive performance. Align visions, leverage diverse skills, and use structured guidance to turn challenges into growth opportunities.

Part 1. The Power of Collaboration

Let's jump into the transformative power of collaboration. When approached strategically, it can amplify your performance and that of your business tenfold. A successful collaboration brings a fusion of knowledge, resources, and skills, creating a synergy where both parties benefit.

Picture this: Two minds, different yet aligned, coming together to create magic. That's the power of collaboration. Now, imagine combining this collaborative power with effective facilitation. Together, these two skills can amplify both personal and company performance.

Collaboration is the hidden tool that opens doors to potential you've never imagined. At its core, it's about aligning vision, strategy, and goals. In fact, for business trailblazers these collaborations aren't just beneficial, they're transformative. But often the challenge lies in choosing the right approach.

Throughout my life, I've sought out collaborators who offer a mutual learning experience, a real demonstration of complementing one another. These collaborations have been a cornerstone of my journey, allowing me to tap into diverse experiences and, in turn, offer my own unique skills for shared success.

Over the years, I've honed a method to identify and engage with the perfect collaborators, and by consistently applying this approach I've unlocked countless opportunities. If you would like to elevate your growth journey, remember that the right collaboration can be your catalyst.

Often there are great advantages to not going it alone. When we dive deep into a potential collaboration, we discover synergies that can supercharge an approach to tackling big challenges, whether they be problems or opportunities. The beauty of collaboration lies in the fusion of shared audiences, the pooling of resources, and the mutual enhancement of added value when taking on any challenge.

The Blueprint: 4 Steps to Effective Collaboration

Here is my go-to strategy for collaborations. I adapt my 3Cs Process to Faster Results to leverage it for success with all my collaborations.

Step 1: CLARIFY Shared Desired Outcomes

It's vital to know what you want from the collaboration—what each person seeks and what you collectively want to achieve. This is what I call the "give and get" phase of your discussions. You document the synergies that are the foundation for what each person can offer, along with the benefits everyone can strive for in return. By having a clear understanding of your goals, you set the tone for a partnership driven by purpose and direction. It's like setting a destination for a journey; you need to know where you're heading.

From the start, establishing trust is key. Collaboration flourishes when all parties are transparent, open to each other's perspectives, and willing to build a trusting relationship. This trust will underpin the entire process, ensuring a strong foundation for everything that follows.

Step 2: CHART a Roadmap to These Outcomes Together

Once the destination is clear, charting the path together becomes essential. It's crucial to identify what I call the non-negotiables for addressing the "give and get" established in Step One and ensure your partner is fully aligned.

This includes outlining what must happen and what cannot happen as you craft and customize your roadmap to success. Effective planning and strategizing, coupled with identifying the right tools and resources, will enable you to communicate clearly and manage expectations throughout the process.

Proactive communication is at the heart of successful execution. Regular check-ins and updates allow you to address potential issues before they escalate and ensure that both sides remain aligned with the overall goals and expectations.

One thing I've learned the hard way through my collaborations is the importance of assigning accountability. Each partner should have someone with the influence and authority within their organization to navigate the silos and ensure timely, successful implementation. In many collaborations, I've found that navigating through organizational silos can delay progress.

It's crucial to have a collaborator who can influence various departments, ensuring that adaptability is built into the process. This not only speeds up implementation but also allows for quicker responses to any roadblocks that arise along the way.

Cultural intelligence is also vital. Understanding and adapting to your partner's decision-making styles, communication preferences, and organizational culture can be the difference between a seamless collaboration, and one filled with misunderstandings. Taking the time to build this intelligence fosters mutual respect and drives smoother implementation.

Equally important is maintaining mutual accountability. Both sides need to regularly revisit the non-negotiables and ensure that the roadmap is being followed, with everyone taking ownership of their role in the overall success.

Step 3: COALIGN with Collaborators on Outcomes and Strategies

This is where the magic happens. Once both parties have clarity on their desired outcomes and have mapped out their non-negotiables and plans, it's time to coalign with all stakeholders you will need for successful implementation. Work together to merge both roadmaps into a cohesive plan with those key stakeholders. It's like two solo travelers deciding to journey together, combining their individual plans to make the trip more enriching.

By coaligning, you create a stronger collaboration where both sides leverage each other's strengths and ideas, allowing for a more robust strategy. This joint effort not only strengthens the partnership but also helps you navigate unforeseen changes that might arise along the way.

Trust plays an even bigger role here. Successful co-alignment requires open communication, transparency, and a willingness to rely on each other's strengths. Building trust at this stage ensures that you can handle any challenges that come your way and keep the collaboration strong.

Step 4: Execute and Evaluate

With a clear plan and aligned objectives, it's time to execute the collaboration. To ensure the partnership remains productive, it's important to establish feedback loops early on. Regularly monitor progress, make adjustments as needed, and continuously evaluate the outcomes.

Encourage open communication throughout the process, creating an environment where both parties can voice concerns or suggest improvements. Feedback isn't just for solving problems; it's also about enhancing collaboration and ensuring long-term success.

Resilience is key in this phase. Collaboration isn't without its challenges, and resilience is essential. Whether you encounter shifting priorities, unexpected roadblocks, or differences in perspective, staying adaptable and committed to the shared goals will keep the partnership on course. Resilience turns short-term setbacks into opportunities for growth.

Celebrate milestones and successes along the way. Recognizing achievements helps sustain momentum and keep everyone engaged. By focusing on ongoing evaluation, you ensure that the collaboration remains dynamic, adaptive, and productive over time.

Finally, remember that collaboration is not just about the current project but about building a relationship that can lead to future opportunities. By executing with precision and continuously evaluating, you set the stage for long-term success and potential ongoing partnerships.

This framework not only provides a structured approach to collaboration but also emphasizes trust, adaptability, cultural intelligence, and resilience. These elements, woven throughout the process, ensure that your collaborations are built on a solid foundation and are prepared to overcome challenges while achieving meaningful results.

Now that we've explored the power and process of collaboration, it's essential to understand the role facilitation plays in making these collaborations successful.

Part 2. Bridging Collaboration and Facilitation

Facilitation is the strategic tool that guides collaborative efforts, ensuring they are productive, focused, and aligned with desired outcomes. Effective facilitation can turn a good collaboration into a great one by providing the structure and support needed to navigate challenges and maximize the benefits of working together.

Facilitation amplifies collaboration by guiding discussions, aligning diverse perspectives, and ensuring that the collective intelligence of the group is harnessed effectively. Without facilitation, even the best collaborations can veer off course, lacking the focus needed to turn ideas into action.

Typically, you and your collaborator already have a full plate within your own areas of responsibility, and now you're adding another initiative to your plates. This is where identifying a facilitator for the collaboration can be the key to amplifying performance and successfully reaching desired outcomes.

The Role of Facilitation in Tackling Big Challenges

A question I often get from entrepreneurs and business leaders is about the use of an external facilitator. Should they use an external facilitator, rely on someone internally, or even try to handle it themselves?

You might be wondering, "What exactly is an outside facilitator, and why should I consider using one?" Let me break it down for you.

An outside facilitator is a neutral party who guides you and your team through a project, discussion, or decision-making process. They offer numerous advantages that can transform your initiative's dynamics and outcomes. Using an external facilitator can truly be a game changer.

One of the critical aspects of a good outside facilitator is their systematic approach. They bring structured, proven methodologies to the table, which can be invaluable when addressing business challenges. It's about having a roadmap that guides you efficiently from Point A to Point B, ensuring no detail is missed and that your team's full potential is tapped into.

Moreover, effective facilitation doesn't just solve today's challenges; it provides your team with the tools, processes, and insights to enhance future collaborations. By learning from the structure and approaches of skilled facilitators, your team can apply these techniques to drive better outcomes long after the current project is complete.

Key Advantages of External Facilitators

Structured Approach

A skilled facilitator brings a systematic approach, using proven methodologies to guide the process. This ensures that every aspect of the challenge is addressed methodically. For example, in a large-scale strategy meeting, they can implement structured frameworks that help the team move from brainstorming to actionable steps without losing momentum.

Neutrality

An external facilitator comes in without any biases, allowing them to guide the conversation objectively. They act as an effective conflict mediator when necessary, ensuring all opinions are heard and considered equally, fostering a truly collaborative process. For instance, in a heated meeting discussion, an external facilitator can step in to refocus the team on core issues, ensuring that diverse perspectives are respected while keeping the conversation productive.

Enhanced Focus

Leaders often find it challenging to balance facilitation and active participation. By bringing in an outside facilitator, leaders can fully engage in the project, contributing their unique perspectives and ideas. This allows leaders to focus on strategy and vision, while the facilitator ensures that the process stays on track and organized.

Specialized Skills

Facilitation is an art in itself. Professional facilitators have the right tools to guide productive discussions, encourage collaboration, and maintain the team's focus. Their expertise in time management helps keep the process streamlined and the team on track. For example, they can effectively manage time during workshops, ensuring that discussions don't veer off course while still allowing for creativity and problem-solving.

Learning Opportunity

Observing an external facilitator at work can be a learning experience for your team, offering valuable insights that can be applied to future challenges. The way they handle conflict, encourage engagement, and steer conversations can become lessons for your own leaders in how to guide future collaborations.

Building Trust and Relationships

Facilitators also play a critical role in building and maintaining trust within the team. By ensuring open communication and encouraging transparency, they help create an environment where strong relationships are forged. This fosters a sense of unity and trust that strengthens the collaboration and lays the groundwork for future partnerships.

Tips for Choosing the Right Facilitator

Now that you understand the key advantages, how do you go about selecting the right facilitator for your needs? Here are some critical factors to keep in mind when choosing a facilitator who can help you achieve the outcomes you desire.

Experience: Look for someone with firsthand operational experience who has been in the trenches, building a company from scratch. A facilitator with practical experience will have a better understanding of the challenges your team faces.

Alignment: Ensure their approach to facilitation aligns with your team's culture and the project's objectives. They should complement your organizational style, whether that's more hands-on or collaborative in nature.

Skill Gaps: Find someone who complements your team's skill sets and brings unique knowledge or experience to the table. If your team lacks specific strategic planning expertise, a facilitator with those skills can provide valuable insights.

Empowerment: Choose facilitators who empower your team, not create dependency. They should focus on providing what you need when you need it, driven by your agenda. A good facilitator leaves your team stronger after the collaboration, ready to take on the next challenge with newfound skills.

Communication Skills: Strong communication abilities are vital. Good facilitators are active listeners and insightful questioners and ensure everyone has an opportunity to contribute. Their ability to read the room and adapt their approach is key to getting the best out of the group.

Broad Experience: Prefer facilitators with a broad scope of business-building experience and the ability to anticipate problems before they become critical issues. A facilitator who has seen diverse scenarios can adapt quickly when unexpected challenges arise.

Flexible Pricing: Consider someone flexible with their pricing structure, offering value that fits within your budget without compromising their expertise. This ensures you get the right fit without straining your financial resources.

Choosing the right facilitator can significantly impact your ability to reach desired outcomes smarter and faster. The next time you're committed to tackling a big challenge, remember the significant advantages that the right facilitator can bring. Their structured approach, impartiality, and focus might just be the keys to unlocking your greatest potential.

Remember, effective leadership sometimes means knowing when to bring in external expertise.

In Summary: Bridging Collaboration and Facilitation

The combination of collaboration and effective facilitation can serve as powerful tools to amplify both personal and company performance. Facilitation provides the structure needed to keep collaboration focused and aligned, while collaboration allows for diverse perspectives and innovation to flourish.

By mastering the art and science of collaboration, and knowing when and how to engage external facilitators, leaders can unlock new levels of potential and drive their careers and organizations to greater heights. Embrace these strategies, and you'll be well on your way to achieving remarkable success.

At the end of the day, the greatest leaders know that success isn't achieved alone. By combining strategic collaboration with the right facilitation, you create new possibilities for growth, innovation, and performance. Don't hesitate to invest in these tools. Your greatest potential lies in how effectively you harness the power of collaboration and facilitation.

Up Next

In the next chapter, we'll summarize key takeaways from this book, highlighting the importance of resilience, adaptability, and strategic planning for effective leadership.

Get ready to integrate these insights into your approach, turning challenges into stepping stones for lasting success.

Chapter 34

Essential Insights for Sustained Growth

Embrace resilience, foster a growth mindset, and focus on
strategic planning and execution.

As we conclude this journey through the diverse experiences, strategies, and insights shared in this book, it's essential to distill the key takeaways that will guide you toward becoming a more effective leader. While there are numerous valuable insights, here are a few essential principles that encapsulate the lessons learned and provide a framework for continuous growth and success.

Embrace Resilience and Adaptability

A common thread throughout the various stories and methodologies explored is the importance of resilience and adaptability. Bouncing back from setbacks and adapting to changing circumstances is crucial. Embrace challenges as opportunities to grow and evolve, and remain flexible in your approach to problem-solving.

Reflect on your journey: How have setbacks shaped your leadership style? What strategies can you implement to become more adaptable in the face of future challenges?

Cultivate a Growth Mindset

A growth mindset is vital for continuous learning and innovation. Constantly seek new ideas, embrace failures as learning experiences, and remain open to new solutions. Cultivating a culture of curiosity and experimentation within your organization can drive innovation and resilience.

What steps can you take today to create more of a growth mindset within your team? How can you create an environment that encourages learning and curiosity?

Focus on Strategic Planning and Execution

Effective strategic planning and execution are the cornerstones of successful leadership. Ensure that your strategic initiatives are data-driven and aligned with your long-term vision. Regularly reassess and refine your plans to adapt to changing market conditions and internal dynamics.

Remember: Strategic success isn't just about planning; it's about disciplined execution. What processes can you improve to ensure your plans are executed precisely?

Prioritize Effective Communication and Collaboration

Strong communication and collaboration are essential for building high-performing teams. Always remember the power of clear communication and the importance of aligning team efforts with organizational goals. Create an environment where open dialogue, feedback, and teamwork are encouraged. Doing so can enhance trust, accountability, and collective problem-solving.

Think about your team: How can you improve communication to build trust and collaboration?

Leverage the Power of Simplicity

Simplifying processes, roles, and strategies can improve efficiency and effectiveness. Reducing complexity in your operations and focusing on core competencies can streamline efforts and improve outcomes. Regularly evaluate and eliminate unnecessary tasks and distractions to maintain a sharp focus on what truly matters.

Consider: What complexities keep your team from achieving their best work? How can you simplify to drive more impact?

Develop Disciplined Thinking and Decision-Making

Disciplined thinking is a critical skill for making informed decisions and achieving desired outcomes. As outlined in the Leader Persona Pathway, approaching problems with rational and objective reasoning can help you navigate challenges more systematically and effectively.

Use tools like the 3Cs process of Clarify, Chart, Coalign to structure your decision-making and ensure alignment with your strategic goals.

Create a Culture of Mentorship and Continuous Learning

Mentorship and continuous learning are vital for personal and organizational growth. As leaders, we should always emphasize the importance of mentoring others and investing in professional development.

Encourage your team members to seek mentors, engage in ongoing learning, and share their knowledge and experiences. This will enhance individual capabilities and strengthen the overall organizational culture.

As a leader, what mentorship opportunities can you create within your team?

Align Personal and Professional Goals

Successful leadership requires aligning personal aspirations with professional objectives. Reflect on your goals, values, and the role you need to play to drive your business forward.

As you navigate the Leader Persona Pathway, ensure that your actions and decisions are consistent with your long-term vision and the values you uphold. This alignment enhances authenticity and drives sustainable success.

As you reflect on these principles—resilience, strategic thinking, and growth mindset—remember how they surface throughout the stories and lessons in this book. These are not just ideas but the core of sustained leadership success.

The journey through this book has given you valuable insights and practical tools. As you move forward, remember to embrace resilience, cultivate a growth mindset, focus on strategic planning, prioritize effective communication, leverage simplicity, develop disciplined thinking, foster a culture of mentorship, and align your personal and professional goals.

By integrating these high-level takeaways into your leadership approach, you can overcome challenges, drive innovation, and achieve lasting success.

Today, reflect on one principle from this chapter that resonates with you most. How will you apply it to your leadership approach starting tomorrow?

Thank you for engaging with this material. Your commitment to personal and professional development is the hallmark of a great leader. Continue to strive, reflect, and grow, turning every challenge into a stepping stone toward more significant achievements.

Up Next

In the next chapter, we'll explore practical strategies and support systems to help you navigate your path to success, enhancing your leadership journey and creating a lasting impact.

BONUS RESOURCES

Visit our Resource Center today to access additional tools designed to support your business growth.

Create your free account at PatAlacqua.com/bonus-resources and unlock these exclusive insights now!

PAT ALACQUA
BUSINESS GROWTH
STRATEGIST

Chapter 35

The Journey to Enduring Success—How I Can Help

Empower yourself through curiosity and intention.
Reflect on your response to challenges and embrace innovation and agility.

Thank you again for engaging deeply with this material. As you continue to strive, reflect, and grow—turning every challenge into an opportunity for more remarkable achievements—your commitment to personal and professional development is the hallmark of a great leader.

I hope the stories, strategies, insights, tips, and lessons learned from the leaders featured in this book have inspired you and ignited a deeper examination of how you confront and navigate your professional challenges. This collection has been crafted to demonstrate that the path to success is rarely straightforward and must be navigated through strategic action and a growth-oriented mindset. Remember, your potential for growth is limitless, and every challenge is an opportunity for you to shine.

As you reflect on these narratives, ask yourself: What motivates your response to challenges? Is it the allure of success or the fear of failure? How does this influence your approach to obstacles?

Empower yourself through curiosity and intention. Consider the role of innovation and agility in overcoming your challenges. Think about applying these lessons to grow in an ever-changing business environment.

How I Can Help

As you continue your career and business-building journey, I offer tailored programs to support you. Whether you are at the inception of your venture, actively scaling, steering an established enterprise, or trying to discover the fastest path to become the leader you aspire to be, my programs are designed to meet you at your point of need and propel you to your desired heights, putting you in the driver's seat of your professional development.

I am here to support you in navigating your path through any challenge or obstacle to success, helping you make informed decisions that will propel your career and business forward and enrich the broader community you serve. Let's craft a strategy together that addresses your immediate challenges and prepares you for future endeavors.

I offer three levels of support designed to meet your diverse needs. Consider which one will most serve your long-term goals for leadership and success.

1. **Self-directed Learning:** For those who prefer to apply new strategies independently.
2. **Selective Support:** For those seeking expert guidance on specific challenge areas.
3. **Full Collaboration:** For those desiring side-by-side help throughout the complete journey when taking on significant challenges.

Your Next Step

Your journey doesn't end here. At PatAlacqua.com, discover a collection of insights, programs, and resources to help you navigate your next steps.

From full collaboration to self-directed learning, there's something for every stage of your leadership journey. Stay curious and continue turning obstacles into opportunities.

While you have a moment, reflect on one principle from this book that resonates with you most. How will you apply it to your leadership approach starting tomorrow?

As a Final Thought

As you close this book, think about the kind of leader you aspire to be. What steps will you take today to ensure your daily actions align with your vision for tomorrow? How will you turn each challenge into a stepping stone toward the legacy you wish to leave?

These questions will shape your success and the lasting impact you create on those who follow in your footsteps. Remember, every action you take has the potential to make a significant difference. You have the power to shape your success and the lasting impact you create on all those who follow in your footsteps.

Every action you take—no matter how small—can propel you toward the lasting success you envision. Start today, and watch the ripple effects of your leadership unfold. You have the potential for great success, and I have no doubt that you will achieve it.

It has been an honor to share this journey with you. Your dedication to growth and leadership is what will set you apart. I'm excited to see how you'll continue to evolve and thrive.

But Wait—There's More!

As you reflect on your leadership journey, I invite you to explore the **bonus resources available at patalacqua.com/bonus-resources. These resources are designed to complement the lessons and strategies you've learned in this book, providing additional insights and tools to further enhance your leadership skills.**

Don't wait. Unlock these powerful tools today and take your next step toward lasting success. From in-depth conversations with top leaders to daily insights and actionable tools that will drive your business forward, these resources meet you where you are and take you where you want to go and who you want to be.

Thank you for being part of this journey. Here's to turning every obstacle into a stepping stone toward your next opportunity!

And remember, leadership is a continuous journey, and this book is just the beginning. Your dedication to growth and leadership is what will set you apart. Keep learning, stay curious, and never stop seeking new ways to turn obstacles into opportunities.

Warm regards,
Pat Alacqua

Acknowledgments

This book is the result of not only my own experiences and insights but also the contributions, support, and inspiration of many remarkable people. I am grateful to all those who walked alongside me throughout my career journey, each one adding their unique touch to bring this work to life.

A heartfelt thank you to C.J. Stewart for writing the foreword and for lending your trusted voice to this book. Your words add invaluable context for readers, setting the tone for what lies ahead. I am grateful for our relationship which has been a two-way journey of learning together. I am proud of the impact you and Kelli have had in your community. I look forward to what is ahead for you, Kelli, and the L.E.A.D. Center For Youth.

To my content development team, whose talent and dedication have been invaluable across the many content creation initiatives we've undertaken over the last few years.

Michael Pallerino, with your decades of experience and award-winning expertise in content creation, you've brought clarity and connection to countless projects.

Sarah Mindlin, your skill for copywriting and brand naming insight has added depth and nuance to all the projects we have worked on together. I'm especially grateful for your help in shaping this book's outline.

Ray Glier, your storytelling ability and commitment to uncovering the essence of every story you've crafted for my projects over the years have set a high standard for the narratives we've shared.

Mayra Velasco, your expertise in digital marketing has been key to ensuring our message resonates across my offerings and digital platforms.

Each of you has been an invaluable part of my content creation process, shaping the legacy we're building through our collective efforts.

My thanks to those who graciously provided testimonials. Your words mean more to me than I can express. It is both humbling and inspiring to know that my efforts have had a meaningful impact. Your support and encouragement add a personal touch to this book and remind me of the value of relationships in everything we do.

To my publisher, Charlie Levin, and his Munn Avenue Press team—thank you for guiding this book to print with expertise and enthusiasm. Your support has made the entire publishing process seamless, and your dedication to the message of this book has made it stronger.

I am grateful to the business partners in my own ventures. Your vision, dedication, and resilience have been instrumental in shaping our successes. Together, we have navigated countless challenges, and the impact of our work speaks to the power of real collaboration.

To the many strategic collaborators who contributed to my journey and helped bring my business goals to life, thank you. Your support, insight, and teamwork have been essential in achieving outcomes that I could not have reached alone. The strength of these partnerships has consistently fueled our shared growth and success.

I also extend my gratitude to the many leaders who shared their stories and allowed me to share their journeys of resilience and growth in this book. Your openness and willingness to pay it forward will help countless others on their paths. Thank you for sharing your insights and for trusting me to tell your stories with integrity.

To my family, who have supported me at every step: my wife, Elaine, whose patience, encouragement, and unwavering support have been my anchor through every challenge and accomplishment. To my daughter, Leigh Ann, and my son, Ross, whose love and belief in me inspire me to keep pushing forward. You are the heart of everything I do, and it's for you that I strive to create something lasting and meaningful.

I am fortunate to have been mentored and guided by so many individuals throughout my career. Though I can't name each of you individually in this chapter, know that your insights, advice, and examples have been invaluable. This book would not exist without the wisdom you shared, and I hope it serves as a tribute to the guidance and lessons I've received along the way.

To everyone who has been part of this journey, directly or indirectly, thank you. Your support has made this work possible, and it is my hope that this book will inspire others as much as you have inspired me.

This book is as much yours as it is mine.

About the Author

Guiding leaders through challenges with clarity, strategy, and alignment—empowering effective execution for accelerated career and business growth.

As a business growth strategist with a track record for operational success in his own businesses and founder of the Entrepreneur to Enterprise Program, Pat Alacqua has been instrumental in guiding leaders at various stages of their career and business-building journeys, helping them overcome challenges and achieve exponential growth.

With a proven track record in startups, rapid growth environments, and company turnarounds, Pat's expertise spans next-level growth, disciplined thinking frameworks, process development, marketing and operational capabilities, product/service strategy development, knowledge product creation, strategic planning, and project management.

Pat created the 3Cs Process to Faster Results. A systematic approach to tackle business challenges and teach business leaders how to apply the right decision-making skills to a set of impactful actions, putting them on the smartest and fastest track to career and business-building success.

These 3Cs are so simple, yet so powerful the more you apply them when tackling each and every one of your big challenges.

- CLARIFYING challenges
- CHARTING your course beyond the challenges to desired outcomes
- COALIGNING your team for successful implementation.

Pat Alacqua's personal mission is to empower entrepreneurs, emerging leaders, and executives to find clarity and confidence as they navigate business challenges. His innovative strategies and solid paths for implementation provide valuable resources for achieving lasting success.

Ready to accelerate your career and business growth?
Connect with Pat today at www.PatAlacqua.com.